STEALING A WOMAN'S TREASURE

How Toxic Body Care, Cosmetics, Hygiene, Synthetic Foods, And Hormones Are Ruining Your Health!

Dr. Botanica© and Anahitta Jafari, Ph.D.

Copyright © 2019 Doc Botanica©, dba Dr. Botanica©, LLC

All rights reserved.

UCC 1-308/1-207

Disclaimer

The information contained in this book is meant to educate the reader, and is in no way intended to provide medical, financial, legal, or any other services for individual problems or circumstances. We encourage readers to seek advice from competent professionals for personal health, financial, and legal needs.

This information is published under the First Amendment of the Constitution of the United States, which guarantees the right to discuss openly and freely all matters of public concern and to express viewpoints, no matter how controversial or unaccepted they may be. Any references for additional information that we may provide are for the reader's benefit only and are not affiliated with Dr. Botanica, Doc Botanica,, Khaliq-Alim-El, Ph.D., Dr. Anahitta Jafari, or any other institution, products, store or professional within the content of this book material, letter in any way, unless otherwise stated.

All information is believed to be correct, but its accuracy cannot be guaranteed. The owner, publisher, and editor are not responsible for errors and omissions.

Dr. Botanica© and Anahitta Jafari, Ph.D.
In Care of: 8212 Page Avenue
Saint Louis, Missouri Zip Exempt near [63130]
www.docbotanica.com
www.womanstreasure.com
Email: dr.botanica@yahoo.com
ISBN 978-0-9600963-0-5
Printed in the United States of America
Library of Congress Number

This information is not intended to diagnose or treat any medical condition and is not intended to replace competent advice from your health care professional. None of the information contained in this report has been evaluated by any regulatory agency such as the FDA or the USDA. While the authors taken every step to ensure that the content within this literature is offering accurate information. If any errors may occur, we urge you to seek additional information from your health care professional or conduct your own research if you have any questions or concerns about the information written.

To Rebecca & Marc
Dr Marc
with Love
Hope the information presented
Here be an Instrument To Your
Health

many Divine Blessings !

1-31-2024

Acknowledgements
Introduction   1

PART ONE
1. A Tribute to those Who Lost the Battle   3
2. The Advent of Glyphosate, Fluoride and Other Chemicals   25
3. Why Is Real Food Hard to Find?   41
4. The Connection Between Toxic Chemicals and Candida   71
5. What's Not So Pretty About Cosmetics and Vanity Products?   77
6. How Advertising Programs Manipulate Your Mind   109

PART TWO
7. How BPA And Plastic Can Make Estrogen The Enemy   123
8. Why the Young Will Be More Vulnerable to Diseases   159
9. Endocrine Disruptors And EMF's: 193
10. A Super Model's Life Is Shock By Tampons and TSS   203
11. Ann Anderson: Persevering Through Medical Disparities   221
12. Chemicals and Lifestyle Can Contribute to Breast Cancer   227

PART THREE
13. Hysterectomies and Hip Replacements   255
14. Why Females Need Organic Sanitary Napkins   271
15. Bio-Identical Hormone Testing: Keeping Hormones in Check   283
16. Why Men Need to Play a Role in Women's Health Care   295
17. You Must Detoxify Before You Purify   311
18. Super Foods and Supplements For A Brand-New Woman   325

REFERENCES   340
INDEX   348
ABOUT THE AUTHORS   351

Acknowledgements
Dr. Botanica©

I am grateful for the compassion to create this book with the support of holistic teacher Dr. Anahitta Jafari, the late great activist, health guru who was like a father and mentor, **Dick Gregory (R.I.P.)** Jonathan Victorian, Kevin Bryant of Conversion Marketing, Dr. Ron Gregory, Alvin Morrow, Barbara McGhee, Jackie Wooten. Special thanks the Kevin Bryant of Conversion Marketing for designing the cover if all my books. The media production work of **Aaron and Richard of AMD Media**. **Valerie O. Walker, M.D.** who is a great medical professional whom I had collaborated with for several years (Thank you for your support). A very special appreciation to Vilmante **Markeviciene, Redas, and Diva** for giving me the opportunity to represent such a phenomenal company.

The book goes out to these significant women: Brienekey, Schaela, Khadija, Hadiya, and Fatima, Granddaughters (Nia, Nija, Nalea, LaKenya), loving Grandmother (Mary Woodberry) Lillie Mae Fleming, Aunt Lizzie, Aunt Cara, Aunt Marguerite, Debra Lee, Ophelia, Cousins, Ruth, Bee (R.I.P.) Regina, Caitlin, Shaina, Ann Anderson, Tracey and my extended family; Marilyn Mack, Velma Victorian, Alicia Young, Debbie (Breast cancer survivor), Delores Hill, Delores, Debra Ingram, Faith Varner, Rae, Sandra Bell (Lung Cancer Survivor), Sharon Shafiq, Delores (R.I.P), Ms. Lucy, Ms. Paulette, Trish, Sheila Mosley, Resie Bryant, Gwen Solomon, Clara Triplett, Betsy Jackson, Jan Bosley, Yvonne Jones, Derica, Joan Gregory, Lillian Gregory and all the Gregory Daughters, Rebecca Cross, Kim Squalls, Vicky McGuire, Laura Wilkerson, Angie Fleming, Lexus, and all the Aboriginal Indigenous sisters of the North and South Amexem, and other ethnic groups of women around the world who represent love, health, faith, charity, and happiness. This book is undoubtedly to the unfortunately premature passing of former friends and clients **Sherry Rich, Velma Victorian, Joyce Porter, Gayle Lessne, Cora Scott-Fleming, Mary Woodberry, Georgia Couch (Like a Grandmother), Joyce Porter, Delores Hill, and Ms. Frazier.**

Great Respect and appreciation go to the late Alvina Fulton, naturopathic pioneer, Charlotte Gerson, daughter of the famous Max Gerson, and the other great pioneers of holistic and western medicine.

Dr. Anahitta Jafari

In the name of the creator of love, knowledge, compassion, truth, kindness, justice, beauty in all conceptions...
I am so blessed to confess to the knowledge I have been given through Love...

So many Blessings throughout my life, first and foremost being born in such a Divine family as mine with so much wisdom, compassion, and love, not just for their children and loved ones but also humanity...

What was taught to us (my sisters and I) with such love, patience, understanding, and never out of anger, is admirable and very hard to find...

To my amazing mother who truly sacrificed her life to teach us true Love for all, sacrifice to reach high and excel, to always be mindful of all our actions before taking steps, and to know that every action we take will affect not only ourselves but the whole cycle of life...

To my father, whom I've always looked up to, such a man that nothing but the highest was expected from his children, thank you for who you are and all you have done...

To my sisters and brother who are so loving, kind, supportive, and exemplary citizens, I Love you all, thank you for being my family...

To all my teachers whom we have crossed the path of learning together, you are certainly admirable for setting up strong pillars of each child you have crossed paths with, I thank you for all you have done...

To my precious daughter Beheshteh, who has been the most amazing gift from the heavens, since the first moment I felt your presence in my body, you are a priceless Gift and Teacher.
Thank you for choosing me as your Mother; it has been a Blessing and Honor. Thank you for spending every moment we share, thank you for all the reminders, and being who you are and who you will become...

To my most Noble teachers, My maternal Grandmother and Great Grandmother, who taught "Traditional Persian Herbalism" with such Love of knowledge and patience, that it not only fed our bodies but our souls...

Thank you all my loving, kind, supportive friends, Rev. Blanca, Rev. Nada, Suzi, Mahvash, Nia so many to name...

Special Thanks to Dr. Botanica for his request of my participation to write in this book the highest Divine Blessing to all readers who have chosen the path of enlightenment

May you be blessed with the most Priceless Gifts of Health, Happiness, Peace & Love

SWT is a personal dedicated one of my closest friends whom I lost to the battle of Breast cancer. Sherry Rich was an immaculate mother, poet, songstress, entrepreneur, a soldier of consciousness, Human Rights, and a woman of Oneness. She will always stay alive in my heart. Dr. Botanica

I also dedicate this book to very noble woman who was very dear to me. Velma Victorian was a beautiful woman and phenomenal mother, with an immaculate character. Her passing has encouraged me to continue to my quest to continue to find answers that can improved the ills of the people.

Introduction

We live in a modern-day matrix that has been created by a system designed to keep us complacent, docile, and naïve. As a result, people find themselves in a state of crisis, proliferated by disease, misery, and chaos because they lack knowledge. The bible scripture of **Hosea 4:6** says, **"My people are destroyed for lack of knowledge"** Our people not only perish for lack of knowledge but also from a lack of desire to seek knowledge. **"Knowledge is Absolute Power."** Those who indeed seek wisdom will find self-empowerment and discover their higher selves.

As sophisticated and advanced as society has become, masses not only still lack knowledge, but consciousness. We continue to endure the diseases and all forms of physical degeneration because the masses' state of mind has been led astray by misinformation and commercial manipulation. Insignificant forms of socialism, entertainment, and political chaos also have an impact on how we think, live, and eat. This phenomenon ultimately comes between the human being and the universal laws of life. To prevent and reduce the risk of chronic and degenerative diseases, we must reconnect with what gives life, and that is only **God's "natural law."**

This book is written to inform the masses of women with the most valuable health information. We have seen our mothers, daughters, close friends, politicians, and even our favorite personalities suffer and succumb to cancer and other systemic diseases. All of these women loved life as well as their families. If that loved one was more informed or educated before the disease, could she be alive today? If more caution was involved in what they consumed, could the disease have been prevented? If alternative modalities and other adjuvant therapies were available at the time of diagnosis, could that loved one be thriving instead of dying?

The above questions are valid because there are ways that diseases like cancer, MS, and Heart Disease can be prevented because of the many modalities that are available. There are undoubtedly alternatives to the toxic chemicals in foods, body care, hygiene, and household products that could have caused the disease.

The world is headed for self-destruction only due to disobedience. The same applies to all who disobeys the laws of nature. As long as we continue to endure synthetic chemicals and corrupt manufacturing practices; our foods, agriculture, body care, and the inhumane way of raising and slaughtering animals will destroy us, expectantly.

We encourage you to read this book and suggest to others to acquire it. Stealing A Woman's Treasure is not only informative, but it is also a guide to protect you with knowledge because knowledge is power. So, study well and help us and other life-promoting organizations to create this new paradigm shift of natural living.

A "Woman's Treasure" is comprised of her womb (uterus), cervix, ovaries, fallopian tubes, and her breast. In order for us to regain the strength that our ancestors once had is to totally reconnect with what is natural and resist anything that is not in harmony with nature. The advent of synthetic foods, GMO's, unfermented soy formulas, and the petrochemical plastics has weakened the physical constitution of the masses.

The woman is the maker of the home, the nation. She the source that has delivered great **Leaders, Scholars, Scientist, Athletes, Pastors, Priest, Musicians, Artist, Poets, Actors, Revolutionaries, and Teachers**, just to name a few. The corporations need to reconsider the types of chemical that are used in manufacturing, which wreaks havoc on the human body, wildlife, and the environment. We hope that this information and education will motivate you to take action for what is natural and only right. We hope that this book can reduce one's risk of premature disease or ill-health.

CHAPTER 1
A TRIBUTE TO THE WOMEN
WHO LOST THE BATTLE

Since 2008, worldwide breast cancer incidence has increased by more than 20 percent. Mortality has increased by 14 percent, according to the World Cancer Research Fund International.

Breast Cancer is the most common form of cancer among women worldwide. Globally, breast cancer now represents one in four of all cancers in women. Every day, many women are not only losing their breasts but uterus, ovaries, cervix, gallbladder, and thyroid due to the enormous exposure and consumption of chemicals. Since the industrial revolution, we have been exposed to the mass production of petroleum by-products. Pesticides, insecticides, herbicides, and other toxic agents end up in our food, water, in practically every consumer product on the market.

Since the advent of the industrial revolution, humans and wildlife have been exposed to thousands of havoc-wreaking chemicals. This magnitude of anti-life production has become the source of breast cancer along with other forms of chronic and degenerative disease among the human race across the globe.

The purpose of this chapter is to remind the reader that it is paramount that we protect our bodies at all costs by becoming consciously selective about what we consume. It would be wise to seek a completely organic lifestyle and consume everything with caution. There should be no exceptions when it comes to the natural balance of our mind, body, and spirit. We have all witnessed the premature death of relatives, friends, colleagues, professional athletes, and entertainers due to cancer and other degenerative diseases. The content of this chapter is not intended to intimidate anyone, but to promote consciousness and awareness.

Our condolences go out to the family members and friends of the women mentioned who have lost the battle to cancer and other degenerative diseases.

A TRIBUTE TO THE FEMALE TREASURES AND ALL OTHER WOMEN ACROSS THE GLOBE WHO LOST THEIR LIVES TO THE ADVENT OF CANCER

Above: *Noreen Fraser, Television producer and Co-Creator of "Stand Up To Cancer" lost a 16-year battle to* **Stage-IV Metastatic Breast Cancer** *in 2017.*

Laura Ziskin, famous film producer and co-creator of "Stand Up To Cancer" lost the battle to breast cancer in 2011.

Above: Sharon Mcghee, Author of **Pocketbook Monologues** *lost the battle to* **ovarian cancer in 2012 at the age of 51.**

Jada Russell, entrepreneur, marketing/PR executive, and community advocate lost the battle to **Breast cancer in 2019 at age 45.**

Above: Dianne Oxberry, BBC television and radio presenter, lost to Ovarian Cancer and age 51

Farrah Fawcett, Award-winning actress (Breast Cancer) in 2009

Above: **Marilou Diaz Abaya,** award-winning director **Breast cancer in 2012.**

Elizabeth Garrett was the president of **Cornell University**, lost her battle in March of 2016 of **Colon Cancer.**

Above: World-renowned R&B Songstress, **Aretha Franklin**, lost her battle with **pancreatic cancer)**

Famous 1970's R&B Songstress **Minnie Riperton** *lost her battle with Breast cancer*

Above: Linda McCartney, musician, activist, and wife of famous singer and musician **Paul McCartney** lost her battle to **Breast cancer in 1998.**

June Jordan, a famous Poet and Political Activist, passed from **Breast Cancer in 2002**

Above: Anca Paghel, Romanian Jazz artist and singer, (Breast cancer, 2008)

Susan Strasberg, film, stage and television Actress, Breast Cancer (1999)

Above: Maryam Mirzakhani, famous Iranian Mathematician and Professor at Stanford University lost her battle to Breast cancer an early age of 30 in 2017.

Coretta Scott King, the wife of *Dr. Martin Luther King, Jr.* and. human rights activist. Passed away from respiratory failure due to end-stage ovarian cancer

Above: Nina Simone, the legendary singer, composer and performer lost a several year battle to **Breast cancer** in April of 2003.

Fatima Ali of Pakistan, former Top Chef Contestant and Chief executive lost her battle to a rare form of **Ewings** cancer at the age of 25 in January 2019

Above: Our condolences go out to the family of **Gwen Ifill**, a famous journalist and PBS anchor who lost the battle to cancer and the age of 61.

*Fox Anchor woman, **Brenda Buttne**r, lost her battle to cancer at 55*

Leah Bracknell: Former actress who lost the battle to lung cancer

Katherine Textorm 60 Minutes Producer lost the battle to cancer at age 45

Henrietta Lacks in the 1940s.Credit...Lacks Family, via The Henrietta Lacks Foundation, via Associated Press

Henrietta Lacks. A symbol Beauty and Nobility that will live for all eternity. African-Americans, to pursue a career in the sciences of life, health, and cancer prevention. A special dedication to immaculate women leaves a phenomenal and scientific legacy. Her spirit and legacy are infinite.

Henrietta Lacks was an African-American woman born in 1920, whose cancer cells were immortalized by being grown in a laboratory. This amazing woman was the mother of five children, economically oppressed, but a very tenacious woman who loved life, but in 1951, she diagnosed with cervical cancer. Like other aggressive malignant virus cells, cervical cancer is not only as aggressive as ants surrounding sweet bread. The aggressive and mutant nature of cancer causes these cells to divide uncontrollably, destroying once healthy tissue.

Henrietta was unable to afford medical care, so she went to Johns Hopkins Hospital, the gynecologists at that time were attempting to develop modalities that could effectively treat cervical cancer. Many women at that time who went through the cancer ward, procedures were conducted without their consent. Henrietta's case was no exception to the rule, and her cancer tumor was removed without her consent.

The doctors at the medical institution discovered that Henrietta's possess cells were not only unlike any other patient, but these were the first human cells to survive outside of the body. The cell's activity was called "HeLa" after the name of Henrietta Lacks. It is an immortal cancerous cell line. It is able to go through the cell cycle infinitely. The surprising fact about the HeLa cell is that they do not require a body to survive.

The cells were cultured and shared among medical researchers and revealed that these abnormal cells could make medical history. One unique medical milestone regarding Henrietta's cells is that the cellular activity halted the spread of polio by assisting in creating the vaccine. This unusual and potentially infinite cell activity could take the place of human cells

Though Henrietta's cells were cancerous, they appeared to thrive like healthy cells in most ways, and soon would be proven vital to creating the polio vaccine, cloning, gene mapping, and countless other medical milestones. The research and experiments were carried out without the consent of Henrietta Lack's family. Unfortunately, Henrietta's cancer metastasized and eventually lost the battle to the aggressive spread of cancer.

Today, some professionals and advocates consider Henrietta's case of not only medical neglect but a violation of human rights. Though Henrietta's cells were unique and presented an opportunity to create better modalities for people with systemic diseases, it was also considered a "selfish form of profit and capitalism."

Henrietta's terminal cancerous condition has helped some to survive a death sentence. The doctor's decision to remove the tumor created a paradigm shift in medical research; it was just unfortunate that doctors and the medical institution withheld this information from her family. We are a creation of a divine order of natural law, and Corporatocracy should never capitalize from The Almighty God's Creation. Human genes and genetic material should not be a commodity for profit but instead used for research and solutions. The profit can always manifest from good work for "natural life."

We advocate for every woman always to seek a "Third opinion", the answers are out there. Seek, and thee shall find, "for our people perish for lack of knowledge." Cancer is one of the most devastating fates of human life. Our advice is to take a proactive approach, consume what is in harmony with the mind, body, and spirit. Seek a health practitioner who is spiritual and puts the Almighty Creator first.

We commend and appreciate Rebecca Skloot for pursuing this historical and scientific epic on Henrietta Lacks. The immortal cell line knows as HeLa that came from a condition of cervical cancer. "The Immortal Life of Henrietta Lacks" is phenomenal with the help of Henrietta's Daughter Deborah who made the book and movie possible. Our gratitude certainly goes out to one of the most talented and tenacious women on the planet, "Ophrah Winfrey." We hope that females of all ethnicities and ages engage and embrace the book, the movie, the history, and the science of Henrietta Lacks. May her soul be pleased with her legacy.

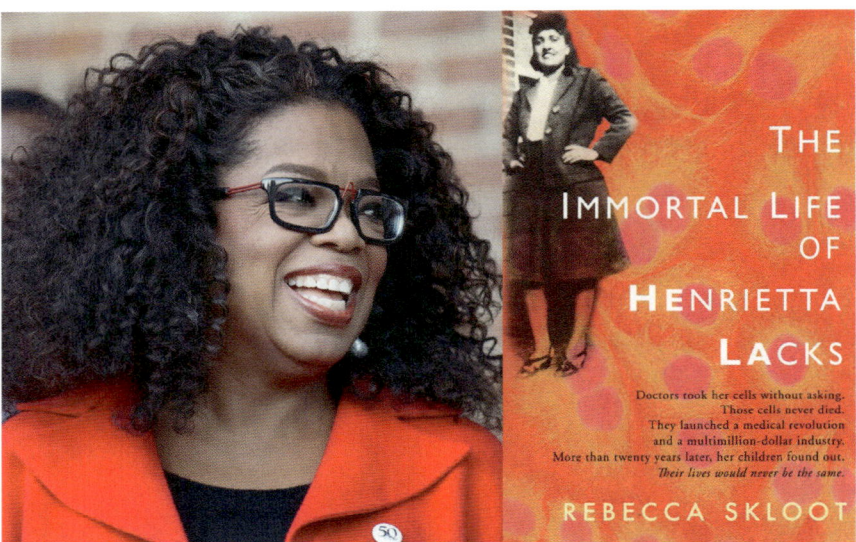

***Oprah Winfrey** gracefully portrayed the role of Deborah in the HBO special "The Immortal Life of Henrietta Lacks. Deborah was the last daughter given birth by the legendary Henrietta Lacks four months before being diagnosed with cervical cancer, a disease that is still prevalent today among women. Thank you, Oprah, for being a part of a legacy that will encourage many young women, especially young*

Henrietta Lacks and the HeLa Cell Timeline

1951 – Cells cultured

1952 – Cells shipped via mail

1952 – HeLa Factory

1952 – HeLa used for Polio Vaccine

1973 – HeLa used to study Salmonella

1984 – HeLa used to prove HPV and Cancer link

1986 – HeLa used to study HIV

1989 – Enzyme discovered that prevents cells from dying

1993 – HeLa used to study TB

2005 – HeLa cells used in nanotechnology research

Why Women Are largely Affected by Cancer.

The unconscious selection of food, water, body care, cosmetics and additives are the cause of many unexpected and premature health challenges. Over the last 30 years, even our offspring (children) have been secretly assaulted by growth hormones, antibiotics, and GMO's through animal proteins, food additives and commercial body care. As a result, girls as you as 9 years of age are now experiencing their reproductive cycle along with the premature and sometimes over developed growth of breast.

In this new synthetic society girls do not have the natural balance that young females had a hundred years ago because of a myriad of artificial foods, GMO's, and vanity products. The food, water, and even clothing in pre-colonial times were in a much purer state than what we consume, use, and wear today. In our industrialized world, it is incredibly hard to find products that are not derived from some sort of petrochemical. The diseases and various forms of ill-health that we see today rarely existed 5 decades ago. Four hundred years ago, human beings could experience the genuine aroma and taste of truly nutrient-rich and chemical-free fruits and vegetables.

We need to take more notice of our environment we live in, take positive actions toward a Healthier, Happier, and Higher Quality Of Life. Many years ago, almost everyone gardened, especially if they lived in small towns or rural areas. They quite effectively used what came from the Earth for personal hygiene and beauty, as women did among many cultures from around the world. People ate what was available seasonally in their area and traded their harvests with each other.

It should be important enough to become more aware of how all the things that we consume are made of, and how they are processed. We need to know what chemicals are added to our water, what is in the air we breathe, what is added to our fabric, and clothing.

We are what we eat; therefore, if you are seeking health, you must be eating what is natural and keeps your body in balance. For those who can afford to invest in healthier foods, it would be wise to do so. Your health and the future state of your offspring depend on your interest in natural living now.

What many people do not know, is that consumer products contribute to health. For example, diabetes is practically an epidemic because of diet and lifestyle, Obesity is practically an epidemic because of diet and lifestyle, and gastrointestinal challenges practically an epidemic because of diet and lifestyle. In order to remedy these chronic forms of ill-health, you need to modify your diet and lifestyle to address these of other conditions that are creating the need for medication and therapy.

Regarding hormonal imbalance and the development of cancer, these conditions are proliferated by not only foods and lifestyle, but by the chemistry composition of the body care, hygiene and cosmetic brands that are used. If the body care is too toxic to consume by mouth, then maybe it should not be used on the surface. Did you know that most synthetic chemicals that are found in body care, hygiene, and cosmetics can elevate estrogen and promote hormone imbalance?

Eating processed foods, such as potato chips, soda, and fast foods can put your health at risk because of the way synthetic chemicals simply don't process well within the human body. Now, because of the tenacity of the human physiology we are able to tolerate and improvise for a time, however if the consumption continues to be repeated throughout the years, there will be repercussions such as diabetes, hormone imbalance, hypertension, and even cancer.

In regard to personal care, those who can redefine their lifestyle absolutely must. To start, one must eliminate as much endocrine-disrupting personal hygiene, body, and hair care as possible. Even for the women who feel bound to a specific personal style, to truly combat the toll misinformation has taken on your bodies, a completely holistic diet and lifestyle are necessary as well. Alcohol, recreational drugs, immunosuppressive drugs, and cigarettes are some of the deadliest things to us, especially women.

Cigarettes and secondhand smoke environments not only contain nicotine but also 600 toxic ingredients, which when burned produce another 7000 chemicals. At least 69 of these chemicals have been confirmed by studies to cause cancer due to extreme toxicity. Addiction is a disease, just as serious as any other physical illness. In a society that not only does not consider that and is built to be full of highly addictive activities and products, but the Traditional Lifestyle is also most definitely not accessible to many. But again, I stress, humans are far more capable than we think; women being the strongest and most capable. To eliminate these things wisely is to save your health and make the conscious decision to care even more about the future of generations to come.

CHAPTER 2
THE ADVENT OF DDT, FLUORIDE, GLYPHOSATE, AND OTHER CHEMICALS

Flying and Biting Bugs on Jones Beach Die in a Cloud of DDT, New Insecticide

A truck-mounted fog generator squirts the poison, mixed with oil droplets, over a four-mile area of the New York City playground. Spread by Army and Navy planes and by hand sprays, DDT routed dangerous disease-bearing flies and mosquitoes on Pacific islands. Dusted on almost the entire population of Naples, it killed lice and halted a typhus epidemic. DDT has a drawback—it kills many beneficial and harmless insects, but does not kill all insect pests. Birds and fish which eat large numbers of DDT-poisoned insects may be casualties, too (page 408).

In 1962 researcher and author Rachel Carson published a landmark book called **"Silent Spring"** that warned us about to advent of industrial toxicity and would eventually lead to necessary government department called the Environmental Protection Agency. We are now faced with the most significant challenge in human history because of "chemical corporatocracy" and the proliferation of chronic and degenerative diseases because of chemically derived foods

CALIFORNIA SAFE DRINKING WATER & TOXIC ENFORCEMENT ACT OF 1986 (PROPOSITION 65)

To meet the requirements of Proposition 65, it is our responsibility to inform you of the following:

WARNING

Some products sold in this store contain chemicals known to the State of California to cause cancer, birth defects or other reproductive harm.

and the horrific care of our farmed produce with the use of insecticides, pesticides, fungicides, and herbicides.

In the case of capitalism and oligarchy, the repercussions of profit are not a concern, because the benefit takes precedence of morals and values among specific species of human. Over one hundred and twenty-five years ago, the Industrial Revolution streamlined the quest to control every species that is known to exist. It was a desire to not only duplicate nature but to alter its position on this planet.

Millions of synthetic chemicals from inorganic substances such as coal, tar, dyes, and petrochemicals are in practically every consumer product. Women are the cornerstones of every nation have endured decades of toxicity, and products that are causing severe harm to their health now more than ever.

One of the primary causes of our many crises is the presence of high levels of synthetic estrogen in the human body, due to industrial toxicity. Young people are developing weaker immune systems, so too are future women going to create a more vulnerable human species because the production of synthetic estrogens has compromised our natural states of health. Women in the U.S. are developing disease faster than any civilization known to date, and this experience of health complications is entirely inexplicable for most.

Glyphosate Today's Talk of Toxicity
"Glyphosate was significantly higher in humans [fed] conventional [food] compared with predominantly organic [fed]

humans. Glyphosate residues were in human urine according to the human health status. Chronically ill humans had significantly higher glyphosate residues in urine than healthy humans"2 –**MONIKA KRUGER, ENVIRONMENTAL & ANALYTICAL TOXICOLOGY.**

Glyphosate is a broad-spectrum herbicide widely used to kill unwanted plants both in agriculture and in nonagricultural landscapes. Estimated use in the U.S. is between 38 and 48 million pounds per year. Most glyphosate-containing products are either made or used with a surfactant, chemicals that help Glyphosate to penetrate plant cells. Glyphosate-containing products are acutely toxic to animals, including humans can include, but not limited to, Symptoms include eye and skin irritation, headache, nausea, numbness, elevated blood pressure, and heart palpitations. The surfactant used in a popular glyphosate product (Roundup) is more acutely toxic than Glyphosate itself; the combination of the two is yet more toxic.

Glyphosate was patented originally to Clean Pipes; like Drano - 1964, Glyphosate is the presumed active ingredient of Monsanto's Roundup weed killer and other commercial glyphosate-based herbicide formulations. It was first patented in 1964 by Stauffer Chemical Company in Westport, Connecticut, as a chelator7, for removing unwanted mineral deposits from metal pipes like Drano. Monsanto Discovers Weed-killing Properties - 1974 A few years later, Glyphosate was also found to be an effective herbicide by Monsanto's

John E. Franz[8] and brought to market by the St. Louis-based company in 1974 as a non-selective, water-soluble herbicide with a specific mechanism of action: the directed interruption of plant development through metabolic poisoning. At least 100 manufacturers use generic glyphosate formulations and found in more than 750 products worldwide, with Monsanto still dominating the market with more than $4.75 billion in sales in 2015 alone.[9]

As with the original pipe cleaning patent, Glyphosate also binds (chelates) vital nutrients such as iron, manganese, zinc, and boron in the soil, preventing plants from taking them up.[10][11][12][13] This could have serious implications for humans, farm animals, and pets that consume genetically engineered Roundup Ready crops, as it could negatively affect the nutritional value of food.

In studies of people (mostly farmers) exposed to glyphosate herbicides, have an increased risk of miscarriages, premature birth, and the cancer non-Hodgkin's lymphoma. Glyphosate has been called "extremely persistent" by the U.S. Environmental Protection Agency.

Glyphosate has also been found in streams following agricultural, urban, and forestry applications. Glyphosate treatment has reduced populations of beneficial insects, birds, and small mammals by destroying vegetation on which they depend for food and shelter. In laboratory tests, Glyphosate increased plants' susceptibility to disease and reduced the growth of nitrogen-fixing bacteria.

The most important agricultural uses are in the production of soybeans, corn, hay, and pasture, and on fallow land.7 Since 1998, Glyphosate has had a growth rate) of about 20 percent annually, primarily because of the recent introduction of crops which are genetically engineered to be tolerant of the herbicide.   In the U.S. about 25 million applications were made yearly on lawns and in yards.9

Glyphosate-based formulations are the most widely sold and used pesticides globally. This dreadful chemical is virtually everywhere in the food chain. As a consequence, Glyphosate is regularly detected in human urine. At these levels and even below, several converging lines of research in laboratory animals suggest that glyphosate-based herbicides may be endocrine disruptors and alter liver and kidney function. It is suspected that Glyphosate is a probable cancer-causing agent used with regularity by farmers, farmworkers, pesticide applicators, and others exposed to the chemical through routine use.

There are specific cancer concerns now associated with Glyphosate:
Non-Hodgkin's Lymphoma • Bone Cancer • Colon Cancer • Kidney Cancer • Liver Cancer • Melanoma • Pancreatic Cancer • Thyroid Cancer. Where Else Has Glyphosate Been Found? Glyphosate

Residues Found in Food, Urine, Breast Milk, Rainwater, Rivers, Tap Water and Tampons – But the FDA Has Never Conducted Proper Widespread Testing.

The Toxic Tales of Fluoride

Fluoride is any combination of elements containing the fluoride ion. In its elemental form, fluorine is a pale yellow, highly toxic and corrosive gas. In nature, fluorine is found combined with minerals as fluorides. It is the most chemically active nonmetallic of all the elements and also has the most reactive electro-negative ion. Because of this extreme reactivity, fluorine is not found in nature as an uncombined element.

Fluorine is a member of group VIIa of the periodic table. It readily displaces other halogens–such as chlorine, bromine, and iodine–from their mineral salts. With hydrogen, it forms hydrogen fluoride gas, which, in a water solution, becomes hydrofluoric acid.

There was no U.S. commercial production of fluorine before World War II. A requirement for fluorine in the processing of uranium ores, needed for the atomic bomb, prompted its manufacture.6 Fluorine compounds or fluorides are listed by the U.S. Agency for Toxic Substances and Disease Registry (ATSDR) as among the top 20 of 275 substances that pose the most significant threat to human health.7 The fluoride compound in "naturally" fluoridated waters is calcium fluoride. Sodium fluoride, a common fluoridation agent, dissolves easily in water, but calcium fluoride does not.9.

The validation of Fluoride toxicity goes back to the Kick Study from 1935 which revealed that sodium fluoride was much more toxic than calcium fluoride.38 The toxicity of Fluoride was recorded for hydrofluorosilicic acid, the compound now used in over 90 percent of fluoridation programs, Hydrofluorosilicic acid is a direct byproduct of pollution scrubbers used in the phosphate fertilizer and aluminum industries. This toxic agent is added to water supplies even though it is also involved in getting rid of its own stockpile of fluoride compounds left over from years and years of stockpiling fluorides for use in the process of refining uranium for nuclear power and weapons.39

According to the Kick study, less than 2 percent of calcium fluoride was absorbed, and this was excreted quantitatively in the urine. But even calcium fluoride is not benign. As the animals' given calcium fluoride also developed mottled teeth, it was clear that such compounds could produce changes in the teeth merely by passing through the body, and not by being "stored in a tooth" or anywhere else. No calcium fluoride was retained.

In 1946 Samuel Chase, one of the authors of the Kick study, became president of the International Association for Dental Research (IADR). This organization promoted the idea that only the fluoride ion in the various fluoridation compounds was of importance. Yet he well knew that sodium fluoride did not behave like calcium fluoride. Unlike calcium fluoride, sodium fluoride was retained in high amounts in the body and was very toxic. Rock phosphate and hydro-fluorosilicic acid experiments yielded the same information.

New areas with "natural" Fluoride appear all over the world, as now all areas not "artificially" fluoridated are considered "natural." The problem is that this "natural" Fluoride is the result of direct water and soil contamination from petrochemical land treatment, uncontrolled fertilizer use, pesticide applications, groundwater contamination from industrial waste sites, rocket fuel "burial grounds," and so forth. Suddenly we have "natural" fluorides showing up in areas previously deemed "fluoride deficient"!

In 1991 the U.S. Public Health Service issued a report stating that the range in total daily fluoride intake from water, dental products, beverages, and food items exceeded 6.5 milligrams daily.42 Thus, the total consumption from those sources alone already greatly exceeds the levels known to cause the third stage of skeletal fluorosis.

Besides fluoridated water and toothpaste, many foods contain high levels of fluoride compounds due to pesticide applications. One of the worst offenders is grapes.45 Grape juice was found to include more than 6.8 ppm fluoride. The EPA estimates total fluoride intake from pesticide residues on food and fluoridated drinking water alone to be 0.095 mg/kg/day, meaning a person weighing 70 kg takes in more than 6.65 mg per day.45b Soy infant formula is high in both Fluoride and aluminum, far surpassing the "optimal" dose 46,47 and is a risk factor in dental fluorosis.48

Fluoride content in tea has risen dramatically over the last 20 years due to industry contamination. Recent analyses have revealed a fluoride content of 17.25 mg per teabag or cup in black tea, and a whopping 22 mg of soluble fluoride ions per teabag or cup in green tea. Aluminum content was also high-over 8 mg. Average steeping time is five minutes. The longer a tea bag steeped, the more Fluoride and aluminum were released. After ten minutes, the measurable amounts of Fluoride and aluminum almost doubled.53

Next to water, tea is the most widely consumed beverage in the world. Tea can be found in almost 80 percent of all U.S. households and on any given day, nearly 127 million people-half of all Americans-drink tea.71

How Fluoride Can Wreak Havoc the Thyroid and Brain

The recent re-discovery of hundreds of papers dealing with the use of fluorides in effective anti-thyroid medication poses many questions demanding answers.73, 74 The enamel defects observed in hypothyroidism are identical to "dental fluorosis." Endemic fluorosis areas have been shown to be the same as those affected with iodine deficiency, considered to be the world's single most important and preventable cause of mental retardation, 75 affecting 740 million people a year.

Iodine deficiency causes brain disorders, cretinism, miscarriages, and goiter, among many other diseases. Synthroid, the drug most commonly prescribed for hypothyroidism, became the top-selling drug in the U.S. in 1999, according to Scott-Levin's Source Prescription Audit, clearly indicating that hypothyroidism is a major health problem. Many more millions are thought to have undiagnosed thyroid problems.

July 25, 2012 – For years health experts have been unable to agree on whether fluoride in the drinking water may be toxic to the developing human brain. Extremely high levels of fluoride are known to cause neurotoxicity in adults, and negative impacts on memory and learning have been reported in rodent studies, but little is known about the substance's impact on children's neurodevelopment. In a meta-analysis, researchers from Harvard School of Public Health (HSPH) and China Medical University in Shenyang for the first time combined 27 studies and found strong indications that fluoride may adversely affect cognitive development in children. Based on the findings, the authors say that this risk should not be ignored, and that more research on fluoride's impact on the developing brain is warranted. The study was published online in *Environmental Health Perspectives* on July 20, 2012.

Research Confirms 9 Ways That Fluoride Disharmonizes The Mind and Body

1. Fluoride Is a Developmental Neurotoxin
A neurotoxin is a substance that's poisonous or destructive to the tissues in the brain, spinal cord, and nervous system. A developmental neurotoxin is one that affects the brain during the most susceptible stages of life – before birth and during early childhood.

2. The Ingestion of Fluoride Lowers IQ in Children
Harvard School of Public Health and China Medical University did a joint analysis of 27 studies on the effects of fluoride and found a strong correlation between fluoride and adverse effects on brain development. (5) Children in high-fluoride areas had significantly lower IQ scores than those living in low-fluoride areas.

3. Fluoride Facilitates the Entry of Aluminum Into the Brain.

In the 1970s, autopsies revealed that Alzheimer's patients had higher than normal concentrations of neurotoxic aluminum in their brains. It's now understood that fluoride may play a role in the aluminum-Alzheimer's connection.

The blood-brain barrier is a semipermeable membrane designed to keep foreign substances – like fluoride and aluminum – out of the brain. When aluminum comes into contact with fluoride, it hitches a ride into the brain as aluminum fluoride, bypassing the blood-brain barrier. The presence of aluminum fluoride in the brain has been linked to Alzheimer's. ([7])

4. Fluoridated Drinking Water Doubles the Risk of Hypothyroidism

Fluoride, especially when added to drinking water, nearly doubles the risk of developing hypothyroidism (underactive thyroid). ([8]) Fluoride binds with iodine receptors in the thyroid, displacing iodine. And when there isn't adequate iodine available, the thyroid can't synthesize thyroid hormones. ([9]). And that is bad news for your brain. Brain fog, memory loss, lack of focus, depression, anxiety, and other cognitive and mental health issues are some of the most problematic side effects of thyroid disorders.

5. Fluoride Causes Nervous System Degeneration

Once fluoride crosses the blood-brain barrier, it causes degeneration to specific parts of the brain – the hippocampus, the neocortex, and the cerebellum. ([10]). The hippocampus is considered the seat of memory and is critical for learning, emotional regulation, and shutting off the stress response.

The neocortex is considered the most evolved area of the brain where sensory perception, conscious thought, and language skills largely take place. The cerebellum is responsible for coordination and balance. The damage from fluoride doesn't stop at your brain; it continues on to your spinal cord and sciatic nerve.

6. Fluoride Impairs Pineal Gland Function

The pineal gland is a pea-sized structure in the brain where melatonin is produced. Melatonin is known mainly as a sleep hormone, but it's much more than that. Melatonin is a potent antioxidant that is especially protective of the brain.

It can offset the damage of serious brain disorders including dementia and Alzheimer's. (11). It may even help you live longer. Melatonin has been shown to work at least as well as antidepressant medications and is particularly useful for a certain kind of depression known as seasonal affective disorder (SAD). (12, 13). The pineal gland is prone to accumulating deposits in a process known as calcification. Calcification, in spite of the name, isn't always caused by calcium. These deposits can be caused by other minerals, including fluoride which is found in strikingly high concentrations in the pineal gland. (14, 15)

This affects melatonin production, contributing to insomnia, depression, and accelerated brain aging. (16). Pineal gland calcification is thought to contribute to dementia and Alzheimer's since it is significantly higher in patients with these diseases. (17)

7. Fluoridated Water Leaches Lead from Pipes and Faucets

If you are as old as we are, you'll remember when paint, gasoline, and water pipes regularly contained lead. Lead is another neurotoxin that posed a serious health threat, leading to a series of bans.

Lead has been banned from paint since 1978, phased out of gasoline in the 1990s, and outlawed in the manufacture of water pipes since 1986. (18, 19, 20) But if you live in a house built before 1986, you may still have lead water pipes. Even new brass or chrome-plated faucets contain some lead. (21). If you have fluoridated water coming through lead pipes and chrome faucets, you have the "perfect neurotoxin storm" since fluoridated water leaches lead and greatly increases the amount of lead in your water – up to 9-fold more. (22)

Young brains are most at risk, but brains of all ages can suffer from lead exposure that can manifest as memory loss, mood disorders, lower IQ, and learning disabilities. (23, 24)

8. An Increase in Rates of ADHD Is Linked to Fluoride

Rates of ADHD skyrocketed about the same time that fluoridation of water supplies was on the rise in the United States. This may not be a coincidence since researchers have found a correlation between water fluoridation and ADHD. (25) States with the largest number of ADHD cases also have the greatest proportion of people drinking fluoridated water.

According to the Centers for Disease Control, 75% of the US population receives fluoridated water, but the numbers vary greatly by state. (26). If you live in Washington DC, the chances of fluoridated water coming out of your tap are 100%. States with the lowest levels of fluoridated water are Montana at 32% and Hawaii at 10%.

If you currently take one of these medications, you may want to discuss switching to a fluoride-free antidepressant or try some **natural ways to relieve depression** instead. **Note**: But do not stop taking any medication before talking to your health care professional.

If you use fluoridated water or toothpaste, even in small amounts, it will increase your aluminum absorption...

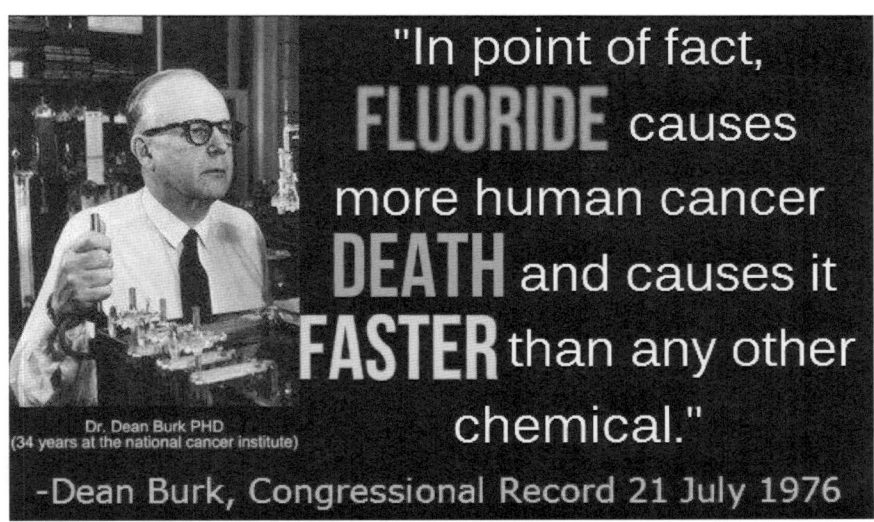

Use Fluoride-Free Toothpaste

Many "natural" personal care companies like Tom's of Maine, Jason's, Nature's Gate, and Kiss My Face carry fluoride-free versions of toothpaste. If you live in one of the handful of countries that regularly add fluoride to their water – the US, Canada, Australia, Ireland, and Brazil – you may be surprised to learn that most of the world does *not* fluoridate their water. Only 5.7% of the world's population drinks artificially fluoridated water. (30)

TOOTHPASTE

DIRECTIONS: Do not swallow. Adults and children 2 years of age in good brushing and rinsing habits (to minimize swa meals or as recommended by a dentist or physician. Superv

WARNING: KEEP OUT OF REACH OF CHILDREN UNDER 6) IF MORE THAN USED FOR BRUSHING IS ACCIDENTALLY S HELP OR CONTACT A POISON CONTROL CENTER RIGHT A

ACTIVE INGREDIENT: SODIUM FLUORIDE (0.24%)

Sodium Fluoride compromises the high science known as common sense. Read and analyze labels before buying and consuming and product.

CHAPTER 3
WHY REAL FOOD IS HARD TO FIND?

"The great enemy of truth is very often not the lie – deliberate, contrived and dishonest – but the myth – persistent, persuasive, and unrealistic. Too often we hold fast to the clichés of our forebears. We subject all facts to a prefabricated set of interpretations. We enjoy the comfort of opinion without the discomfort of thought." – **John F. Kennedy**

"For the first time in the history of the world, practically every human being has consumed some form of toxic chemical through food. It appears that the human body is becoming in the bodies of the vast majority of human beings, regardless of age. They occur in the mother's milk, and probably in the tissues of the unborn child." 1 – Rachel Carson, **SILENT SPRING**

Over a one-hundred years ago, the human diet was not nearly as complicated as it is today in this overly processed and factory food society. The food at that time unadulterated and cattle was adequately raised and slaughtered, whereas the meat that the masses purchase and consume today is pumped full of growth hormones, antibiotics, and fed chemical-based grains. The vegetable produce of yesterday was grown organically without the contamination of pesticides, insecticides, or herbicides; also, the fruit that did not last for weeks without spoiling.

The food we eat today in the US can be a significant source of environmental estrogens. These estrogen-mimicking agents can be found in the commercial meats and dairy products we've been consuming our whole lives. Farm factories give their livestock estrogen and growth hormones so they will grow faster and gain the maximum amount of weight before they get slaughtered. The commercial Dairy cows are also given hormones such as rBGH/Bovine Growth hormones and continuously impregnate them so they will produce more milk, constantly!

Even if the factory farms had not deliberately pumped the animals full of hormones, their meat and milk would still contain xenoestrogens from GMO soy and corn, the two grains often used as animal feed in addition to farm fertilizers, all of which contain estrogenic chemicals. These two grains are also the most likely to be genetically modified.

The commercial fruits and vegetables we eat aren't any better, because they are treated with estrogen-mimicking chemicals. According to the Agency for Toxic Substances and Disease Registry, polycyclic aromatic hydrocarbons (PAHs) are the by-products of the incomplete burning of coal, gas, and oil, and are used to make many of the pesticides sprayed on food crops. Studies show that PAHs can cause tumors through inhalation, via food, or through prolonged contact with the skin. PAHs are xenoestrogens and easily bind to estrogen receptor sites on our cells and actually trigger breast growth in those who naturally lack breasts, as well as contribute to prostate cancer. **Special note**; this synthetic chemical influence is also behind the development of breasts in those with external genitalia, here meaning most men.

What Is Real Food?

Real food is what the human body or mammal thrives on to sustain optimal health. Real food is in a base of vitamins, minerals, trace elements, essential fatty acids, co-factors, and enzymes. Food is in harmony with nature, made without any chemicals or additives).

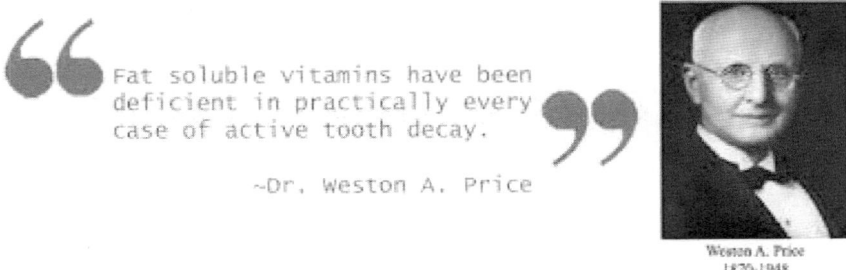

" Fat soluble vitamins have been deficient in practically every case of active tooth decay. "

~Dr. Weston A. Price

Weston A. Price
1870-1948

Real food is food that has stood the test of time (meaning previous generations ate the food, back to ancient civilizations). Real foods nourish our bodies and minds and make us feel good after we eat it (not like we need a nap or a toilet within our line of sight at all times).

Most of all, real food is medicine because it improves and revitalizes our health, not destroys it. Unfortunately, it is hard to find real food, evening in the health food stores. That is why it is vital to find real supplements because the foods that most people consume have been altered, depleted in minerals, and preserved with chemicals.

If our land were not destroyed, buy artificial fertilization, and had the synthetic corporation left the land like it was over a hundred years age, real food would be BETTER than medicine. Real food comprised of natural rice, beans, legumes, herbs, spices, roots, nuts, berries, and seeds can heal the body faster than any synthetic. Real food can heal because the molecular structure of what is natural is in harmony with nature. If it contains life, it will give life, unlike prescription medication, which masks symptoms

Dr. Weston Price: Nutrition and Physical Degeneration

In the 1930's Dr. Weston Price a doctor of Dentistry who is famous for the publication **"Nutrition and Physical Degeneration"** would travel the world and demonstrated with great clarity that the foods of modern commerce do not provide humans with sufficient nutrients to allow the body to reach its maximum genetic potential.

A sufficient amount of nutrients is needed to reach the complete development of the bones in the body and the head, nor the fullest expressions of the various systems that allow humankind to function at optimal levels of immune system nervous system digestion reproduction. So, what is it about the foods of today that wreak havoc on our bodies to the point that humankind develops, reproductive, intestinal, heart, and other organ diseases? It is practically everything we find on our grocer's shelves, in our refrigerators and food cabinets: refined sugar, table salt, white flour, jams, jellies, cookies condensed milk, commercial dairy, butter, canned vegetables, pastries, refined grains products, margarine, and vegetable oils. This includes; the unpredictable ingredients that are in the fast-food chicken, burgers, beverages, and condiments. This also includes the "fine dining" restaurants.

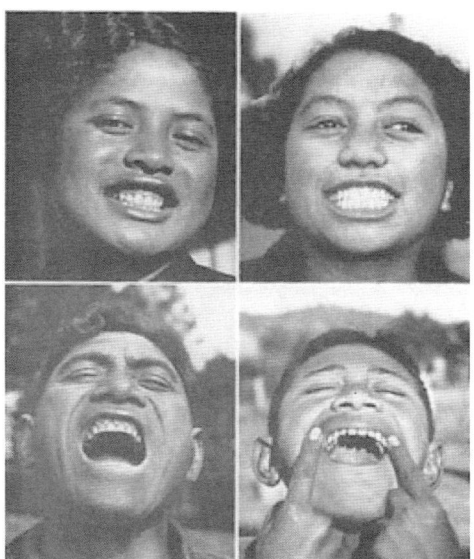

Above: Before the advent of adulterated foods like white flour, white sugar, polished rice, and other refine foods, the indigenous people had the finest dental arches and teeth. Below: After repeated consumption of refine foods, these indigenous people suffered from tooth decay and infections.

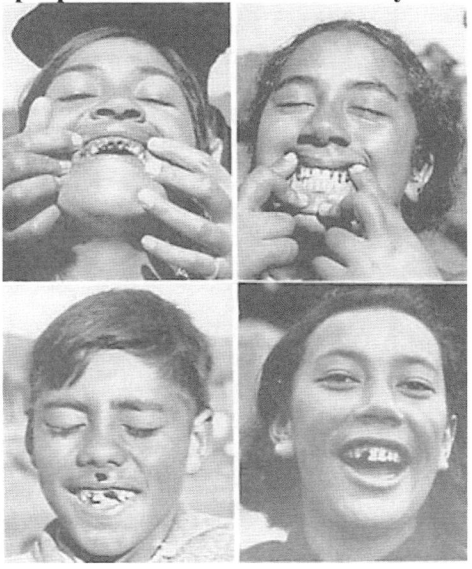

After the topsoil was destroyed, the advent of refined and adulterated foods of commerce became the underlying cause of tooth decay, bone deformities, and other forms of today's mental and physical degeneration among children and adults. Courtesy of Weston Price Foundation and Sally Fallon.

Adulteration is the act of intentionally altering the natural molecular structure of nature made substances that would normally be considered as food. This by a synthetic creation of a mixture of inferior substances that replaces what was already created by nature, thus the natural source loses its organic value. Since the industrial revolution, food adulteration has become one of the most serious problems in modern society. The repeated consumption of adulterated food has been shown to be the underlying causes of gastrointestinal problems like Crohn's diseases, Irritable Bowel Syndrome (IBS), Acid reflux, obesity, psoriasis, diabetes, heart disease, cancer, etc.

Most people are not yet familiar with the term "food adulteration." However, it is certainly important to know just what we are eating. That being said, it's important to know where our food comes from and what ethical practices are used in the manufacturing process of the food that we consume. As the "organically grown" movement expands, more people are becoming aware that there is a problem with what they call food and grocery. Salmonella, Escherichia coli (E. coli) and are now household names because of the carelessness and pathogenic oversights of food manufacture, now contaminated foods, beverages, snacks, and other food matter have become common sources of infection. Among the more common infections that one can get from contaminated foods and drinks are typhoid fever infections, shigellosis or bacillary dysentery, giardiasis, cryptosporidiosis, another salmonellosis, cholera, rotavirus infections, also a variety of worm infestations. Many of the infectious diseases transmitted in food and water can also be acquired directly through the fecal-oral route.

Commercial food-preservation has very extensive use, which often constitutes adulteration. Salt is the classic preservative but is seldom classified as an adulterant. Preservative Agents like salicylic, benzoic, and boric acids, and their sodium salts, formaldehyde, ammonium fluoride, sulfuric acid, and its salts are among the principals of expanding the shelf life of foods on the commercial market.

We are experiencing a new generation of foods not like ever before. The bulk matter or foodstuffs in the commercial arena are now considered as factory foods because these products are often made with multiple processed ingredients, GMO's, gums, flavors, colors, preservatives, and other additives. Some products also include a novel, genetically engineered ingredients like the "heme" secreted from genetically engineered yeast to make fancy meatless burgers and hotdogs.

Various **"processing aids"** are made from organisms (like genetically engineered bacteria, yeast, and algae) that produce proteins, and chemicals to extract proteins. For example, chemicals like hexane are used to extract components of food like proteins (peas, soy, corn) or compounds (from genetically engineered bacteria) to make xanthan gum. Unfortunately, the disclosure of these ingredients is not required and of course, is not labeled on the box, while other processing aids (e.g., bacteria, yeast, algae) also include genetically engineered proteins. Because this secret list of ingredients is not disclosed on-package labeling, it makes the lack of transparency not only mysterious but also potentially dangerous to the "risk-taking consumer."

For hundreds of years, people from different ethnicities and cultures have incorporated plant-based proteins such as tofu into their diets. The problem associated with today's commercialized plant-based menu could be as questionable and as dangerous as the increasingly industrial hazards in cattle and fish factory farming. Though, the lifestyle of vegetarian and vegan can be a very healthy lifestyle by replacing animal proteins with organic produce, whole grains, legumes, and beans. The attempt to mimic animal-based products should be cautioned because of the unpredictable process ranging from animal tissue grown from animal cell cultures with animal serum, to plant proteins produced by genetically engineered corn, algae, and yeast.

One of the modern-day cautions is what we will call "the new magical foods" when the prime ingredient of the meat alternatives contains genetically engineered yeast to produce an actual "plant blood" (leghemoglobin "heme" protein). This is becoming an appeal to the meatless consumer in the fast-food market because of its "bleeding plant-based??"

There is also a very interesting shellfish alternative that also contains genetically engineered algae to produce a protein "algae-based shrimp." Now, there are several other animal replacement products planned for the meatless consumer market that will contain ingredients derived from genetically engineered yeast, including new types of gelatin and egg white replacements.

Whether these commercial foodstuffs are made from genetically engineered yeast or through in vitro processes, this upcoming generation of animal replacement products is manufactured in resource-intensive factories that are not in harmony with nature whatsoever! Altering any natural organism at the genetic level can create unexpected changes in the organism, as well as in the compounds it produces. Therefore, organic plant and natural animal replacement through genetic engineering may pose unforeseen health risks starting at the cellular levels of our body.

GMO'S STANDS IN THE WAY OF REAL FOOD

Genetically engineered crops paved its way into America market in the mid 90s. With the help from the provocateur's of "corporatocracy", product brand didn't require additional labeling, due to their concept of "substantial equivalence," the consumer was none the wiser. At the time, the Food and Drug Administration didn't find it necessary to inform consumers of about the use of GMO's through labeling because they didn't see any significant difference between GMOs and conventional crops.

The vast majority of the Standard American Diet contains, Genetically Modified Ingredients and other synthetic chemicals. In the America, over 80% of all processed foods contain these toxic agents. Be aware of commercial foods and grains like rice, corn and wheat; legumes like soybeans and soy products; vegetable oils, soft drinks; salad dressings; vegetables and fruits; dairy products including eggs; meat, chicken, pork and other animal products; and even infant formula plus a vast array of hidden additives and ingredients in processed foods (like in tomato sauce, ice cream, margarine and peanut butter). Consumers don't know what they're eating because labeling is prohibited, yet the danger is clear. Independently conducted studies show the more of these foods we eat, the greater the potential harm to our health.

According to several reports, experimental studies of genetically engineered foods and their effects in the body are disturbing, to say the least. Biologist David Schubert of the Salk Institute has stated that children are the most likely people to experience the adverse effects of GMOs, noting that apart from adequate safety studies, children become "the experimental animals". In truth, every citizen is a guinea pig when genetically altered organisms are introduced into the food supply without adequate safety studies let alone honest labeling.

Unfortunately, the people are kept in the dark and are part of an uncontrolled, unregulated mass human experiment the results of which are unknown. Yet, these food risks are enormous, it will take years to learn them, and when we finally know it'll be too late to reverse the damage if it's proved conclusively that genetically engineered foods harm human health as growing numbers of independent experts believe. Once GM seeds are introduced to an area, the genie is out of the bottle for keeps. There is nothing known to science today to reverse the contamination already spread over two-thirds of arable US farmland and heading everywhere unless checked.

Today, consumers eat these foods daily without knowing the potential health risks. In 2003, genetically modified foods researcher Jeffrey Smith explained them in his book titled "Seeds of Deception." He revealed that efforts to inform the public have been quashed, reliable science has been buried, and consider what happened to two distinguished scientists - UC Berkeley's Ignacio Chapela and former

Scotland Rowett Research Institute researcher and world's leading lectins and plant genetic modification expert, Arpad Pusztai. They were vilified, hounded, and threatened for their research, and in the case of Pusztai, fired from his job for doing it.

Pusztai, conducted the first ever independent one on GMO's anywhere and was shocked by his findings. It was discovered that the lab rats fed GM potatoes developed smaller livers, hearts, testicles and brains, damaged immune systems, and showed structural changes in their white blood cells making them more vulnerable to infection and disease compared to other rats fed non-GMO potatoes.

It was discovered that the Thymus and spleen was also damaged; enlarged tissues, including the pancreas and intestines; and there were cases of liver atrophy as well as significant proliferation of stomach and intestines cells that could be a sign of greater future risk of cancer. The test results showed up after 10 days of testing, and they persisted after 110 days that's the human equivalent of 10 years.

The shocking discoveries made by Pusztai on GMO's other independent studies were confirmed and published in a 2007 book Jeffery Smith called "Genetic Roulette,: The Documented Health Risks of Genetically Engineered Foods." The book is encyclopedic in depth, an invaluable comprehensive source, and this article reviews some of the shocking data in it.

There are two notable books that highlights the clear and present danger of GMO's and the commercial foods on the market - Jeffrey Smith's **"Genetic Roulette: The Documented Health Risks of Genetically Engineered Foods." "Seeds of Destruction: The Hidden Agenda of Genetic Manipulation."**

Genetically engineered foods saturate our diet today. In the US alone, over 80% of all processed foods contain them. Others include grains like rice, corn and wheat; legumes like soybeans and soy products; vegetable oils, soft drinks; salad dressings; vegetables and fruits; dairy products including eggs; meat, chicken, pork and other animal products; and even infant formula plus a vast array of hidden additives and ingredients in processed foods (like in tomato sauce, ice cream, margarine and peanut butter). Consumers don't know what they're eating because labeling is prohibited, yet the danger is clear. Independently conducted studies show the more of these foods we eat, the greater the potential harm to our health.

To find out more about GMO's, visit website. Prepare to blow chunks, this list is shocking. A few general observations: The availability of Non-GM food vs. GM food is about 50/50. Most "brand name," products and corporate giants genetically modify their foods. Most foods listed under the "non-genetically modified," section are not well known and are not considered "mainstream."

In Search for The Better Vegan Diet

Vegan New Flash!!!

GMO IMPOSSIBLE BURGER POSITIVE FOR CARCINOGENIC GLYPHOSATE
POSTED BY ZEN HONEYCUTT 2726.40GS ON MAY 16, 2019
GMO IMPOSSIBLE BURGER TESTS 11X HIGHER FOR GLYPHOSATE WEED KILLER RESIDUE THAN BEYOND MEAT BURGER

Updated July 8, 2019

A Monsanto trial jury awarded the plaintiffs over $2 billion dollars, for the connection between the glyphosate-based herbicide, Roundup, and their cancer. Today, Moms Across America announces that the Impossible Burger* tested positive for glyphosate. The levels of glyphosate detected in the Impossible burger by Health Research

Institute Laboratories were 11 X higher than the Beyond Meat Burger. The total result (glyphosate and its break down AMPA) was 11.3 ppb. Moms Across America also tested the Beyond Meat Burger and the results were 1 ppb.

"We are shocked to find that the Impossible Burger can have up to 11X higher levels of glyphosate residues than the Beyond Meat Burger according to these samples tested. This new product is being marketed as a solution for "healthy" eating, when in fact 11 ppb of glyphosate herbicide consumption can be highly dangerous. Only 0.1 ppb of glyphosate has been shown to alter the gene function of over 4000 genes in the livers, kidneys and cause severe organ damage in rats. I am gravely concerned that consumers are being misled to believe the Impossible Burger is healthy." stated Zen Honeycutt, Executive Director of Moms Across America.

The Impossible Burger is a new genetically modified (GM) plant-based product that was prominently featured at the Natural Products Expo West. Hundreds of fast food chains and restaurants now serve this new and tasty phenomenon to the meatless enthusiasts. **It does not have to be labeled or described as GM on the menu.** The Impossible Burger is made of GMO soy, which has been shown to cause organ damage in animal studies and has been shown to be significantly different from non-GMO soy. The GM ingredients of the Impossible Burger, which includes a genetically modified yeast and GM soy leghemoglobin proteins, 46 of which are undisclosed and untested, are even more concerning to many consumers than the long-term health effects from glyphosate because of the reported immediate allergic reaction potential, which is acknowledged by the manufacturer. The part of the genetically modified soy used in the Impossible Burger has never before been allowed in the human food supply and has not been properly safety tested.

Although the leghemoglobin soy is claimed to be "identical to soy heme which has been consumed for thousands of years", the following question posed by Consumers Report's Michael Hansen has never been answered: "How could the heme in the Impossible Burger be 'identical' to the heme humans have been consuming for hundreds of thousands of years in meat and other foods if you genetically engineer it?"

Soy, sugar, and cotton are commonly sprayed with glyphosate herbicides as a drying agent before harvesting. The "natural" product - *which could contain more than 80% GMO ingredients-* also contains potatoes, which may be genetically modified, and could also absorb the chemical through the soil after pre-planting herbicide applications. Glyphosate does not wash, dry, or cook-off and was listed on the Prop 65 California EPA list of carcinogens in 2017.

Glyphosate herbicides have not only been proven to be carcinogenic, but they are also neurotoxic, endocrine disrupting, cause DNA damage and liver disease at ultra-low levels, lower than what was found in the Impossible Burger.

According to the American Liver Foundation over 100 million people in America, (that's about 1/3 of Americans) are estimated to have non-alcoholic fatty liver disease.

The impact glyphosate and GMO have on products can no longer be ignored. Honeycutt considers, "If Bayer goes bankrupt due to the outcome of about 14,000 lawsuits filed against them for the carcinogenic effects of glyphosate herbicides, who will become liable for harm to the public? I wonder if it will be retailers and food brands who continue to expose the public to toxic glyphosate herbicides."

Moms Across America calls upon consumers to ask their restaurant and grocery stores not to sell this product and to sell/buy/eat whole, organic, plant-based, *real* food instead. They also request public comments be made to the EPA to cancel the license for glyphosate. Glyphosate herbicides have been severely restricted or banned in 34 countries.

Moms Across America hopes that companies like Impossible Foods are not only honest about their ingredients and make safe food- but that they work with other food manufacturers and farmers to pressure the EPA to stop allowing toxic chemicals like glyphosate to poison the food supply.

Will Impossible Foods ask the EPA to ban glyphosate and prevent the contamination of their product?

Moms Across America is a 501c3 non-profit whose mission is to educate mother and others to transform the food industry and environment, creating healthy communities together. Their motto is "*Empowered Moms, Healthy Kids.*"

According to the ingredient investigation, here is are the Impossible Burgers list of Ingredients: (All ingredients in red could be GMO OR sprayed with glyphosate herbicides as a drying agent) Water, Soy Protein Concentrate, Coconut Oil, Sunflower Oil, Natural Flavors, 2% or less of: Potato Protein, Methylcellulose (possibly from cotton), Yeast Extract, Cultured Dextrose, Food Starch Modified, Soy Leghemoglobin, Salt, Soy Protein Isolate, Mixed Tocopherols (Vitamin E), Zinc Gluconate, Thiamine Hydrochloride (Vitamin B1), Sodium Ascorbate (Vitamin C), Niacin, Pyridoxine Hydrochloride (Vitamin B6), Riboflavin (Vitamin B2), Vitamin B12.

PROMOTION OF GM IMPOSSIBLE BURGER AT EXPO WEST BRANDED 'DECEPTIVE'

By
Jim Manson
April 18, 2019

THE PRESENCE OF THE GMO-DERIVED IMPOSSIBLE BURGER AT THE 2019 YEAR'S NATURAL PRODUCTS EXPO WEST EVENT – THE WORLD'S LARGEST NATURAL FOOD TRADE SHOW – HAS BEEN CRITICISED BY PROMINENT US INDUSTRY INSIDERS AND FOOD CAMPAIGNERS.

POULTRY PROBLEM

JUST HOW BIG ARE TODAY'S CHICKENS?
Average weight of chicken breeds at 56 days old

1957
905g

1978
1,808g

2005
4,202g

At one point or another, some of us may have heard that poultry is injected with hormones to promote growth. Some concerns consuming such tainted poultry products could lead to the development of cancer, as well as early menarche and premature sexual development in young girls.

An epidemic of precocious development in Puerto Rican children.
Sáenz de Rodríguez CA, Bongiovanni AM, Conde de Borrego L.

An alarming incidence of premature sexual development has been reported in Puerto Rico during the last seven years. A significant increment of premature the larche, premature pubarche, prepubertal breast enlargement in boys, and precocious pseudo puberty in girls has been observed throughout the island. Several food specimens analyzed by chromatography and cytosol receptor assay revealed significant levels of estradiol equivalent in some meat samples. We suspect that early sexual development is caused by exogenous estrogen contamination in the food ingested by the children and by their mothers. J. Pediatr.. 1985 Sep;107(3):393-6.

Chicken Wings and Ovarian Cysts

Do growth hormones used in poultry cause ovarian cysts in women who consume chicken wings?

Are you a woman with a history of ovarian cysts? Do you also enjoy eating delicious and spicy foods like chicken wings? If you answered "yes" to these questions, then you'll want to continue reading on to get our top three reasons for why you should stop eating chicken wings right now. Many women who have ovarian cysts – or who deal with the chronic pain of ovarian cysts but haven't been diagnosed – may not realize how spicy foods such as chicken wings can inflame their cysts and cause discomfort. Read our guide listing the three top tips for why chicken wings should be out of your diet for good – and feel relief and health in the future:

Commercial Chickens Are On Steroids

Chickens sold on the mainstream market have been injected with steroids. The only way to avoid "steroid injected chickens is to buy only free-range, grass-fed chicken, which can be expensive. Factory Farmed chickens receive an injection in their wing during the growth process, so the highest concentration of steroids is in the wings —

which is what consumers are be eating! Steroids can cause ovarian cysts.

According to researchers, high amounts of artificial sugar often can be found in the sauces used to coat chicken wings, which it adds to the health problem. These sauces are used to marinate the chicken for hours at a time, which means that one is getting a higher dose of sugar per serving.

For those who indulge in the chicken wing cuisine, we suggested chickens that are caged-free, organic, or free-range. Chemical-free chickens can be purchased in the health food grocery store and some chain stores. Read the labels when purchasing store-bought or pre-made chicken wings. When preparing wings at home, select a natural source of sweeteners and natural sauce that creates a more wholesome, healthier meal. This will reduce the risk of toxicity.

DES AND THE RISKS OF GROWTH HORMONES

As early as the 1930s, it was realized that cows injected with material drawn from bovine (cow) pituitary glands (hormone secreting organ) produced more milk. Later, the bovine growth hormone (bGH) from the pituitary glands was found to be responsible for this effect. However, at that time, technology did not exist to harvest enough of this material for large-scale use in animals.

In the 1980s, it became possible to produce large quantities of pure bGH by using recombinant DNA technology. In 1993, the Food and Drug Administration (FDA) approved the recombinant bovine growth hormone (rbGH), also known as bovine somatotropin (rbST) for use in dairy cattle. Recent estimates by the manufacturer of this hormone indicate that 30% of the cows in the United States (US) may be treated with rbGH.

What Type of Hormones Are Used In Today's Meat and Dairy Industry?

According to Cornell University, there are six different kinds of steroid hormones that are currently approved by FDA for use in food production in the US: **estradiol, progesterone, testosterone, zeranol, trenbolone acetate, and melengestrol acetate.** Estradiol and progesterone are natural female sex hormones; testosterone is the natural male sex hormone; zeranol, trenbolone acetate and melengesterol acetate are synthetic growth promoters (hormone-like chemicals that can make animals grow faster). Currently, federal regulations allow these hormones to be used on growing cattle and sheep, but not on poultry (chickens, turkeys, ducks) or hogs (pigs). The above hormones are not as useful in increasing weight gain of poultry or hogs. The FDA does allow the use of the protein hormone rbGH to increase milk production in **dairy cattle.** Accord to the report, this protein hormone is not used on **beef cattle.**

THE OBESOGEN THEORY and THE EPIDEMIC OF OBESITY

"Obesogens are compounds that disrupt the function and development of adipose tissue or the normal metabolism of lipids, leading to an increased risk of obesity and associated diseases.[1] Obesogens are defined functionally as chemicals that inappropriately alter lipid homeostasis to promote adipogenesis and lipid accumulation."[2]

Right now, between 12-13 million U.S. children are obese – that's one out of every six children – and millions more are overweight, with the CDC estimating that more than 30% of children 2–19 years old fall into this category. Obese children have an increased risk of high blood pressure, high cholesterol, sleep apnea, bone and joint problems, as well as asthma and type 2 diabetes. They're at increased risk of bullying and even mental illnesses like depression. It's a shame that more than 200,000 American children have type 2 diabetes.

Obesity Global Statistics

- **Worldwide obesity has nearly doubled since 1980.**
- **In 2008, 35% of adults (>20yrs old) were overweight and 11% were obese.**
- **65% of the world's population live in countries where overweight and obesity kills more people than underweight.**

Organotins

Organotins also include chemicals like tributyltin (TBT), a wood preservative and marine antifouling paint and fungicide, which is now banned, in part because of its habit of turning female snails into males. TBT's obesogenic effects are thought to be due largely to its ability to bind with hormone receptors called PPARγ (peroxisome proliferator-activated receptor gamma) receptors that play an important role in turning pre-fat cells into mature fat cells, a process known as adipogenesis.

This binding to the PPARγ receptor also affects fat storage and glucose metabolism. It also impacts other hormone receptors, such as retinoid X receptor (RXR), and the thyroid gland. Thus, TBT promotes obesity by increasing the number of fat cells, the storage of fat in existing fat cells, changing the metabolic rate, altering hormonal control of appetite or satiety, or shifting energy balance to calorie storage, meaning it can either directly or indirectly lead to increased fat accumulation and weight gain.

In one study, showed that *tributyltin* and *triphenyltin* developed more and bigger fat cells. The animals treated with these chemicals didn't eat a different diet than the ones that didn't get fat. They ate the same diet, but still got fatter. **Obesogens'** effects are not strictly limited to fat metabolism and weight gain. They also affect fertility, particularly in males, increase the risk of genital malformation, reduce male birth rates, trigger precocious puberty, impair immune function, and increase the risk of miscarriage, behavior problems, brain abnormalities, various cancers, and cardiovascular disease.

Prenatal obesogen exposure has been shown to tilt a type of stem cell in the body in the direction of fat cell development at the expense of other cell types (bone or muscle as examples). Thus, *in utero* and early postnatal obesogen exposure predisposes a child to obesity by influencing all aspects of adipose tissue growth, starting from multipotential stem cells and ending with mature adipocytes. Some evidence suggests that the intrauterine environment has a significant and lasting effect on the long-term health of the growing fetus and the development of metabolic disease in later life. Metabolic diseases have been associated with epigenetic changes that occur without changes in the DNA sequence, such as cytosine methylation of DNA (these epigenetic modifications can be reversed by the addition of methyl donors, such as dietary folic acid, which I explain in greater detail at the end of this article).

we can't continue to frame the obesity discussion simply in terms of calories in and calories out, or by only examining the nutritional content of food. Given the proliferation of industrial pollutants, a paradigm shift in thinking is needed. A heightened understanding of the effects of these endocrine-disrupting chemicals is key to freeing ourselves from weight gain. Without it, we remain stuck in the insidious cycle of weight loss and weight gain.

How Can We Protect Ourselves from Obesogens?

Try only purchasing plastic items you really need, which may help keep BPA out of your house dust and off your skin, not to mention help eliminate it from our waterways. I never put plastic in the oven or the microwave. Heat damages plastic and increases leaching. Avoiding plastic-wrapped meat is also a good idea since most varieties contain mostly PVC (the plastic wrap most folks use at home is increasingly made from polyethylene). PVC contains phthalates that, according to animal studies, may lower testosterone levels. In humans, lower testosterone leads to weight gain as well as a decrease in muscle mass and sex drive. Go to a butcher who uses paper instead.

Despite all we know about the underlying causes of extreme weight gain, many scientists remain unconvinced, even ignoring other critical factors affecting the nation's obesity spike. I'm still surprised how few scientists, and physicians, pay attention to, or even know about the most significant factor underlying extreme weight gain: A class of natural and synthetic endocrine-disrupting chemicals, which we know as *obesogens*. Bruce Blumberg, professor of developmental and cell biology and pharmaceutical sciences at the University of California, Irvine first coined the term "obesogen" and it is any chemical that promotes weight gain by:

- Increasing the number of fat cells.
- Increasing fat storage in existing fat cells.
- Changing the metabolic rate.
- Altering hormonal control of appetite or satiety.
- Shifting energy balance to favor the storage of calories.

Consume a diet high in folic acid.

There are now a number of studies that show that consuming a diet high in folic acid (dark leafy greens, asparagus, broccoli, citrus fruits, beans, peas, lentils, seeds and nuts, just to name a few) can actually reverse *in utero*-induced epigenetic changes in adult animals. When attempting to lose weight, these items are a definite "plus" in the diet and should help with overcoming some obesogen-induced disadvantages. If necessary, you can also add a high-quality folic acid supplement. But please be sure to check the manufacturer. Not all brands have equal bioavailability

Keep protein intake high when dieting.

One of the reasons why high protein, low carbohydrate diets are so successful is that they may reverse some *in-utero* epigenetic changes. This may be one of the reasons why people who try Atkins, Paleo, and other high-protein, low-carb diets have early success.

Try to maintain a diet with adequate L-methionine.

Once again, animal data show that adults with previous epigenetic changes can reverse these changes by supplementing with methionine, an amino acid that favors DNA methylation. Foods high in this amino acid include eggs, lean beef, lamb, Brazil nuts, parmesan cheese, and soybeans (even if roasted).

The source of this information was gathered from Steward Lanky, **M.D.**
Stewart Lonky, M.D., is a physician, toxicologist, and biomedical engineer. www.stewartlonky.com

The cereal and snack that you consume the most may contain Glyphosate and other human carcinogens. Consider investing in better health and buy only Bona fide, certified organic or consult with holistic product specialist.

INGREDIENTS: POTATOES, VEGETABLE OIL (CONTAINS ONE OR MORE OF THE FOLLOWING: CANOLA, CORN, COTTONSEED, SAFFLOWER, OR SUNFLOWER), SEA SALT.

ALLERGENS: NONE

MANUFACTURED IN A FACILITY THAT ALSO PROCESSES MILK PRODUCTS.

WARNING: CONSUMING THIS PRODUCT CAN EXPOSE YOU TO CHEMICALS INCLUDING ACRYLAMIDE, WHICH ARE KNOWN TO THE STATE OF CALIFORNIA TO CAUSE CANCER. FOR MORE INFORMATION GO TO WWW.P65WARNINGS.CA.GOV/FOOD.

THE BUREAU OF CHEMISTRY
A Department that Really Protected The Consumer

Around 1902. Dr. Harvey Wiley the Chief Inspector of the Bureau of Chemistry and group of healthy men volunteered as the "Poison Squad." William R. Carter [standing] would be in charge of the food preparation. These men would volunteer to taste the effects of new foods of commerce. This agency would confirm the potential risk of adulterated foods.

Unlabeled stimulants, artificial sweeteners in soft drinks., growth hormones in meat and milk, plastic shavings and wood chips in fast foods, formaldehyde – used as a common food preservative. The American food industry was once a wild and dangerous place for the consumer, and still is in 2019, thanks to the provocateurs and their chemical engineers of synthetic additives.

In 1883, **Harvey W. Wiley, M.D.**, was appointed chief chemist at **USDA**. Wiley devoted his career to raising public awareness of problems with adulterated food, developing standards for food processing, and campaigning for the Pure Food and Drugs Act, also known as the "Wiley Act." [1]

Back in the 1880s, when Wiley began his 50-year crusade for pure foods, America's marketplace was flooded with poor, often harmful products. With almost no government controls, unscrupulous manufacturers tampered with products, substituting cheap ingredients for those represented on labels: Honey was diluted with glucose syrup; olive oil was made with cottonseed; and "soothing syrups" given to babies were laced with morphine.

All through the 1880s and 1890s, pure-food bills were introduced into Congress--largely through his work-- and all were killed. Powerful lobbies had established themselves. To bring his cause to the public, and with a budget of $5,000, Wiley organized in 1902 a volunteer group of healthy young men, called the Poison Squad, who tested the effects of chemicals and adulterated foods on themselves. Women banded together, notably in the Federated Women's Clubs, for political clout. Major canners became supporters of the legislation and voluntarily abandoned the use of questionable chemicals. Finally, the battle was won on June 30, 1906, when President Theodore Roosevelt signed the Pure Food and Drugs Act, largely written by Wiley, who was then appointed to oversee its administration.

Above: *Wiley called these his "hygienic table studies." But they soon became known popularly as **"the Poison Squad."** Credit: The U.S. Food and Drug Administration/<u>Flickr</u>/Public Domain*

On the previous page, **William R. Carter** was the waiter and cook for the "**Poison Squad.**" When access to Harvey Wiley was cut off, reporters began to interview Carter through the kitchen window to get each day's menu. He was popular with the men, who described him as "courteous and tactful" even as "appetites were sometimes ravenous and sometimes rebellious and often tempers were short and strained." Carter later became a lab technician and retired in April 1946 with the longest tenure of any of the FDA's "charter members." Credit: The U.S. Food and Drug Administration/Flickr/Public Domain

Dr. Harvey Wiley. Credit: U.S. Food and Drug Administration/**Flickr**/Public Domain

AFTER 29 YEARS... When he died in 1930, at age 86, Harvey Wiley was given a patriot's funeral at Arlington Cemetery. [2]. The battle had been won--but not the war. Wiley had many adversaries in Congress and in the food and patent-medicine industries, and in 1912 he left his government post. A headline of the day read: **WOMEN WEEP AS WATCHDOG OF THE KITCHEN QUITS.**

Because of the acceleration of patents, safety assessments specific to these genetic engineering techniques could be inadequate because there is no mandatory regulatory oversight in place to conduct several years of testing and observation in human consumption such as the "poison squad that was once used under the auspices of Dr. Harvey Wiley and the U.S. Bureau of Chemistry back in the early 1900's.

Don't Forget About Acrylamide

Food should deliver all the ingredients necessary for the organism to function properly. Organic and inorganic compounds present in food are used by the organism as energetic, regulatory and/or building substances. Unfortunately, food consumed by people is often a source of harmful substances. Acrylamide (AA) is one of the most common toxins in food. It occurs in food containing high concentrations of hydrocarbons subjected to high temperature (Mottram *et al.* 2002). High concentration of acrylamide may be found in food products such as potato chips, fried potatoes, cornflakes or bread. Thus, acrylamide is present in everyday diet of most people. To make matters worse, some of the products containing acrylamide are attractive to children and young people.

Acrylamide, whose presence in some foods was discovered in 2002, occurs naturally. It is not added to food, nor is it part of food packaging. The major food sources of acrylamide include French fries, French toast, Grill Cheese, potato chips, baked goods, canned black olives and coffee. Levels vary depending on the manufacturer, cooking time and temperature.

Genotoxicity and cytotoxicity of acrylamide

Oxidative imbalance induced by exposure to acrylamide may lead to cytotoxic and genotoxic effects. Free radicals may cause damage to mitochondria and other cell organelles. They induce apoptosis and cause oxidation of DNA bases, leading to fragmentation of the double strand. All of these may cause cell death or neoplastic transformation (Valko *et al.* 2004).

The ROS related mechanism of cytotoxicity and/or mutations is attributed to all the factors capable of inducing oxidative stress.

In 2001, the Scientific Committee on Toxicity, Ecotoxicity and the Environment demonstrated its neurotoxicity, genotoxicity, carcinogenicity and reproductive toxicity (Keramat *et al.* 2011, Carere 2006).

Here is a list of real food, along with some notes about what to look for when shopping for real food:

- **Fruits & Vegetables**: local, seasonal and/or organic when possible.
- **Whole Grains**: must be 100% whole grain; ancient, gluten- and wheat-free grains preferred.
- **Beans & Legumes**: including green beans, snap peas and lentils; soaking helps with digestion, BPA-free cans when possible.
- **Seeds & Nuts**: raw, unsalted, unsweetened and/or organic when possible (sprouting helps with digestion).
- **Spices, Herbs & Seasonings**: fresh/dry/ground; minimally processed and organic when possible.
- **Unrefined, Virgin, Cold-Pressed Oils & Fats**: coconut oil, olive oil, grass-fed butter, ghee, palm shortening and rendered animal fats, like tallow and lard.
- **Natural, Unrefined Sweeteners**: honey, maple syrup, coconut palm sugar and dates (raw when possible).
-

Non-Vegetarians (For those who still indulge in Animal Protein, should only eat sparingly) Reducing your meat consumption will allow your body to thrive further.

- **Meat & Seafood**: wild, grass-fed, pastured and/or humanely raised without hormones or antibiotics when possible.
- **Dairy & Eggs**: full-fat, grass-fed, pasture-raised when possible (raw and/or unpasteurized preferred).

CHAPTER 4
THE CONNECTION BETWEEN FOOD, CHEMICALS, AND CANDIDA

It is estimated that 85% of Americans have a Candida Yeast infection. Most people don't realize that they have a Candida Yeast overgrowth, and most men think that only women develop candida/yeast infection. Wrong, ladies have your significant other get checked out. The **"Standard American Bulk Matter"** *such as the* **"five whites Sins" (White Flour, White Sugar, White Potatoes, White Rice, Dairy) hydrogenated oils, farmed factory meats, fast foods, inorganic produce, makes any one a candidate for candida.** *This includes; and chemically produced, soaps, bath gels, fragrance sprays, toxic tampons and sanitary napkins.*

Candida (YEAST INFECTION) has become a significant crisis within women throughout America within the last 30 years in recent decades. Because of the inflammatory nature, candida/slash yeast infection proliferates annoying heat, thus creating itching of the vaginal area, and that's just the beginning. More serious are the gastro-intestinal problems that it causes and a wide range of diseases and conditions when it invades the bloodstream. More often than not, we may not even realize that our health problems are due to Candida and other microbes and parasites. Autoimmune diseases, allergies, asthma, arthritis, chronic fatigue, anxiety and depression, hyperactivity, and attention deficit are all closely related to Candida and other microbes. From an eastern perspective, the presence of Candida can be a result of spleen imbalance, Liver Stagnation, Kidney imbalance, Phlegm Obstruction, Toxic Blood Heat, or even damp heat in the large intestine.

What is Candida Albicans?

Candida is a part of our natural Microflora or Microorganisms that generally reside in our bodies. It can be mostly found in our GI tract, Mouth, and Vagina. Candida Albicans is the most common cause of fungal infections in humans.

Thrush is a form of infection caused by Candida.
There are many different types of infections caused by Candida Albicans, Here are some of the most common one:
1: Urinary Tract Infection (UTI), produced by taking several courses of Antibiotics or Medical devices such as a catheter.
2: Diabetes caused by a weekend Immune System, which includes infection and inflammation within the pancreas, spleen, or both Symptoms can consist of: Increased need to urinate, painful or burning sensation when urinating, abdominal pressure and pain or pelvic, also blood in the urine.
3. Genital Yeast Infection
Usually, an excellent Probiotic complex keeps the amount of Candida in the area under control. However, if the Probiotic levels are disrupted, Candida can overgrow and cause an infection.

Believe it or not, one may also develop a genital candida infection after having oral sex.

Although Healthy individuals can get Genital Infections, some groups are at higher risk than others:
- Individuals that have taken antibiotics recently
- Individuals with uncontrolled Diabetes
- Individuals with Suppressed Immune System
- Pregnant women
- Individuals are on Hormone Therapy or taking Oral contraceptives

What to look for;
- Burning while having sex or urinating
- Itchy or painful in or around the vagina
- Vaginal discharge that could be watery, or thick and white and having an offensive odor
- Rash on the Penis
- Rash around the Vagina

Candida can also infect your skin:
- Wearing tight or synthetic undergarments, poor hygiene, not changing underwear frequently.

Another major contributing factor to the rise of Candida in the women of America is the toxic presence within sanitary napkins, tampons, commercial soaps, and fragrances. Though the commercial sanitary napkins appear to be white, clean, and pristine, the inorganic products contain dioxin, plastic fibers, chlorine, inorganic cotton, and even old newspaper pulp. This type of material causes positive ions, which breed bacteria and sets off a disharmonizing PH level in the vaginal tract, thus exasperating the colony of candida. This is why it is not an option to invest in a natural product brand sold in the health food stores.

When the natural state of intestinal flora is compromised by antibiotics and antibacterial prescription other drugs, Candida can significantly increase and occur in the intestinal tract. This tends to cause gastrointestinal symptoms with digestive problems, discomfort, and bloating. The infection can quickly spread to other parts of the gastrointestinal tract, causing thrush around the anus, inside the mouth and vagina.

Vaginal yeast infections, also called Vaginal Thrush, cause intense vaginal itching, burning during urination, and often a cheesy white or yellow vaginal discharge. In the mouth, it may form a white tender and easily bleeding cover on cheeks and tongue. In mild cases, it may just result in cracks in the corners of the lips. It can also be a cause of canker sores and bad breath.

If left untreated, Candida soon develops a new form with long, burrowing legs (rhizoids). The condition starts growing into and through the mucous membranes of the intestinal tract and may cause severe pain. Gradually the abdominal wall deteriorates and allows partially digested proteins and the Candida organism itself to travel into the bloodstream and cause toxicity and immune reactions. This condition is called Leaky Gut Syndrome and is connected with Irritable Bowel Syndrome or Inflammatory Bowel Disease, Crohn's Disease, Ulcerative Colitis, food disharmony, and multiple allergies. Other microbes and parasites are often present as well.

Candida and related fungi or mycoplasmas are the underlying factor in autoimmune diseases, such as lupus erythematosus, multiple sclerosis, rheumatoid arthritis, Raynaud's syndrome, scleroderma, and thyroid diseases. Also, most or all children with hyperactivity and attention deficit disorder seem to be affected by fungus overgrowth. Candida overgrowth is the leading cause of the multiple allergies that trigger hyperactive periods and short attention spans. It is similar to asthma and eczema, which also commonly have candida as the underlying primary cause.

The toxicity of candida to the nervous system is primarily due to the excessive production of acetaldehyde. This substance is formed when yeast cells metabolize sugars, and oxygen is deficient. Acetaldehyde can also develop from ingested alcohol. Depending on other contributing factors, candida can manifest with different symptoms in different bodies. You may have any combination of these yeast-related symptoms, and in mild cases, you may not even notice anything. Furthermore, these symptoms may be due to other causes and illnesses, as well. As a group, most at risk of developing candida infections are diabetics, pregnant women, and obese individuals.

A Suggested Candida Protocol

You must avoid White bleached simple carbohydrates, eat Several servings of Organic fresh green leafy vegetables each day, Drink a half Gallon of High-quality Alkaline Water, avoid sweets, candy bars, cookies, cakes, donuts, and all refined products. Drink Organic unsweetened 100% Cranberry juice diluted with water, 32 oz. a day, unless otherwise not advised by your physician.

Take high-quality Organic Vegan Vitamin supplements in addition to a parasite cleanse to empower your immune system to get rid of the infections people who have taken the supplements listed below, have experienced quick recovery, followed by an Organic diet.

IMMUNO PLEX+PLUS by Parsi Herbs • Hanna Kroeger (Rascal)
BRAIN COCKTAIL+PLUS by Parsi Herbs• Black Walnut and Wormwood.
SUPER BODY ZIBA+PLUS by Parsi Herbs
Extra Virgin Coconut Oil (internally)
SUPER MEAL+PLUS
OXY PARSI+PLUS by Parsi Herbs

Detox formulas and Antifungals

Parsi Herbs; Formula
Grapefruit Seed Extract.
Clarkia (Black-Walnut extract, Cloves extract, Wormwood extract)
Extra-Virgin Coconut Oil
Colloidal Silver (500ppm)
Echinacea/Golden Seal/Pau D' Arco teas
Garlic
Clear Heat (**Health Concerns**)
Astra Isatis (**Health Concerns**).
Diatomaceous Earth (DE) (Food grade only!!)
Cape Aloe (**Priority-One Professional line**) or Aloe Vera Juice
Coconut Oil (Virgin/unprocessed)
20-100 billion professional probiotics
L-Glutamine powder
Quercetin (**Allergy** Research)
Artmensia (Allergy Research).
Super Foods Acai, Goji, Chlorella, Spirulina
35% Food Grade Hydrogen Peroxide (see special instructions, it is considered a Hazardous Material) So use with caution.
Raw Pumpkin Seeds
Camu Camu or from a non-GMO corn source. Professional lines:
Pure Encapsulation, Allergy Research, Doctor's Research Magnesium Life extension, Now, Natures Life, Douglas Labs, Doctor's Research, Priority-One, Thorne, Innate Response Mega Foods, Protocols for Life, Metagenics, Amazing Grass CV Sciences.

CHAPTER 5
WHAT'S NOT SO PRETTY ABOUT COSMETICS AND VANITY PRODUCTS

"If you use commercial shampoo, leg shaving cream, deodorant, lotions hair dyes, eyeliners, lipstick, blush, cosmetic care, and soaps, you are likely exposing yourself to estrogenic chemicals daily. One type of estrogen mimic called nonylphenols created during the breakdown of certain chemicals found in shampoos, hair dyes, and leg shaving cream. Nonylphenols are persistent in the environment suspected of creating health, the State of infertility, and reproductive development in both men and women.

Long-term exposure also influences the proliferation of breast tissue, possibly leading to a higher risk of developing cancer of breast cancer, uterus, and ovaries; thus, it will have a similar impact on men as well increasing their risk of breast and prostate cancer.

Mineral oil, Sodium laureth sulphate, Propylene glycol, shampoo, spray deodorant, commercial, sodium fluoride. This chemicals are full of carcinogens and are so toxic that they cause liver, kidney abnormalities and causes cancer. These products are the base ingredient in you soaps, hair shampoo, body lotion, makeup, toiletries and toothpaste and this products are marginally making you ill.

Over that last several decades, personal care products have indeed appeared to be poisoning your body with parabens are another type of xenoestrogen that was commonly apart of commercial shampoo and conditioner, but still could be lurking in the bathroom. Though these preservatives are phased out of personal care products, the damage from years of use has already wreaked havoc on the physiology, therefore requiring particular natural detoxification.

Many manufacturers still use them in all sorts of commercial products—even though studies show they have estrogenic potencies comparable to bisphenol-A. Avoid any products that contain methyl-, ethyl-, and propyl- or butyl-parabens. Phthalates (pronounced "thay-lates") are another class of estrogen mimics. These chemicals are found in colognes, deodorants, hair gels, and body lotions, long-term exposure is suspected of causing damage to the kidneys, liver, and reproductive organs. Check the ingredient label and avoid any product that contains dibutyl phthalate or diethyl phthalate. Another product packed with estrogenic chemicals in the popular sunscreen. In a widely publicized study, researchers at the Swiss University of Zurich tested six common compounds in sunscreen. They found that five of the chemicals (benzophenone-3, homosalate, 4-methyl-benzylidene camphor (4-MBC), octyl-methoxycinnamate, and octyl-dimethyl-PABA) these created a strong estrogen presence and caused cancer cells to accelerate more rapidly than usual.

More than 10,000 ingredients are allowed for use in personal care products -- and the average woman is immediately exposed to at least 20% of those ingredients daily according to a 2009 British study that looked at the routines of over 2,000 women. The mass public has very little information about the health effects of these chemicals. More than 90% have never been tested for their impact on human health, and complete toxicity data are available for only 7% of them.

Some personal care products contain chemicals that are linked to cancer, birth defects, and reproductive diseases. While the US FDA bans nine ingredients from cosmetics - the E.U. has banned over 1,000 due to health concerns.

Some FD&C colors are carcinogenic or contain impurities that have been shown to cause cancer when applied to the skin. Allergens and irritants are suspected carcinogen, its compounds and derivatives include triethanolamine (TEA), which can be contaminated with nitrosamines. Nitrosamines have been shown to cause cancer in laboratory animals. Animal studies have shown that carcinogens, reproductive toxins to exacerbate asthma and other respiratory ailments.

Hazardous to the reproductive system, other effects include anemia and irritation of the skin, eyes, nose, and throat. EGPE, EGME, EGEE, DEGBE, PGME, DPGME, these are associated with the chemical base name "methyl.". [Strong animal and human evidence] Lead damages the nervous system, leading to decreased learning ability and behavioral deficits.

Mercury, believe it or not, is an actual component is a body and personal care. It is toxic to physical development, as well as to the nervous system promoting damage to the respiratory system, the kidneys, and gastrointestinal and reproductive systems. Other constituents of mercury, Methyl-, ethyl-, propyl-, butyl-, isobutyl- and different parabens have shown hormonal activity. The most common preservatives used in cosmetics. Recently found in tissue samples from human breast tumors. Propylparaben affects sperm production in juvenile rats.

[Suggestive animal and human evidence] PPD are mutagenic and reasonably anticipated to be a human carcinogen. It has been banned in Europe. It is also linked to skin irritations and respiratory disorders. [Compelling animal evidence] liver and kidney lesions: reproductive abnormalities, including testicular atrophy, altered development of reproductive tissues, and subtle effects on sperm production (maybe through endocrine disruption); cell line transformations; and cancers, including those of the liver, kidney, and mononuclear cell leukemia. These effects are generally quantitatively, though not qualitatively different between phthalates. The developing male reproductive system appears to be sensory organs. [Strong animal evidence; suggestive human evidence; some children evidence through exposure via medical devices]. The cosmetics industry says it is safe to put toxic chemicals into personal care products because the amount in each product is too small to matter.

According to the FDA's Office of Cosmetics and Colors, the government agency that regulates cosmetics, "...a cosmetic manufacturer may use almost any raw material as a cosmetic ingredient and market the product without an approval from FDA" (FDA 1999). While some cosmetic ingredients may appear to be benign, others can cause or suspected of causing harmful health effects such as cancer, mutations, and allergic reactions, respiratory problems as well as developmental and reproductive problems.

According to the CDC, everyone is exposed to phthalates 5, a family of chemicals commonly used in cosmetic products, food containers, wraps, and synthetic seals. Though evidence from animal studies indicates that phthalates may affect reproduction, growth, and development, conscious people can certainly see the difference in the growth and development of young people. The CDC also tested for exposure to heavy metals with well-known health effects such as lead and mercury that can cross the placenta and can damage the fetal brain, as well as affect the nervous system of growing children and even adults.

The skin is a highly absorbent organ, and toxins absorbed directly through the skin bypass the liver detoxifying enzyme system & go straight into the bloodstream. So, every potentially toxic chemical in personal body care or hygiene will wreak havoc. U.S. Food Drug & Cosmetic Act 1 defines cosmetics as "1) products intended to be rubbed, poured, sprinkled, or sprayed on, introduced into, or otherwise applied to the human body or any part thereof for cleansing, beautifying, promoting attractiveness, or altering the appearance, and (2) articles intended for use as a component of any such articles; except that such term shall not include soap." This definition includes a myriad of products used by men and women: skin-care creams, lotions, powders and sprays, perfumes, lipsticks, fingernail polishes, eye, and facial make-up, permanent waves, hair colors, deodorants, baby products, bath oils, bubble baths, and mouthwashes.

According to industry estimates, on any given day, a consumer may use as many as 25 different cosmetic products containing more than 200 different chemical compounds. Almost exclusively, a self-policing industry safety committee, the Cosmetic Ingredient Review (CIR) 2 panel, evaluates the toxicity of product ingredients. Did you know that testing is voluntary, controlled by the manufacturers, and many ingredients in cosmetics products are not safety tested at all? 89% of 10,500 ingredients used in personal care products have not been evaluated for safety by the CIR or anyone else (FDA 2000, CIR 2003). In the Skin, Deep investigation3 by the Environmental Working Group, 99.6 percent of the 7,500 products examined contain one or more ingredients never assessed for potential health impacts by the CIR.

The absence of government oversight 4 for this industry leads to companies routinely marketing products with ingredients that are poorly studied, not studied at all, or worse, known to pose potentially dangerous health risks: cancer, birth defects, reproductive and developmental problems, allergies and respiratory ailments, and other health problems on the rise in the U.S. Many of these chemicals have been detected in our bodies and children, even human breast milk.

THE TOXIC SIDE OF NAIL FASHION

When nail care products claim to be free of unsafe chemicals, despite how the label reads, just the opposite is often exact. In May of 2011, staff from the Department of Toxic Substance Control (DTSC) conducted a limited-scale sampling of nail products offered for sale in the San Francisco Bay Area. Nail products are known to contain toxic chemicals, such as dibutyl phthalate (DBP), toluene, and formaldehyde, that are healthy and safety concerns for about 121,000 nail salon workers in California. DBP and toluene are known to the State of California as developmental toxins. Formaldehyde is a known carcinogen.

These three chemicals are commonly called the "toxic-trio." They have been at the center of ongoing public attention over nail product safety and potential health risks for nail salon workers. A small number of nail product manufacturers claim to have removed some or all toxic-trio chemicals from their goods. DTSC's objective in sampling the products were to (a) verify if toxic-trio related claims were valid, (b) determine baseline levels of some chemicals of current public interests, and (c) explore trends of ingredient substitutions. Twenty-five products, representing six product categories, were randomly collected from six distributors who supply products to nail salons. Of the 25 products collected, 12 claimed to be free of at least one toxic-trio chemical. Seven products claimed to be free of all three toxic-trio chemicals.

Thirteen products did not make any toxic-trio related claims. In this report, products that made no such claims are referred to as "traditional." Toluene was found in higher concentrations in products with toxic-trio related claims than in traditional products. Ten of the twelve products with "toluene-free" claims did contain toluene. Products that claim to be free of all three toxic-trio are called "three-free."

A study found that five of the seven "three-free" product claims could not substantiate. Chemicals were also detected whose purpose, property, human toxicity, and environmental fate, are unknown to DTSC. Based on the report's findings, DTSC recommends manufacturer disclosure of nail product formulations. Additionally, DTSC urges increased collaboration and coordination among interested stakeholders, along with expanded outreach and education and training of nail salon owners and workers.

When the regulations were finalized, 26 chemicals, which included the toxic-trio and 23 other chemicals were discovered (6, 7). These chemicals are known or suspected carcinogens, reproductive toxins, acute skin, and respiratory irritants, or toxicants that may cause other adverse health conditions. DTSC staff conducted a limited scale-sampling project in May of 2011.

This project was designed to investigate the accuracy of "three-free" claims, provide information on hazardous chemicals used in these products, and offer further support to SFE's nail salon recognition program. DTSC staff believes that a successful SFE nail salon recognition program may serve as a model for other municipalities and communities throughout the State. Consumer demand for safer nail products may ultimately stimulate the industry to innovate and reformulate using safer chemical ingredients.

Dibutyl Phthalate In products making a toxic-trio related claim, DBP was found in higher concentrations than in products not claim at all. For example, in one product claiming to be three-free, DBP levels presented at 8.2%. Similarly, in products claiming to be free of at least one toxic-trio chemical, DBP levels ranged from 6.2% to as high as 8.8%. In traditional products, those that made no toxic-trio claims, concentrations of DBP ranged from 1.4% to 4.2% (Tables 4 and 5). The percentage of samples testing positive for DBP is similar for both products with toxic-trio related claims (33%) and traditional products (38%). However, median DBP concentration in products making toxic-trio claims was higher than median DBP concentration in traditional products (Table 5).

Butyl acetate is found in nail strengtheners and nail polishes. Health Hazards: - Butyl acetate vapors may cause dizziness or drowsiness. Continued of a product containing butyl acetate may cause the skin to crack and become dry. Butyl acetate is found in a variety of cosmetics, and it is an antioxidant that helps slow the rate at which a product changes color over time. It is used to control itching and to scale to soften skin, and it is also a human carcinogen. It is currently used as a disinfectant and preservative found in nail polish, soap, deodorant, shaving eyelash adhesive, and shampoo. It is found in a variety of cosmetics, and it is an antioxidant that helps slow the rate it may cause skin and eye irritation.

Lead is associated with multiple health challenges such as respiratory tract inspection and eye irritation, cancer, immune system damage, genetic damage, and triggering asthma. The word "Fragrance" may be used to indicate any number of chemicals in a personal care product. Many fragrances are toxic. Some of these may be phthalates, which can act as obesogens and may compromise the endocrine system, including reproductive health. Phthalates may cause developmental defects and delays. Lead typically occurs as a contaminant, such as in hydrated silica, an ingredient in toothpaste.

Lead acetate is an ingredient often used in lipstick, and it is a neurotoxin. The chemicals have been shown to contribute to cerebral/brain malfunction even in low concentrations. The use of mercury compounds has been allowed to creep into the consumer market. Eye make-up at concentrations up to 65 parts per million, the preservative Thimerosal, a form of mercury found in most mascaras' products.

These ingredients are associated with a host of health concerns, including allergic reactions, skin irritation, toxicity, neurological damage, and environmental damage. These chemical additives are prohibited for use in cosmetics in the European Union; however, the chemicals are found in several U.S. brands of mascara, foot-odor powder, and other products. Be cautious of all products that contain names such as "petroleum" or "liquid paraffin." 4. Propylene Glycol (P.G.) (PEG) (PROPANEDIOL, DIHYDROXYPROPANE, METHYLETHYLENE GLYCOL, and PROPANE) as a wetting agent and solvent, this ingredient is the active component in antifreeze.

There is no difference between the P.G. used in industry (brake & hydraulic fluid, paint, floor wax) and the P.G. used in personal care products. It is used in industry to break down protein, and cellular structure (what the skin is made of) stripping the Natural Moisture Factor, yet is found in most forms of make-up, hair products, lotions, after-shave, deodorants, mouthwashes, and toothpaste. It is also used in food processing. Because of its ability to quickly penetrate the skin, the EPA requires workers to wear protective gloves, clothing, and goggles when working with this toxic substance. Skin contact, dermatitis, kidney damage, and liver abnormalities can inhibit cell growth in human tests and can damage membranes causing rashes, dry skin, and surface damage. There is no warning label on products such as stick deodorants, where the concentration is greater than that in most industrial applications, leaving the immune system vulnerable. They are also potentially carcinogenic.

Even though government agencies are aware of the health hazards of some ingredients, such as hydroquinone or phthalates, they are still allowed in personal care products. It is important to be familiar with the most common hazardous ingredients so that you can check your cosmetic labels and see if they are there. Hazardous ingredients are usually present in conventional products, but they may also be found in some "alternative" products, which try to be more health conscious. Note, though, that some chemicals about which there are serious concerns such as fragrance ingredients or contaminants found in certain chemicals will not show up on labels, so reading labels won't tell you everything you need to know.

Scientists can monitor minute quantities of chemicals in our bodies by taking samples of urine, blood, breast milk, and tissue. Studies from around the world confirm that all people carry household, agricultural, and industrial chemicals (or their breakdown products) in our bodies, often referred to as the "body burden of chemicals." One of the underlying causes of this crisis is the unconscious buying and consumption of commercial products; women overlook the possibilities of toxicities in the beauty, body, hair, and hygiene products.

These highly favored product brands, unfortunately, contain toxic chemical ingredients that are absorbed through the skin, inhaled, or ingested? These unnatural ingredients are linked to cancer, lymphatic toxicity, neuro-damage, and other female health problems. No commercialized body care, lotion shampoo, deodorant, make-up, or cosmetic is exempt from the United States of America Corporation's synthetic and artificial influence of unnatural ingredients that wreak havoc on the physiology of the women.

According to the Advocates For Safer Cosmetics and Body Care most secret chemicals revealed in fragrance testing have not been assessed for safety 80% 70% 60% 50% 40% 30% 20% 10% 0% Secret chemicals found in product tests Chemicals listed on labels 19% have not been assessed for safety 66% have not been assessed for safety the 17 name-brand fragrances tested in this study contained nearly equal numbers of secret and labeled ingredients, with 14 chemicals kept secret but found through testing, and 15 disclosed on labels. Widespread exposure and a long-standing culture of secrecy within the fragrance industry continue to put countless people at risk of contact sensitization to fragrances with poorly tested and intentionally unlabeled ingredients (Schnuch 2007).

According to EWG analysis, the fragrance industry has published safety assessments for only 34% of the unlabeled ingredients (for details of the analysis, see Methods section). The under-evaluated chemicals range from food additives whose safety in perfumes has not been assessed to chemicals with limited public safety data such as synthetic musk fragrances, which accumulate in the human body and may be linked to hormone disruption.

Percentage of chemicals not assessed for safety by the fragrance industry. Source: EWG analysis of product labels, tests commissioned by the Campaign for Safe Cosmetics, and industry reports of safety assessments by the Personal Care Products Council and International Fragrance Association in the past 25 years.

This complex mix of clandestine compounds in popular colognes and perfumes makes it impossible for consumers to make informed decisions about the products they consider buying. The federal government is equally uninformed. A review of government records shows that the U.S. Food and Drug Administration has not assessed the vast majority of these secret fragrance chemicals for safety when used in spray-on personal care products such as fragrances. Nor has the safety review panel of the International Fragrance Association or any other publicly accountable institution evaluated most. Fragrance secrecy is legal due to a giant loophole in the Federal Fair Packaging and Labeling Act of 1973, which requires companies to list cosmetics ingredients on the product labels but explicitly exempts fragrance. By taking advantage of this loophole, the cosmetics industry has kept the public in the dark about the ingredients in fragrance, even those that present potential health risks or build up in people's bodies. Ingredients not in a product's hidden fragrance mixture must be listed on the label. As a result, manufacturers disclose some chemical constituents on ingredient lists but lump others together in the generic category of "fragrance." In fact, "fragrances" are typically mixtures of many different secret chemicals, like those uncovered in this study.

EWG analysis of 91 chemicals in 17 products - including 51 chemicals listed on product labels, and 38 unlabeled chemicals found in tests commissioned by the Campaign for Safe Cosmetics - combined with analysis of chemical hazard and toxicity data from government and industry assessments and the published scientific literature.

Common Hazardous Chemicals found in Personal Care Products Eye and Face Make-up (revised Spring 2011) Blush Concealer Eye Liner Eye Shadow Face Powder Foundation Lip Gloss, Balms and Protectors (see skin products section) Lip Products Make-up Remover Mascara Dental and Oral Hygiene (Spring 2011) Dental Floss Denture Cleaners Mouthwash Toothpaste Tooth Whiteners Feminine Hygiene (Spring 2011) Douches Tampons, Pads and other Menstrual Products Hair Care (Spring 2011) Conditioner Hair Coloring Hair Oils and Pomades Hair Relaxers and Straighteners Hair Styling Mousse (see Hair Styling) Permanent Waves.

In February 2003, the European Union adopted an amendment to the Cosmetics Directive 76/768/EEC that prohibits the use of known or suspected carcinogens, mutagens, and reproductive toxins (a.k.a. CMRs) from cosmetics 9. As of September 2004, cosmetics sold in European Union countries must be free of these CMR chemicals, including two phthalates, DEHP and DBP, this is in addition to 451 substances already covered by the Directive - bringing the list of substances banned in cosmetics to over 1000 in Europe. Examples of banned substances include formaldehyde and its releasers (common in shampoos), lead and its compounds (an ingredient in

Grecian formula), acrylamide polymers (found in foundation and skin lotions), and some phthalates (commonly found in a large variety of products).

Contrary to the commercial guidelines of the USDA, FDA, or any other governing structure that is supposed to be the consumer's watchdog over products that pose a threat to internal, external, and environmental toxicity, the women cosmetics industry is certainly in need of product manufacturing reform.

A News Article Concerning African American/Aboriginal Indigenous Women

By Nneka Leiba, VP, Healthy Living Science, and Paul Pestano, Former Senior Database Analyst

THURSDAY, AUGUST 17, 2017

Women of "Color" use more beauty products and are disproportionately exposed to worrisome chemicals compared to white women, according to a new study.

The study, published in the American Journal of Obstetrics & Gynecology, calls on health care providers to become more aware of how exposure to environmental chemicals may impact the reproductive health of vulnerable populations.

Ami R. Zota, an assistant professor of environmental and occupational health at the George Washington University Milken Institute School of Public Health, and Bhavna Shamasunder, a scientist in the Urban and Environmental Policy Department at Los

Angeles' Occidental College, recommend further study into the potential effects of exposure to chemicals through beauty products. They also suggest this may be an important area of intervention, especially for women of color who are likely most affected by toxic ingredients in these products.

"Pressure to meet Western standards of beauty means Black, Latina and Asian American women are using more beauty products, and thus are exposed to higher levels of chemicals known to be harmful to health," Zota wrote in a news release.
Women of color spend more on cosmetics that include skin-lightening creams, hair straightening, and relaxing treatments, and feminine cleansing and hygiene products.

In 2015, the same researchers published a study in the journal Environmental Health that found differences among races and ethnicities in both feminine hygiene practices and exposure to phthalates.

"Our findings showing that women of African or Aboriginal American descent may be at higher risk is important," said Zota. "It shows that some subpopulations are disproportionately exposed, and that personal care product use may be driving these exposure disparities."

In December 2016, EWG assessed almost 1,200 products marketed specifically to Black women and concluded that fewer products made without hazardous ingredients are available for this group. According to market data, Black women buy and use more personal care products than other demographic groups.

Women of childbearing age should limit their exposure to hormone-disrupting chemicals that can harm the reproductive system and fetal development. Preservatives like parabens have been linked to diminished fertility, lowered thyroid levels, and other reproductive problems. Some of the adverse reactions associated with exposure to toxic formaldehyde-releasing preservatives include hair loss, a blistered scalp, neck and face rashes, nosebleeds, and other long-term health problems. In 2011, the U.S. government designated formaldehyde as a known human carcinogen.

The fragrance is by far the most widely used ingredient, found in more than half of the products EWG evaluated. Fragrance mixtures can be comprised of any number of more than 3,000 ingredients and can trigger allergic reactions such as asthma, wheezing, headaches, and contact dermatitis. Some of the ingredients used in these formulas mimic the hormone estrogen and are associated with harmful thyroid effects.

Obstetricians and gynecologists should consider environmental exposures to beauty products, and the disparities across racial and social demographics when providing treatment or counseling patients. "Beauty product use is a critical but underappreciated source of reproductive harm and environmental injustice," Zota said.

The Food and Drug Administration should be testing the ingredients used in all personal care products to ensure cosmetics are as safe and healthy as possible. Right now, there aren't even basic safety assessments. And while some companies have voluntarily reformulated their products because of consumer feedback, much more work needs to be done. Federal standards governing the safety of personal care products have not been updated since the 1930s. Sens. Diane Feinstein, D-Calif., and Susan Collins, R-Maine, recently introduced the Personal Care Products Safety Act, which would significantly strengthen the FDA's authority to address the health risks of cosmetics.

The bill would require the FDA to regularly review the safety of cosmetics ingredients and require bans or special labeling of chemicals found to be harmful. The agency also would have the recall authority to take dangerous products off store shelves.
"For women who live in already polluted neighborhoods, beauty product chemicals may add to their overall burden of exposures to toxic chemicals," Shamasunder, coauthor of the new study, wrote in a statement.

There is much more work to be done. EWG agrees that the medical community should consider reframing the issue of harmful exposures from everyday use of personal care products as a health disparity for women of color. Study: Women of Color Exposed to More Toxic Chemicals in Personal Care Products

Study: Women of Color Exposed to More Toxic Chemicals in Personal Care Products

Most chemicals has its purpose for the modern-day woman, but when women over indulged in the use of foreign chemicals like ... in hair color rinses, body rubs, hand lotions, after-shave lotions, fragrances, and many other cosmetics, it can proliferate an adverse effects like headaches, flushed skin, dizziness, mental depression, nausea, and other mystic symptoms.

Dangers of Deodorants

Deodorant and antiperspirants: prohibit sweat from being secreted. However, sweating is one of the body's methods of detoxification. Blocking perspiration can cause toxins to back up in the body. For this reason, it is not advisable to use any sweat blocking agents, to allow the body to eliminate toxins naturally. Billions of people around the planet rely on the particular hygiene guard to protect them from perspiration and eventful a body odor. The human underarm is among the most delicate areas of warmth and moisture areas on the surface of the human body. The sweat glands provide moisture, which when excreted, has a vital cooling effect, though some people do not expire as much as others, it should be a caution to consume the cleanest foods and use the purest of body care and hygiene. In women that have limited perspiration will find their lymphatic system in much of a more toxic state because of trapped impurities over time.

When adult armpits are cleaned with alkaline pH soap, the skin loses its acid mantle (pH 4.5 - 6), raising the skin pH and disrupting the skin barrier.[9] As many bacteria thrive in this high pH environment, this makes the skin susceptible to bacterial colonization. The bacteria feed on the sweat from the apocrine glands and dead skin and hair cells, releasing trans-3-Methyl-2-hexenoic acid in their waste, which is the primary cause of body odor. Underarm hair wicks the moisture away from the skin and aids in keeping the skin dry enough to prevent or diminish bacterial colonization. The hair is less susceptible to bacterial growth and therefore is ideal for preventing bacterial odor. Deodorants are classified and regulated as cosmetics by the U.S. Food and Drug Administration (FDA) and are designed to eliminate odor. Deodorants are usually alcohol-based. Alcohol initially stimulates sweating but may also temporarily kill bacteria. Deodorants can contain other persistent antimicrobials such as triclosan, or with metal, chelate compounds that slow bacterial growth. Deodorants may contain perfume fragrances or natural essential oils intended to mask the odor of perspiration.

Deodorants, combined with antiperspirant agents, are classified as drugs by the FDA.[1] Antiperspirants attempt to stop or significantly reduce perspiration and thus reduce the moist climate in which bacteria thrive. Aluminum chloride, and aluminum-zirconium compounds, most notably and aluminum, are frequently used in antiperspirants. Aluminum chloralhydrate and aluminum zirconium tetrachlorohydrate glycol are the most common active ingredients in commercial antiperspirants. Aluminum-based complexes react with the electrolytes in the sweat to form a gel plug in the duct of the sweat gland.

The plugs prevent the gland from excreting liquid and are removed over time by the natural sloughing of the skin. The metal salts work in another way to prevent sweat from reaching the surface of the skin: the aluminum salts interact with the keratin fibrils in the sweat ducts and form a physical plug that prevents sweat from reaching the skin's surface. Aluminum salts also have a slight astringent effect on the pores, creating contraction to inhibit sweat from reaching the surface of the skin. The blockage of a large number of sweat glands reduces the amount of sweat produced in the underarms; this may vary from person to person.

In 1941, a new kind of deodorant was developed, which addressed the problem of the excessive acidity of aluminum chloride and its excessive irritation of the skin, by combining it with a soluble nitrile or a similar compound. According to Time Magazine By the 1950s, this Deodorant Spray called Stopette became a top-selling deodorant. Soon after, a Right Guard produced by Gillette's hit the market in the

1960s. Aerosols sprays appear to be convenient because the user would release the spray without coming in contact with the underarm area. By the end of the 1960s, approximately half of all the antiperspirants sold in the U.S. were aerosols.

By the late 1970s, the adverse effects of the Aerosol spray began to become noticed, and by 1977 the FDA the Food and Drug Administration (FDA) banned the active ingredient used in the aerosol. Due to hazardous concerns, a chemical called aluminum zirconium was found to wreak havoc of humans after long-term inhalation. Aerosol sprays appear to be notorious for the estrogen balance in women and testosterone in men.

In 1977 Then, Environmental Protection Agency (EPA) limited the use of chlorofluorocarbon (CFC) propellants, a gas found in aerosols that created a toxic impact on the Earth's Ozone layer. Because the average consumer is unaware of the chemical toxicity in commercial products, they purchase base on the social media/advertising programming.

Though odor altering deodorants are needed, there is a caution women and men should take because if the chemical influence on the physiology. So, whether popular of Dollar value, commercial underarm deodorants and antiperspirants can with tight wire-strapped bras to cause blockage of the lymphatic system and lymph nodes in the breast/chest area (underarms) resulting in painful lumps in the armpits or underarms, and worse, cysts in the breasts. LIFESTYLE Commercial pharmaceutical brands of birth control are 100% toxic!

They may curb or inhibit conception, but the side effects may prove insalubrious and fatal in many cases.

Because advertising has a way to convince the consumer to buy without question, women sometimes spontaneously buy and use fragrance sprays, and talc applies to the vaginal area to present freshness during a workday or just for religious purposes. The chemical residue can seep into the vaginal area and travel to the uterus, cervix, and ovaries, causing a host of adverse health challenges.

Here just some other of the disharmonizing ingredients to look out for that can take a healthy woman out of not only a hormonal imbalance but proliferate other mystical symptoms that can become ill-health: Dibutyl Phthalate, Formaldehyde, Methylene glycol, Toluene, Methyl Methacrylate.

Eye and Face Make-up

Since the time of Ancient Egypt, cosmetics have relished the beauty of all ethnicities of both women and men. From fashion to war, the creativity of body and face makeup representing a significant occasion, yet it was a natural component of berries, insects, herbs natural henna, and other ingredients directly from what in harmony with nature. Today, people followed the same beauty pattern, but with risky results.

Ancient Egyptians outlined eyes with kohl, a poisonous substance made from antimony. Greeks and Romans liked the pale look, achieved by applying white lead and chalk to their faces. During the

Renaissance, the pale look was again popular with a white lead and vinegar mixture applied to face, neck, and bosom. Lips and cheeks were tinted bright red with vermilion, a paint containing mercuric sulfide. A heavy coating of powder, often based on talc, kept everything in place. When women noticed that their lead cosmetics caused a variety of skin problems, some applied a facial peel made from mercury. It is a known fact that mercury is highly toxic.

Today, the average woman uses approximately 20 different personal care products containing several hundred ingredients every day. And, even now, many of the commercial ingredients are highly toxic due to textile waste, petrochemicals, and toxic dyes. Colors in conventional cosmetics are often chemically synthesized from coal tar.

While they're less expensive than natural compounds to produce, certain coal tar colors have been shown to cause cancer in animals, and many are toxic to the nervous system.
Impurities like arsenic and lead in some coal tar colors have been shown to cause cancer not only when ingested, but also when applied to the skin. Because it is a contaminant in colors, lead, for example, has been found in many popular brands of lipstick. As well, conventional cosmetics may contain as many as five different synthetic preservatives. Parabens, which mimic estrogen in the body and have been linked with breast cancer, are currently the most popular preservatives used in makeup. Another concern is the introduction of nanoparticles into just about every type of personal care product on the market, including sunscreen, shampoo,

conditioner, anti-wrinkle cream, foundation, face powder, lipstick, blush, eye shadow, and nail polish.

The only labeling you are likely to see is "micronized," which may indicate that companies have used nanoparticles of certain ingredients in the product, or "no nano" from companies that have made a choice to avoid their use. Nanoparticles are tiny manipulated versions of existing chemicals, but they present new risks that have not been evaluated and are not yet understood. Because of the lack of information about nanoparticles and their use in personal care products, particularly sunscreens and mineral makeup, products that are identified as "best" or "good" would not qualify in those categories if their ingredients were known to be in nano form.

Everyone Is Impacted By Chemical Fragrance
The Campaign commissioned a laboratory analysis of men's and women's fragrances as well as scented products marketed to teens of both genders; all products tested contained a range of ingredients associated with health concerns, such as allergic sensitization, and potential effects on the endocrine system or reproductive toxicity. Most people who live in North America use between 17 and 21 scented products per day, exposing themselves to a random chemical soup with unknown health effects.

According to the U.S. Food and Drug Administration, fragrances cause 30% of all allergic reactions, and 70% of all asthmatics develop respiratory symptoms when exposed to perfumes. Natural Fragrances Companies, which manufacture products with all-natural ingredients often, use natural fragrances for added scent. Some companies who use both natural and synthetic ingredients have chosen to substitute natural fragrances for synthetic ones. In both cases, this eliminates some of the toxic chemicals found in synthetic fragrances, like toluene and phthalates. However, some people become ill when exposed to natural fragrances, so natural fragrances are not a good choice for a scent-free environment.

Numerous other products used daily, such as shampoos, lotions, bath products, cleaning sprays, air fresheners and laundry and dishwashing detergents, also contain strongly scented, volatile ingredients that are hidden behind the word "fragrance." Some of these ingredients react with ozone in the indoor air, generating many potentially harmful secondary air pollutants such as formaldehyde and ultrafine particles (Nazaroff 2004). People have the right to know which chemicals they are being exposed to. They have the right to expect the government to protect people, especially vulnerable populations, from hazardous chemicals.

Here is a list of the top 20 unwanted ingredients commonly found in your skin products, with their side effects.

1. **Isopropyl Alcohol** - This is a solvent and denaturant (poisonous substance that changes another substance's natural qualities). Isopropyl alcohol is found in hair color rinses, body rubs, hand lotions, after-shave lotions, fragrances, and many other cosmetics. This petroleum-derived substance is also used in antifreeze and as a solvent in shellac. According to A Consumer's Dictionary of Cosmetic Ingredients, inhalation or ingestion of the vapor may cause headaches, flushed skin, dizziness, mental depression, nausea, vomiting, narcosis, and coma.

2. **Antibacterial** - Overuse of antibacterial can prevent them from effectively fighting disease-causing germs like E. coli and Salmonella enterica. Triclosan, widely used in soaps, toothpaste, and deodorants, has been detected in breast milk, and one recent study found that it interferes with testosterone activity in cells. Numerous studies have found that washing with regular soap and warm water is just as effective at killing germs.

3. **Mineral Oil** - Baby oil is 100% mineral oil. This derived substance, a commonly used petroleum ingredient, coats the skin just like plastic wrap covers any given vessel. The skin's natural immune barrier is disrupted as this plastic coating inhibits its ability to breathe and absorb (moisture and nutrition). Your skin's ability to release toxins is impeded by this "plastic wrap," which can promote acne and other disorders by slowing down normal cell development causing the skin to prematurely age. Petroleum distillates are possible human carcinogens. They are prohibited for use in cosmetics in the European Union but are found in several U.S. brands of mascara, foot-odor powder and other products. Look out for the term's "petroleum" or "liquid paraffin."

4. **Propylene Glycol (PG) (PEG) (PROPANEDIOL, DIHYDROXYPROPANE, METHYLETHYLENE GLYCOL, PROPANE)** Is a wetting agent and solvent, this ingredient is the active component in antifreeze. There is no difference between the PG used in industry (brake & hydraulic fluid, paint, floor wax) and the PG used in personal care products. It is used in industry to break down protein and cellular structure (what the skin is made of) stripping the Natural Moisture Factor, yet is found in most forms of make-up, hair products, lotions, after-shave, deodorants, mouthwashes, and toothpaste. It is also used in food processing. Because of its ability to quickly penetrate the skin, the EPA requires workers to wear protective gloves, clothing, and goggles when working with this toxic substance. Skin contact, dermatitis, kidney damage, and liver abnormalities can inhibit cell growth in human tests and can damage membranes causing rashes, dry skin, and surface damage. There is no warning label on products such as stick deodorants, where the concentration is greater than that in most industrial applications, leaving the immune system vulnerable. They are also potentially carcinogenic.

5. **Imidazolidinyl Urea and DMDM Hydantoin** - These release formaldehyde into your body. The Mayo Clinic says formaldehyde

can irritate the respiratory system, cause skin reactions, trigger heart palpitations, immune system toxicity, and cancer in humans. Exposure may cause joint pain, allergies, depression, headaches, chest pains, ear infections, chronic fatigue, dizziness and loss of sleep. It can also aggravate coughs and colds and trigger asthma. Yet it still turns up in baby bath soap, nearly all brands of body products, antiperspirants, nail polish, eyelash adhesive, and hair dyes.

6. **Bronopol - (2-Bromo-2-nitropropane-1, 3-diol)** may break down in products into formaldehyde and also cause the formation of carcinogenic nitrosamines under certain conditions. It is found in expensive over-the-counter products, but also "natural" products.

7. **Sodium Lauryl Sulfate (SLS) and Sodium Laureth Sulfate (SLES)** Used as detergents and surfactants, these closely related compounds are found in car wash soaps, garage floor cleaners, and engine degreasers. Yet both SLS and SLES are used more widely as one of the major ingredients in cosmetics, toothpaste, and hair conditioner and about 90% of all shampoos and products that foam. According to the American College of Toxicology, both **SLS and SLES** can cause malformation in children's eyes, and damage to the immune system, especially within the skin. Skin layers may separate and inflame due to its protein denaturing properties. It is possibly the most dangerous of all ingredients in personal care products.
Research has shown that SLS when combined with other chemicals, can be transformed into nitrosamines, a potent class of carcinogens, which causes the body to absorb nitrates at higher levels than eating nitrate-contaminated food. According to the ACOT, "SLS stays in the body for up to five days..." Other studies have indicated that SLS easily penetrates the skin and maintains residual levels in the heart, the liver, the lungs, and the brain.

8. **DEA (diethanolamine) MEA (monoethanolamine) TEA (triethanolamine) - DEA and MEA** are usually fisted on the ingredient label in conjunction with the compound being neutralized. Thus, look for names like Cocamide DEA or MEA, Lauramide DEA, etc. These are hormone-disrupting chemicals and are known to form cancer-causing nitrates and nitrosamines. These are commonly found in most personal care products that foam, including bubble baths, body washes, shampoos, soaps, and facial cleansers. On the show, CBS This Morning, Roberta Baskin revealed that a recent

government report shows DEA and MEA are readily absorbed in the skin. "Repeated skin applications of DEA-based detergents resulted in a major increase in the incidence of two cancers - liver and kidney cancers." Diethanolamine (DEA) is a possible hormone disruptor, has shown limited evidence of carcinogenicity and depletes the body of choline needed for fetal brain development. DEA can also show up as a contaminant in products containing related chemicals, such as cocamide DEA.

9. **1,2-Dioxane in Surfactants/detergents** A wide range of personal care products including shampoos, hair conditioners, cleansers, lotions, and creams, besides household products such as soaps and cleaners, contain surfactants or detergents such as ethoxylated alcohols, polysorbates, and laureates. These ingredients are generally contaminated with high concentrations of the highly volatile 1,4 dioxane, which is both readily inhaled and absorbed through the skin. Epidemiological studies on dioxane-exposed furniture makers have reported suggestive evidence of excess nasal passage cancers. It is a known animal carcinogen and a possible human carcinogen that can appear as a contaminant in products containing sodium lauryl sulfate and ingredients that include the terms "PEG," "-xynol," "ceteareth," "oleth" and most other ethoxylated "eth" ingredients. The FDA monitors products for the contaminant but has not yet recommended an exposure limit. Manufacturers can remove dioxane through a process called vacuum stripping, but a small amount usually remains. A 2007 survey by the Campaign for Safe Cosmetics found that most children's bath products contain 10 parts per million or less, but an earlier 2001 study by the FDA found levels above 85 parts per million.

10. **Parabens - (methyl-, ethyl-, propyl-, butyl-, isobutyl-) Parabens**, which have weak estrogenic effects, are common preservatives that appear in a wide array of toiletries. A study found that butylparaben damaged sperm formation in the testes of mice, and a relative, sodium methylparaben, is banned in cosmetics by the E.U. Parabens break down in the body into p-hydroxybenzoic acid, which has estrogenic activity in human breast cancer cell cultures.

11. **Nanoparticles** - Tiny nanoparticles, which may penetrate the skin and damage brain cells, are appearing in an increasing number of cosmetics and sunscreens. Most problematic are zinc oxide and titanium dioxide nanoparticles, used in sunscreens to make them

transparent. When possible, look for sunscreens containing particles of these ingredients larger than 100 nanometers. You'll most likely need to call companies to confirm sizes, but a few manufacturers have started advertising their lack of nanoparticle-sized ingredients on labels. For a more complete discussion, see Screen Test: Reading the Micro-Fine Print. (a link on your computer)

12. **Lead and Mercury** - Neurotoxic lead may appear in products as a naturally occurring contaminant of hydrated silica, one of the ingredients in toothpaste. Lead acetate is found in some brands of men's hair dye. Brain-damaging mercury, found in the preservative thimerosal, is used in some mascaras and until recently, in many vaccinations.

13. **P-Phenylenediamine** - Commonly found in hair dyes, this chemical could damage the nervous system, cause lung irritation and cause severe allergic reactions. It is also listed as 1,4-Benzenediamine; p-Phenyldiamine and 4-Phenylenediamine.

14. Artificial Colors, Dyes & Coal Tar is a known human carcinogen used as an active ingredient in dandruff shampoos and anti-itch creams. Coal-tar-based dyes such as FD&C Blue 1, used in toothpaste, and FD&C Green 3, used in mouthwash, are carcinogenic in animal studies when injected under the skin. Some artificial colors, such as Blue 1 and Green 3, are carcinogenic. Impurities found in commercial batches of other cosmetic colors such as D&C Red 33, FD&C Yellow 5, and FD&C yellow 6 have been shown to cause cancer not only when ingested, but also when applied to the skin. Some artificial coal tar colors contain heavy metal impurities, including arsenic and lead, which are carcinogenic. The use of permanent or semi-permanent hair color products, particularly black and dark brown colors are associated with an increased incidence of human cancer including lymphoma, myeloma, and Hodgkin's disease.

15. **Hydroquinone** - Found in skin lighteners and facial moisturizers, hydroquinone is neurotoxic and allergenic, and there is limited evidence that it may cause cancer in lab animals. It may also appear as an impurity not listed on ingredients labels.

16. **Talcum Powder** - TALC, is carcinogenic. Inhaling talc and using it in the genital area, where its use is associated with increased risk of

ovarian and lung cancer, are the primary ways this substance poses a carcinogenic hazard.

17. **Lanolin** itself is perfectly safe. But cosmetic-grade lanolin can be contaminated with carcinogenic pesticides such as DDT, dieldrin, and lindane, in addition to other neurotoxic pesticides.

18. **Chlorine** - Exposure to chlorine in tap water, showers, pool, laundry products, cleaning agents, food processing, sewage systems and many others, can affect health by contributing to asthma, hay fever, anemia, bronchitis, circulatory collapse, confusion, delirium diabetes, dizziness, irritation of the eye, mouth, nose, throat, lung, skin and stomach, heart disease, high blood pressure and nausea. It is also a possible cause of cancer.

19. **Fragrance** - The catchall term "fragrance" may mask phthalates, which act as endocrine disruptors and may cause obesity and reproductive and developmental harm. Avoid phthalates by selecting essential-oil fragrances instead. "Fragrance" is present in most deodorants, shampoos, sunscreens, skin care, body care, and baby products. Many of the compounds in fragrance are carcinogenic or otherwise toxic. "Fragrance on a label can indicate the presence of up to 4,000 separate ingredients. Most of all of them are synthetic. The FDA reports have included headaches, dizziness, rashes, skin discoloration, violent coughing and vomiting, and allergic skin irritation. Exposure to fragrances can affect the central nervous system, causing depression hyperactivity, irritability, inability to cope, and other behavioral changes".

CHAPTER 6
HOW ADVERTISING PROGRAMS AND MANIPULATES YOUR MIND

American Tobacco Company ad

PR must "create news . . . in order to appeal to the instincts and fundamental emotions of the public"

Crystallizing Public Opinion (1923), p. 171

uncle Siggy (1856-1939)   "torches of freedom"

The masses are unaware of the unseen strings behind the veil of consumer manipulation through advertising and public relations. This powerful instrument of consumer persuasion has been used to sway everything from political opinion to weight loss trends. One of the most profound advents of public relations was the introduction of fluoridated water through the creator of public relations founder, "Edward Bernays," a nephew of Sigmund Fraud.

    Edward Bernays saw that the minds of the masses could be indoctrinated and shape to conformity regardless of one class. One of the most famous examples is the War of Worlds, a psycho media campaign and experiment that was created by Orson Wells. The War of the Worlds was fictional live radio broadcast about the planet

Cowardice asks the question, "Is it safe?"

Expediency asks the question, "Is it politic?"

And Vanity comes along and asks the question, "Is it popular?"

But Conscience asks, "Is it right?"

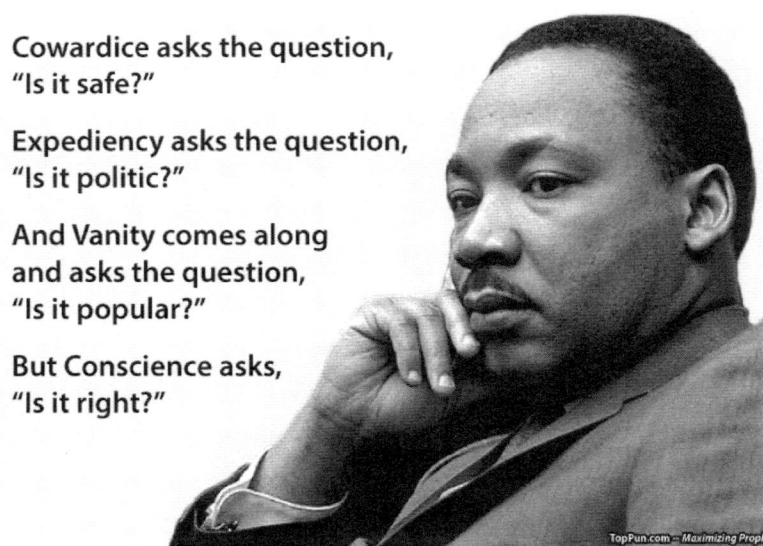

Nothing – no, nothing – beats better taste – and

LUCKIES TASTE BETTER!

Cleaner, Fresher, Smoother!

You can even see why Luckies taste better—cleaner, fresher, smoother

Ask yourself this question: *Why do I smoke?* You know, yourself, you smoke for enjoyment. And you get enjoyment only from the taste of a cigarette.

Luckies taste *better*—cleaner, fresher, smoother! You can see *why* when you strip the paper from a Lucky by tearing down the seam.

First, you see that your Lucky is *made better*, because it remains a perfect cylinder of fine tobacco—round, firm and fully packed.

Second, you see Luckies' famous fine tobacco itself—long strands of fine, light, truly mild tobacco with a rich aroma and an even better taste. Yes, L.S./M.F.T.—Lucky Strike *means* fine tobacco.

Nothing—no, nothing—beats better taste, and Luckies taste better—cleaner, fresher, smoother. So...

Be Happy-**GO LUCKY!**

Earth being attacked by Martians. The audio sounds of sirens, crashing noises, and screaming had some people so frantic that they were jumping out of buildings, taking up arms, and some even left their home and headed for the hills. All because of a broadcast of hype, with no thorough investigation, people demonstrated just how naïve they were, and still are.

Advertising is a convenient form of ideology in a capitalist society. "Advertising is the most influential institution of socialization in modern society" (Jhally 1990: p.1), thus, to critically assess the view that advertising is a convenient form of ideology in a capitalist society, we need to understand the social and economic value of consumer brands.

The 1950's epoch was the beginning of a consumerist culture, as multi-national corporations were faced with the competing ideologies of 'supply and demand.' It became a universal phenomenon as it began to materialize in Hollywood film and television. Thus, people became passive consumers. Many advertisements in the mass media convinced viewers that they needed a life that would go beyond regular consumers to increase on the social ladder; they needed to buy more than just 'regular' products. The commercials implied that cars, clothes, and even their brand of cosmetics that they possess could represent their social status. Commodities have become a means for promoting self beyond talking. Advertising, economic, and social engineering have a very structured way to conform the masses into a profitable belief system, that some call the matrix. Thus, if we look at modern society, we can see how the system of public relations persuades the minds of the consumer. Advertisers now know that status is psychological anxiety.

It is very interesting how public relations and the influence of authority can have an effect on the massed of people. For example; Did you know that the bacon and eggs was a socially engineered concept? Though, the bacon and eggs association with the American breakfast is barely a century old. Before this, the majority of Americans ate more modest, often meatless breakfasts that might include fruit, a grain porridge (oat, wheat or corn meals) or a roll, and usually a cup of coffee.

In the 1920s, Bernays was approached by the Beech-Nut Packing Company - producers of everything from pork products to the nostalgic Beech-Nut bubble gum. Beech-Nut wanted to increase consumer demand for bacon. Bernays turned to his agency's internal doctor and asked him whether a heavier breakfast might be more beneficial for the American public. Knowing which way his bread was buttered, the doctor confirmed Bernays suspicion and wrote to five thousand of his doctor's friends asking them to confirm it as well. This 'study' of doctors encouraging the American public to eat a heavier breakfast - namely **'Bacon and Eggs'** - was published in major newspapers and magazines of the time to great success. Beech-Nut's profits rose sharply thanks to Bernays and his team of medical professionals.

This is bacon, egg and biscuit dish is still considered the breakfast of choice by many people. in America.

"Until the Second World War, excessive indulgence in cigarettes was considered un-ladylike, and those who did smoke were expected not to inhale too deeply" (Hughes, 2003: p.116). Smoking was not associated with the female etiquette, as women were confined to smoke in the private sphere of their homes. If a woman were to smoke in public, she would be deemed un-ladylike; thus, her social status would be at the bottom.

Edward Bernays's Torches of Freedom campaign was the first major advertising success, as a group of young women marched down New York's Fifth Avenue to light up "Lucky Strike cigarettes." It was a successful celebration of women challenging the "taboos" of the women smoker in the 1920's America and juxtaposing the act of smoking Lucky Strike cigarettes with equality and liberation, as the issues were very much at the forefront of women's rights at the time.

Bernays was the first to take Freud's idea that we were driven by our unconscious desires, and use them to manipulate the masses, thus, he was the first to show American corporations how to make people want things they didn't need by linking their unconscious desires to mass-produced goods" (Gable, 2010:p.108). Edward Bernays created ways of exploiting the unconscious desires of the consumer's innermost feelings by offering solutions to our repressed desires. Subliminally, women were convinced that the cigarette was a symbol of the penis. Thus, this masculine sexual power was given to the cigarette to challenge the existing male-dominant authority; hence, if a woman smoked, it made her feel in control.

The idea that smoking made women free was irrational, but it made them feel more independent. "This meant that irrelevant objects could become powerful and emotional symbols of how you wanted to be seen by others" (Curtis, 2002). Advertising should not attempt rational or logical explanations of a product's usefulness; on the contrary, it should deal entirely on the level of feelings and human emotions. Bernays stressed that consumer products should make us feel better by engaging with hidden and irrational emotions, and so, "manipulation of public opinion was necessary to overcome the chaos and conflict in society, thus, the manipulation was for our own good, and the only way that democracy can work efficiently" (Bernays, 2005:p.37-41).

When Cigarette Companies Used Doctors to Push Smoking

This photo of legendary actress Lucille Ball represents a simple but effective public relation, and trendsetting advertising approach that tells the female consumer smoking can represent a woman of confidence and authority.

The cigarette industry used many persuasive adds to convince that it was safe for practically any one to indulge in the pleasures of smoking. The young, pregnant, and nursing mother was no exception.

Today, the promotion of smoking cigarettes as healthy (even to youth and pregnant moms) and the use of doctors' endorsements may appear horrifying. Yet before 1950, medical industry denied that there wasn't good evidence showing that cigarette smoking was bad for one's health, even pregnant or nursing moms.

Cigarettes had become a mass-produced commodity for a mass audience, and now, "the cigarette marks the convergence of corporate success, technology, mass marketing, and in particular the impact of advertising. These forces induced new modes of individuality and group behavior, thus with the rise of consumerism, a new behavioral ethic was defined." (Hughes, 2003: p.118).

Doctors were paid to endorse the lifestyle of smoking among pregnant women. Consumer products were now not about their usefulness, instead, the commodity becomes a symbol to represent another's identity or uniqueness, which then turns a want into an emotional need. "We must shift America from needs to a desires culture, and people must be trained to desire and to want new things. Even before the old have been entirely consumed, we must shape a new mentality in America" (Haring and Douglass, 2012: p.17). This signifies that the novelty of advertising is no longer about watching someone consume a product, or what the product can do, but rather it's about "social manipulation creating inferiority and false problems that could only be resolved by submission to purchase" (Haring and Douglass, 2012:p.12). Having a celebrity consume a product used to be enough to make anyone buy the product now; corporations were selling an idea of a particular lifestyle.

Nike, Adidas, Under Armor, and Converse are Sports Corporation's that don't compete in the commodity market. It wasn't about their clothing, their trainers, or the slogan trend. They wanted to sell an idea that was symbolic of the nature of sports and pure athletic capability, for example, this is how, Michael Jordan "became a Nike guy" (Katz, 1994: p.6), he became the icon or metaphor of the American dream. "The Nike commercial 'Jordan flight' was replayed often in 1985, as Michael Jordan became more famous as Air Jordan: the Nike guy who could fly" (Katz, 1994: p.7). Nike was selling a brand that presented the consumer with the idea of invincibility and a lifestyle of athletic capability. Thus, if you purchased a Nike product, you would become a Nike kind of person like Michael Jordan.

Multi-national corporations were selling a product by connecting it to a belief, or an action to the product: the community was used to sell McDonald's, revolution and the idea of doing things differently was used to sell the iPhone, and peace and love were used to sell the famous Coca Cola. These Iconic brands of America became elite because "they understood that a brand wasn't just a mascot or a catchphrase or a picture printed on the label of the company's product: the company as a whole could have a brand identity or a corporate consciousness" (Klein, 2000:p.7). What advertising did was think about what the consumers were thinking and experiencing whilst consuming the product.

Theodor Adorno argued that cultural corporations "manipulated the masses, as popular culture was seen as a reason why people become passive because of the easy pleasures available through consumption of popular culture made people docile and content" (Adorno and Horkheimer, 2002: p.63-94). Popular culture may seem to offer the freedom of choice in aid of self-expression, but for Adorno, this is an ideological illusion: a phenomenon he terms pseudo-individualization. People merely imitate ideas and lifestyles from someone else that they admire; hence, why people are vulnerable to manipulation and socially engineered into a matrix of illusions. Meanwhile, the game of advertising continues to play games on our insecurities, fears, needs, and anxieties, especially in the industry of vanity, i.e., the cosmetic market.

Black Flag, long preferred by housewives everywhere for quickly killing flies and mosquitoes on contact, now does *double duty*. The amazing DDT ingredient now in Black Flag stays on walls, floors, doorways to *keep on killing flies for weeks!* To use wonderful DDT *safely and effectively* in your home use only a well-known and reliable insecticide—ask for Black Flag.

The power of advertising can manipulate our consciousness and our decision making. Strong public relations can potentially influence how we should look and feel, similar to the way politics manipulate the masses; slogans like a steak at every dinner table, no new taxes, and no child left behind are practically nothing but emotional forms of persuasion that conform opinion and belief.

The masses don't thoroughly analyze the complete composition of a cosmetic, body lotion, shampoo, or sanitary napkins when shopping, because of time constraints. For example, when the average consumer is looking for toothpaste, their focus is not on whether the brand is fluoride-free or not; however, if the consumer is not aware of the adverse effects on sodium fluoride, therefore toothpaste is just toothpaste. It is evident that people are not concerned about the adverse effects of brushing

When popular brands run an ad, most consumers are convinced that this is a brand that should be purchased, because it appears to be safe. Otherwise, why would it be advertised in the first place? Consumers have no desire to be undesirable in public; therefore, they need a deodorant that will suffice, one will purchase the product regardless of the chemical composition or the integrity of the product.

Another example is digestive disorders; because of the Standard American Dietary consumption, many people have acid reflux, bloating, colitis, irritable bowel syndrome (IBS), and Crohn's disease, so there is needs symptom reliever. Consumer buys an over the counter drug hoping for relief based on the commercial ad. Though there a warning of possible adverse reactions, the consumer's objective is to find relief for their repeated human dietary error. Manufacturers know how naïve the average consumer is, and it is not to necessarily take advantage of the consumer; it just business.

In 1964, a gynecologist named Robert Wilson published a book called Feminine Forever, 'told women that menopause was a disease, women were no longer feminine after menopause, and that horse estrogen was the "Magical Cure" for these conditions. Then Ann Walsh, in 1965, followed up with her book "The Pills to Keep Women Young" and emphasized the same approach. Unfortunately, both of these completely undocumented books were monumental successes. Many corporations, who profited from these internationally prescribed hormone replacement drugs, were even more successful.

Marketing does not have a responsibility for improving societal attitudes or breaking down gender stereotypes. Marketing is responsible for - and paid for - the brand that is attempting to persuade a specific target market with a particular message. Some ethical guidelines and rules apply to how this is achieved, but certain realities dictate how marketing campaigns represent certain groups. Here is the origin of product and campaign manipulation:

In the 1950s, Marlboro undertook a campaign to associate its cigarette with masculinity and being a 'real man.' Its message was pretty clear: the post-Liberation woman became strong, empowered, and equal to her male, Marlboro-smoking counterpart. To prove it, she had her own equally addictive cigarettes, created just for her. "When the restless, isolated, bored, and insecure housewife fled the feminine mystique for the workplace, advertisers faced the loss of their primary consumer."

CHAPTER 7
BPA and Plastic The Chemical That Is Clearly Behind Estrogen Dominance

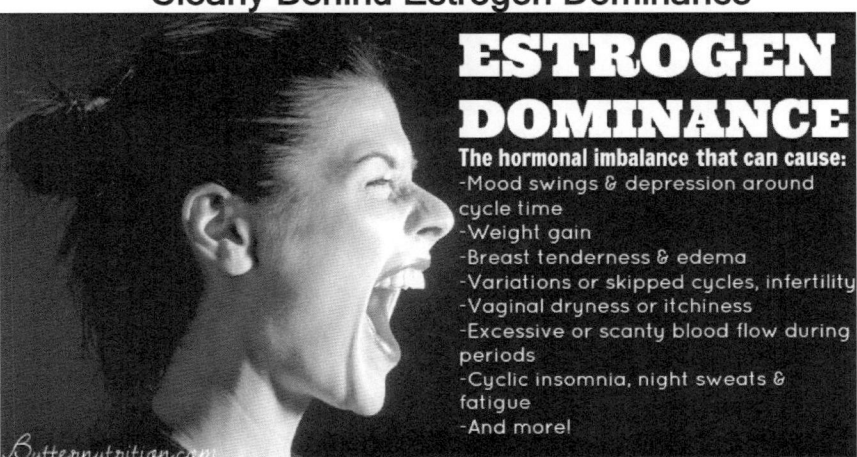

In the past 40 years, we have seen a dramatic rise in illnesses never before seen in history. Today, we see the age of puberty (menarche) dropping precipitously to as low as sometimes 8 years of age, endometriosis afflicting 10% of all perimenopausal women; Premenstrual Syndrome (PMS), rising and afflicting close to 30% of perimenopausal women, uterine fibroids affecting close to 25 % of women from age 35 to 50, and breast cancer afflicting close to 10% of women. Being a woman in the 21st century is undoubtedly a high-risk existence.

The two primary hormones secreted by the ovaries are estrogen and progesterone. The properties of one offset the other, together they are maintained in optimal balance at all times. Too much of one hormone or the other can lead to significant physical and emotional imbalances. During the 1970s, one of the great medical pioneers, Dr. John R. Lee, went beyond the mainstream of western medical methodologies and discovered one of the contributing factors of today's women-related epidemic was linked to estrogen dominance and progesterone deficiency.

Estrogen dominance is associated with the increased development of not only fibroids and endometriosis, but the increase of uterine, breast, ovarian, and cervical cancer. Even women who diligently workout, have a higher incidence of fibroid development due to the exposure of estrogen-mimicking chemicals.

In 1981 Dr. John R. Lee discovered an article produced by John Hopkins University that showed women who had normal levels of progesterone had only 1/10th of the risk of various cancers. Though it was literally in the medical literature, it was not being taught in medical school. Then he began studying the reports of xenogenous estrogens and why species like amphibians and fish were also at risk of becoming extinct. Then they realized that the synthetic estrogen that was used 30 or more years ago was not estrogen, but DiEthylStilbestrol (DES) a potent estrogen-mimicking agent that was found to increase breast cancer risk in women. When given to pregnant mothers, there was an increased risk of cervical cancer in their newborns with internal reproductive anatomy.

Estrogen is the most powerful, but most dangerous of all human hormones, which is why it is referred to as the "Angel of Life and "Angel of Death." Estrogen also helps protect the bones, heart, and balance your mood. When in harmony, estrogen levels are kept in check by two other hormones, which are progesterone and testosterone. Progesterone is a hormone that is produced in the adrenal glands and testicular tissues. It is a precursor to the stress hormone cortisol, testosterone, estrogen, and other hormones. The roster of hormonal balance helps keep bones strong, blood vessels healthy, and energy at its peak.

Estrogen

When estrogen levels increase beyond what is usual for a given human, certain symptoms may develop. These symptoms include mood swings, depression, vision problems, changes in voice tone, decreased libido, skin elasticity, hair loss, acne, weight gain, and even largely extended belly and abdominal fat. This is the reason why Bioidentical hormone testing is imperative in today's society, however this is not to be confused with any other type of replacement. *See more on Why Bioidentical Testing Is Important, which will be discussed in Chapter 18*

Estradiol

For those who have internal reproductive systems, estrogen is produced in the ovaries; it regulates the menstrual cycle, promotes cell division, and is mainly responsible for the development of secondary sex characteristics during puberty, including the growth and development of the breast and pubic hair. Estrogen, therefore, affects all reproductive organs, including the ovaries, cervix, fallopian tubes, vulva, and breast. As a general rule, estrogen promotes cell growth, including signaling the growth of the blood-rich tissue of the uterus during the first part of the menstrual cycle and stimulates the maturation of the egg-moving follicles outside the ovaries.

Estrogen produced in the body is not a single hormone but a trio of hormones working together. The three components of estrogen are estrone (E1), estradiol (E2), and estriol (E3). Estrogen is a pro-growth hormone. Since too much of anything is generally not good, the body has another hormone to offset and counterbalance the effects of estrogen, which is progesterone.

Women who live in rural, countryside areas in countries overseas do not experience high rates of osteoporosis, heart disease, arthritis, hot flashes, cancers, and other problems because they are not as exposed to xenoestrogens. They have been shown to have generally lower levels of estradiol and estrone, and higher levels of estriol and progesterone. Western women overall have excessive estradiol and estrone levels from eating so much saturated fat, alcohol, coffee, sugar, artificial sweeteners, creamers, carbonated beverages, highly refined carbohydrate intake (potato chips, corn chips, dairy, and GMO snacks.

Women in America and Europe generally have excessive estrogen levels (even after menopause). Have you noticed how very few menstruating women refilled their estrogen prescriptions? For ERT, horse estrogen was the most prescribed drug for women in the world, with 45 million prescriptions a year. In 2002, it was found to be a dismal and dangerous failure. Nevertheless, it is still a popular drug even though it has been scientifically discredited. Horse estrogen is extracted from the urine of pregnant mares. Unbelievable! Horse estrogen is composed of about half estrone and estradiol, and half equilin and other equines (horse) estrogens.

There is a cascade of unnatural factors that can create or chronically elevate your estrogen levels. Here is some of the reason to be concerned about estrogen dominance:

• **Medications** - This includes estrogen-containing drugs, steroids, ulcer medications, some antibiotics (tetracycline, ampicillin, etc.), antifungal medications, and antidepressants. According to testimonials, you have to take the extra precaution of the new aged antibiotic, Levaquin.

• **Unfavorable Diet** - The type of food that you consume influences the conversion of testosterone into estrogen. Different natural body types are widely ranged, as well as both healthy and unhealthy body fat. Fat cells, especially those in the abdominal region, can produce an enzyme known as "aromatase." This enzyme is key in converting testosterone into estradiol. With a substantial amount of unhealthy fat in the body, more testosterone is converted into estradiol, causing an imbalance and leading to further estrogen dominance.

- **Alcohol** - Excessive can increase the body's conversion of testosterone into estrogen, especially in fat cells. It can also block the liver from effectively eliminating excess estrogen.

- Toxic chemical and environmental exposure - produce that is laced with pesticides, insecticides, and herbicides have the potential to mimic and elevating estrogen. This is why we need to support the natural food stores and demand mainstream grocery stores stock more affordable organic and hormone-free products in addition to a national organic non-GMO movement.

Bisphenol A Plastic and Xenoestrogens

Just One Word, Ben..." Plastics!"
In the 1967 movie "The Graduate," Mr. McGuire (Walter Brooke) gives Ben party..." Plastics."

Plastics! Unfortunately, this fractionally distilled substance used to create petrochemical plastics is inescapable in our environment. From canned food liners to the toothbrush, this unbreakable toxic substance has truly altered the environment for plants, humans, and animals. It has become a detriment to our health.

One of the primary causes of our many crises is the presence of high levels of synthetic estrogen in the human body, due to industrial toxicity. Young people are developing weaker immune systems, so too are future women going to develop a weaker human species because our natural states of health have been compromised by the production of synthetic estrogens. Women in the U.S. are developing disease faster than any civilization known to date, and this experience of health complications is completely inexplicable to most. So, the symptoms continue until the diagnosis of fibroids, candidiasis, endometriosis, cancer, and autoimmune diseases are finally determined by invasive tests.

These current and future Matriarchs are society's honored storytellers, healers, advisors, sages, and parents; they are the pillars of society despite not being recognized as such. But society has disenchanted the health potential of most women, because of the limited proactive campaigns (like the EWG and Campaign for Cosmetics health advocates) are intercepted by political campaigns, television programming, and other forms of distraction from around the world. In the meantime, the manufacturing of harsh chemicals that mimic estrogen continues uninterrupted.

BISPHENOL A

$$HO-\text{C}_6H_4-\underset{\underset{CH_3}{|}}{\overset{\overset{CH_3}{|}}{C}}-\text{C}_6H_4-OH$$

One prime compound in plastic that has received global notoriety is Bisphenol A (BPA). Did you know that when the clear toxic chemical was developed in the 1930s, it was discovered to have the ability to mimic estrogen, so BPA was actually a drug candidate for menopausal women with low estrogen levels?   While it never made it on the roster as a prescription drug, the chemists discovered that, when you string BPA together into a long chain, it makes a very resilient plastic known as polycarbonate. This launched BPA as a leading ingredient in consumer products, bringing this estrogen mimic into every American home. It's so pervasive that a government study found BPA exposure in 95% of the study participants.

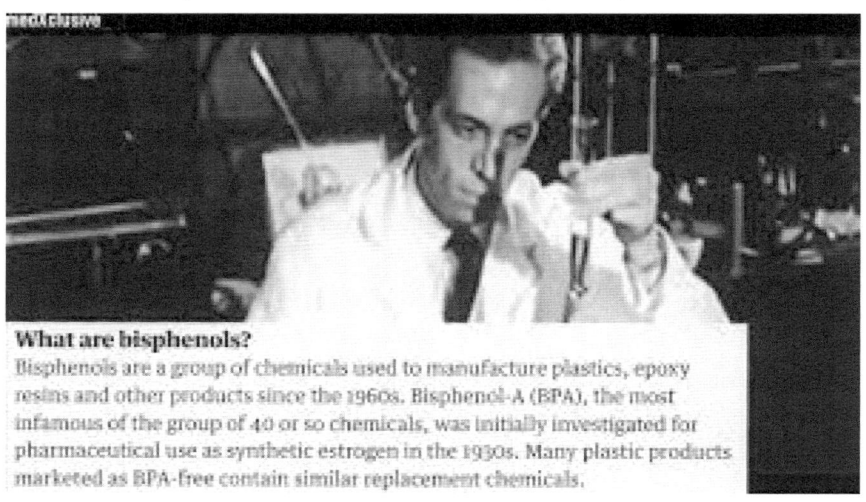

What are bisphenols?
Bisphenols are a group of chemicals used to manufacture plastics, epoxy resins and other products since the 1960s. Bisphenol-A (BPA), the most infamous of the group of 40 or so chemicals, was initially investigated for pharmaceutical use as synthetic estrogen in the 1930s. Many plastic products marketed as BPA-free contain similar replacement chemicals.

BPA, a petrochemical constituent that is wreaking havoc on the human body and our environmental resources, is linked to devastating endocrine disruption and hormonal imbalances. People who consume foods and beverages contained in plastic bottles, plastic wraps, and food seals are exposed to the bisphenol A (BPA) toxin every day. BPA is also found in the lining of canned food as well as on store receipts. Absorption through the skin and ingestion are the two most effective ways to enter the body. Even inhalation is also a possibility because of the sheer volume produced, which is around 1.6 billion pounds annually.

PHTHALATES A Toxic Component of Plastics

Are a class of plasticizers used to soften polyvinyl chloride (PVCs), add fragrance to a product, or enhance pliability in plastics and other products. Phthalates are classified as low molecular weight (3-6 carbon backbone) and high molecular weight (>6 carbon backbone), with the low molecular weight classes thought to pose the most significant health risks. Phthalates act by interfering with androgen (testosterone) production. Because androgens are critical to male development, including genital development, boys are thought to be most vulnerable to exposure. However, androgens also play important roles in females, making phthalates relevant to both sexes. **Use of some phthalates has been restricted from toys since 1999 in the EU and 2008 in the US. Phthalates are found in:**

> *Shampoos, lotions, nail polish and other personal care products; Cosmetics; Baby products including lotion, shampoo, powders and teethers; Toys; Scented products such as candles, detergent and air fresheners; Automobiles (phthalates are responsible for the 'new car' smell); Medical equipment including tubing, blood bags, and plastics in the NICU; Building materials including vinyl flooring, wallpaper, paint, glue and adhesives; Enteric coatings of pharmaceuticals; Art supplies including paint, clay, wax and ink. Phthalate exposure is linked to: Genital abnormalities in boys; Reduced sperm counts. Decreased 'male typical' play in boys; Endometriosis; Elements of metabolic disruption including obesity.*

This synthetic estrogen mimicker was first discovered in 1891 as a significant building block in what is now known as polycarbonate plastic. It was first found to be estrogenic back in 1936. One of the main problems with bisphenol-A is that it is a reproductive toxin. Not only does it affect the female ability to reproduce because of its estrogenic nature, but also it has been shown to affect men as well. The industry argues that the amounts of bisphenol-A humans are exposed to and assimilate minute and, therefore, not a significant threat to health. They cite a single study. Other researchers are bewildered by this assertion as the number of studies showing quite the opposite effect is numerous.

BPA is a large business, and though there are environmentalists, clinician, health and holistic organization they oppose the production of it, the aftermath of BPA still has a mighty presence regarding the toxic damage hormonal hysteria.

What makes matters worse is that BPA is with other chemicals like bisphenol S and F, which has had limited and may not be deemed any less toxic than bisphenol-A. In summary, it is still plastic, and it is still a petrochemical derivative.

While the provocateurs of greed and power continue to manufacture synthetic materials, the people are ingesting and an extraordinary amount of estrogen, which is why breast cancers and ovarian cancers are running rampant?   It all comes back to the culprit of the production of synthetic chemicals mimicking estrogen.

Phthalates are a group of chemicals used to soften and increase the flexibility of plastics. They are also heavily used in personal care products, especially those that are scented. Bisphenols are in air fresheners that use heat to release the aroma. Even if these sources are avoided, phthalates are still prevalent do not bind very tightly to the plastics and therefore are released into the atmosphere quite quickly.

Several recent studies have revealed that many of the metabolites of phthalates (DEP, DnBP, BBzP, and DEHP) are found extensively in the general population. There is evidence that the exposures also have socioeconomic and socio-demographic divides, which place a more significant burden on children of the poor. One of the mechanisms behind phthalate toxicity is its depression of testosterone. Growing evidence shows that phthalate exposure may express its effect on reproductive health, especially in developing males. It has also known to cause miscarriages and congenital disabilities. Arguments against phthalate's toxicity include its relatively short half-life, which is less than twenty-four hours.

Women with polycystic ovary syndrome (PCOS), the most common hormone imbalance in women of reproductive age, may be more vulnerable to exposure to the chemical bisphenol-A (BPA), found in many plastic household items, according to a new study.

The study found that BPA, a known hormone disrupter, is elevated and associated with higher levels of male hormones in the blood of women with PCOS compared with healthy women. These findings held for both lean and obese women with PCOS, said Evanthia Diamanti-Kandarakis, MD, Ph.D., study co-author and professor at the University of Athens Medical School in Greece.

"Women with the **polycystic ovary syndrome** should be very cautious regarding this environmental contaminant's potential adverse effects on reproductive aspects of their health problem," she said.

Excessive secretion of androgens -- masculinization-promoting hormones -- occurs in PCOS. The syndrome raises the risk of infertility, obesity, Type 2 diabetes, and heart disease. Past studies show that women who have had recurrent miscarriages have shown traces of BPA in their blood. This chemical can leach into the bloodstream from food and beverage containers that are made of polycarbonate hard plastic or lined with epoxy resins, or from some dental sealants and composites.

In the new study, the researchers divided 71 women with PCOS and 100 healthy female control subjects into subgroups matched by age and body composition (obese or lean). Blood levels of BPA, compared with those of controls, were nearly 60 percent higher in slim women with PCOS and more than 30 percent higher in obese women with the syndrome.

Additionally, as the BPA blood level increased, so did the concentrations of the male sex hormone testosterone and androstenedione, a steroid hormone that converts to testosterone, Diamanti-Kandarakis reported. Fluoride: Have We Been Deceived?

The truth is now becoming increasingly evident that fluoridation and the proclaimed benefit of Fluoride as a way of preventing dental decay is perhaps the most significant "scientific" fraud ever perpetrated upon an unsuspecting public.

The primary estrogen used in birth control pills is Ethinyl estrogen and is very dangerous even at low doses. Synthetic estrogens do not exist in nature; however, It is more potent than estradiol (E2). Find another means of contraception, and do not use the Pill to avoid pregnancy. The long-term use results in severe side effects, including various forms of cancer. BPA was also suggested as a form of birth control.

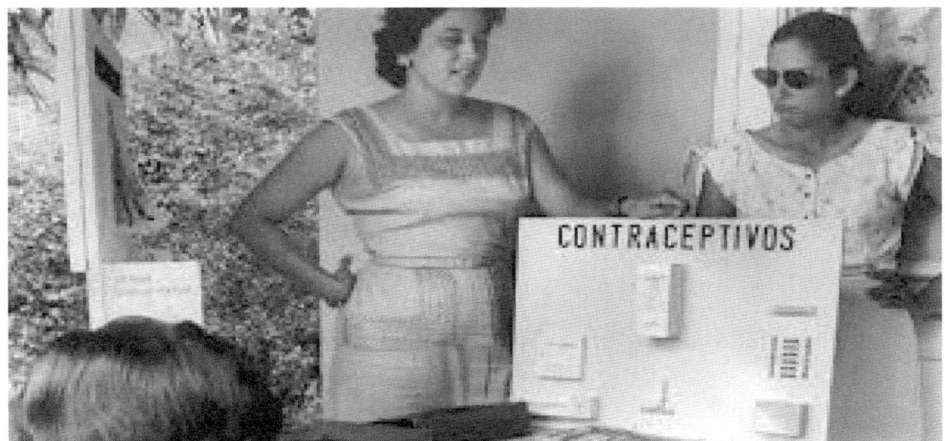

The contraceptive was not only prescribed for birth control but fibroids.

Food additives may also be another addition to estrogen dominance. Italian researchers recently screened 1,500 food additives and found that two had estrogenic properties. The first is propyl gallate, a preservative used in baked goods, shortening, candy, dried meats, pork sausage, mayonnaise, and dried milk. The second, 4-hexylresorcinol, is used to prevent shrimp and other shellfish from discoloring.

Estriol: The Forgotten Estrogen

Estriol is the most prominent of all estrogens and comprises about 80% of human and mammal estrogen. It is a kind and friendly estrogen and has many benefits. This is an orphan or forgotten hormone (along with pregnenolone). The research on estradiol and estrone is not only overwhelming but often unnecessary and repetitious. More work still needs to be done on estriol, especially for various diseases and conditions.

The research has been most impressive. The more we learn about this essential hormone, the more benefits we are going to find for deficient women. Even though most of the research was conducted with oral doses, the doctors still got dramatic results. They will get even better results when they use the proper sublingual and transdermal forms. Estriol is rarely deficient in men; by the way, men do not need to test this. Deficiencies in women, especially over the age of 40, are all too common. You can even find estriol deficiencies in teenage girls, especially those who are overweight.

Western women are generally low in estriol, while high in estradiol and estrone. Doctors do not have the word "estriol" in their vocabulary. This lack of knowledge includes endocrinologists, gynecologists, naturopaths, holistic, and life extension specialists. Pharmacies do not carry it and cannot even special order the oral tablets. Ask your physician or licensed holistic practitioner for advice before estriol, estradiol, estrone, progesterone, or testosterone along with any other medication or herbal supplement. Some medical professionals feel that Oral estriol is not effective.

Progesterone and estrogen require a counterpart, a pro-growth hormone. Since too much estrogen can promote a problem, the body develops another hormone to offset and counterbalance the effects of estrogen. It is called progesterone. As its name implies, progesterone is a hormone that is pro-gestation. In other words, it favors the growth and wellbeing of the fetus. Without a proper amount of progesterone, there can be no successful pregnancy. It protects us against the "growth effect" of estrogen. When progesterone is secreted, further ovulation is prevented from taking place in the second half of the menstrual cycle, and thick mucus that is hostile to sperm is produced that prevents its passage into the womb.

Progesterone is made from **pregnenolone**, which in turn comes from cholesterol. Production occurs in several places. In those who can become pregnant, it is primarily made in the ovaries just before ovulation and increasing rapidly after ovulation. It is also made in the adrenal glands in all sexes and the testes in those with external reproductive anatomy. In menstruating women, its level is highest during the luteal period (especially from day 19-22 of the menstrual cycle). If fertilization does not take place, the secretion of progesterone decreases, and menstruation occurs 12 to 14 days later under normal conditions. If fertilization does occur, progesterone is secreted during pregnancy by the placenta. This is an important activity because it prevents spontaneous abortion. About 20-25 mg of progesterone is produced per day during a given monthly cycle. During pregnancy, up to 300-400 mg of progesterone is produced.

According to **Dr. John Lee, M.D.**, an authority on natural hormone therapy, the key to hormonal balance is the modulation of progesterone to estrogen ratio. For an optimum state of health in women who menstruate, the progesterone to estrogen ratio should be between 200 and 300 to 1. From age 35 to 50, there is a 75% reduction in the production of progesterone in the body. Estrogen, during the same period, only declines by about 35%. By menopause, the total amount of progesterone made is extremely low, while estrogen is still present in the body at about half its pre-menopausal levels.

The body needs natural progesterone to counter the estrogen effect. Synthetic progesterone's are far from the natural form. While some studies show that estrogen does not cause cancer in the short-term, but in menstruating women taking estrogen and/or a synthetic progestin for more than ten years, there appears to be a significantly elevated risk of breast, ovarian, and uterine cancers.

Because there is a lucrative potential, one has to question if hormonal imbalance and HRT is becoming a stock commodity along with the hysterectomy procedure. According to a book called "Bad Medicine," written by an author, John Archer revealed that about 600,000 hysterectomies are performed each year in the U.S., and about 45,000 in Australia and all were taking Hormone Replacement Therapy (HRT). Most menstruating women are encouraged to get on and remain on the HRT Treatment.

The History of Estrogen Replacement Therapy

When it comes to making a decision on ERT, many women become quite confused when they have been ultimately thrown into a radical state of menopause, because they no longer have an innate ability to produce estrogen, especially if all parts of the internal reproductive system have been removed; losing not only the uterus, but the cervix and ovaries as well.

ERT is touted as the most appropriate idea since the concept of oral contraceptives – even though statistics over the years revealed the risk of taking Birth Control Pills (BCP) included health hazards ranging from cardiovascular disease to cancer development while protecting them from unwanted pregnancy.

ERT has a strange history that goes back to the 1930s with the research of Dr. Serge Voronoff. His research involved the implant of freshly severed monkey testicles into the scrotums of men, with limited effectiveness. Eventually, promoting the audacity of grafting monkey ovaries in women, which created dire consequences, thus causing several fatalities in both the women and the monkeys, later creating a new concept of synthetic estrogen? Due to World War II, the research was halted.

Over the years, there have been many professional advocates of synthetic estrogen, as well as many other medical and 'professional' crusaders continue to arrogantly alter the natural life cycle by using anti-life protocols and products that would "save" pre-menopausal women from the horrors of "unnatural" menopause and accelerated aging.

For example, in **1966 a book titled Feminine Forever** was written by **Gynecologist Dr. Robert Wilson** hit the bestseller list raving about the benefits of estrogen replacement therapy, and that it rescued pre-menopausal women from the maladies of menopause, rescuing women from so-called hormone "hysteria" as well as promoting "better" health. His book sold over 100,000 copies in the first year, promoting the ERT as a new youth phenomenon. He argued that women on the verge of menopause need hormone drugs to be delivered from the inevitable "horrors" that menopause brings.

Still, there has been no legitimate research regarding the safety of estrogen therapy and its long-term effects. The unopposed estrogen concept fizzled of vogue when it became apparent that ERT shortens the lifetime of its users. In 1975, the New England Journal of Medicine investigated the statistics of endometrial cancer that were using estrogen. The investigation revealed that the risk was seven and a half times greater for the ERT users, and for women who have used the ERT for seven years or longer were 14 times more likely to develop malignant activity (Cancer).

Another professional, **Dr. Lynette J. Dumble**, Senior Research Fellow at the University of Melbourne's Department of Surgery at Royal Melbourne Hospital, believed that HRT not only exacerbates a woman's current health challenges but also contributes to the acceleration of aging. Based on Dr. Dumble's expertise and research, the prime motive for HRT was to commercialize it to the masses to maximize profits, even though the acclaimed benefits of HRT were unproven.

Another landmark study involving **121,700** *women* appeared in a 1995 report in the New England Journal of Medicine concerning the startling effects of HRT. The report warned women who decided to use ERT to buffer symptoms of menopause should be aware of the increased risk of developing breast by 30 to 40 percent if taken beyond five years. Women between the ages of 60 and 64, the risk jumped to 70 percent beyond five years. The report from the NEJM also concluded that 45 percent of the women who used it would be more likely to die from breast cancer than women who refrained from HRT or discontinued the use prior to five years.

The Advent of Fibroids and Endometriosis

Across the globe, many women are at risk of benign tumor growth within the internal reproductive system called **Myoma**, a medical term used for fibroids. It is a benign growth of smooth muscle in the wall of the uterus, a solid tumor made of fibrous tissue; hence, often called fibroid tumors. The growth may vary in size and multiply, are most often slow-growing and usually cause no symptoms in the beginning. According to research, fibroids grow in some women and will grow faster than others depending on the factors of lifestyle, diet, stress, chemical exposure, and level of detoxification that will cause symptoms and need medical treatment.

Myomas or **fibroids** may grow as a single nodule or in clusters and may range in size from pea size to beyond the size of a medium-sized melon. Myomas are the most frequent type of tumor found in the internal reproductive system, and the most common reason for a woman to have a hysterectomy. Although they are recognized as tumors, they tend not to be cancerous. According to western medicine, the cause of fibroids is still unknown, but most benign tumors develop in women during their reproductive years. Even women in their senior years had been found to have fibroids.

Fibroids tend to proliferate during pregnancy when the body is producing extra estrogen. Once menopause has begun, they generally stop growing and can begin to shrink due to the loss of estrogen. (http://www.uterine-fibroids.org)

Myectomy is the surgical removal of fibroids from the uterus. It allows the uterus to be in place and, for some women, makes pregnancy even more likely than before. The Myectomy is the preferred fibroid treatment for women who want to become pregnant. After this surgery, female chances of pregnancy may be improved but are not guaranteed.

Before myomectomy, shrinking fibroids with gonadotropin-releasing hormone analog may reduce blood loss from the surgery. GnRH-a therapy lowers the amount of estrogen the body makes. If you experience bleeding from a fibroid, GnRH-a therapy could also improve anemia before surgery by stopping uterine bleeding for several months. (http://women.webmd.com)

The myomectomy is a medical procedure in which uterine fibroids are surgically removed from the uterus. According to research, uterine fibroids (also known as myomas) affect over 30% of women. While many women tolerate fibroids for long periods, some women may experience various symptoms visit (http://www.myomectomy.net) for more information.

Myomectomies are performed less than 40,000 times a year in the U.S. Possibly as many as 80% of all women have uterine fibroids, though the symptoms may be tolerated by some 1 in 4 ends up with symptoms severe enough to require treatment. (http://www.nuff.org/health_statistics) especially if they develop chronic symptoms of prolonged or heavy menstrual bleeding, pelvic pressure or pain, and in rare cases, reproductive dysfunction.

Uterine fibroids are also medically termed, as uterine leiomyoma is non-cancerous tumors consisting of fibers or fibrous tissue that arise in the uterus. It is the most common tumor within the internal reproductive system, and these growths are highly sensitive to estrogen. They develop following the onset of menstruation; enlarge during pregnancy, and decrease, often disappearing after menopause when the estrogen level decreases by half. They can be as small as a golf ball, or commonly grow to the size of an orange or grapefruit. The largest fibroid on record weighed over 100 pounds. It afflicts many women, mainly from ages 35 to 50. The increasing growth of fibroids increases discomfort by pressing on the bladder, thus promoting heavy menstrual bleeding. One in four women in the U.S. has at least some evidence of fibroids.

In cases where the tumor size compromises other bodily functions such as compression of the bladder or excessive bleeding, surgery may be necessary. The most common surgery is a hysterectomy. Many hysterectomies, however, are performed way before the patient reaches this stage. Over 500,000 hysterectomies are performed every year in the U.S. alone, as mentioned earlier. These lesions disrupt the functions of the uterus and cause excessive uterine bleeding, anemia, defective implantation of an embryo, recurrent pregnancy loss, preterm labor, obstruction of labor, pelvic discomfort, and urinary incontinence and may mimic or mask malignant tumors.

Many menstruating women, who are subjugated by this invasive treatment, are reluctant to take their prescriptions and continue with ERT because of the most unpleasant side effects. The vast majority of women in American are, in fact, excessive in estradiol and estrone, but deficient in estriol and progesterone during their cycles, when approaching and after menopause.

By 1975 women on estrogen replacement therapy (ERT) were getting up to 800% more uterine cancer, among many, many other problems. The promoters were compelled to change this to HRT (hormone replacement therapy) by adding unnatural progestin analogs instead of real human progesterone. Since progesterone cannot be patented, this was done purely for profit. Now even wilder, and more extravagant claims were made - again with no scientific basis at all, and side effects were often denied. Of course, the side effects were every bit as severe as before, only different, since progestins themselves are toxic and dangerous.   Many doctors today use the terms "progesterone" and "progestin" interchangeably as if they were the same hormones!

Possibly the biggest medical fallacy going is that estrogen levels in women drop severely after menopause.   These low levels are directly responsible for the many female complications, which include everything from depression to hot flashes. Countless clinical tests prove quite the opposite. Doctors ignore all other essential hormones. The fallacy continues that horse estrogen is the "Magic Answer", and you don't even have to.

Once a medical protocol fails, and the woman's symptoms persist, the patient will often return to their Gynecologist to seek other treatment options. According to many medical studies, most women are familiar with only surgical options like (myomectomy, surgically removing some of the fibroids or hysterectomy, surgically removing the uterus) from their Gynecologist.

While a hysterectomy is an option for some women suffering from fibroids and it does result in an elimination of the woman's symptoms, it is at a very significant and steep price (i.e., the loss of her uterus and perhaps her ovaries as well). Hysterectomy has a profoundly negative effect on many women. It can affect them psychologically (like male castration), sexually (loss of libido, loss of orgasm), increases their risk for significant bone loss (osteoporosis), and there is even data to suggest an increased cardiovascular risk. A study in the Journal of Women's Health in 2013 looked at approximately 1,000 pre-menopausal adult women suffering from fibroids.

Their findings included:
Average time waited to seek treatment 3.6 years, with 25% over five years. When asked why they waited so long, over 50% did not want a hysterectomy, and 75% wanted a treatment option that avoided surgery altogether (but were not given one). Hysterectomy is unnecessary to treat fibroid-related symptoms effectively.

By the time they reach 50 years of age, nearly 70% of Caucasian women and more than 80% of "African American or Aboriginal Indigenous women will have had at least one fibroid; severe symptoms develop in 15 to 30% of these women. Uterine fibroids in women of African or Aboriginal Indigenous descent is significantly larger at diagnosis than women of European descent, are diagnosed at an earlier age, and are characterized by more severe symptoms and a more extended period of sustained growth. Approximately 200,000 hysterectomies, 30,000 myomectomies, and thousands of selective uterine artery embolization's and high-intensity focused ultrasound procedures are performed annually in the United States to remove or destroy uterine fibroids.

The annual economic burden of these tumors is estimated to be between $5.9 billion and $34.4 billion. Fibrous tissues are sensitive to estrogen dominance, the more estrogen and synthetic estrogen, the faster the fibroid grows and the higher the risk of cancer. While a fibroid in itself does not usually lead to cancer or become cancerous, it signals a severe underlying imbalance in a woman's reproductive and hormonal system. Specifically, there is an estrogen dominance and progesterone deficiency. Such imbalance does not only affect the uterus but affects other hormone-sensitive tissues such as breast, cervix, ovaries, and the vagina as well.

Fibroids located in the front of the uterus will compress the bladder to cause increased urinary frequency and nocturia (causing a woman to wake up in the middle of the night to urinate; often multiple times each night). These fibroids are located more laterally will press on pelvic nerves to causing pelvic pain, which can radiate across the pelvis onto the lower back, hips, buttocks, and even down her extremities. Sub-serosal fibroids in other locations of the uterus can cause dyspareunia (painful intercourse), constipation, or hydronephrosis (blockage of the kidney). This condition can be an underlying cause of infertility, extreme menstrual pain. A standard imaging tool to diagnose fibroids is the pelvic ultrasound exam, and there are two conventional probes used for this exam:

Transabdominal: is a small amount of gel placed at the end of this probe, and scanning occurs across the skin of her lower abdomen and pelvic regions.

Transvaginal: A gel-coated condom that is placed over the thin probe. Gel is placed on the end of the condom, and then scanning procedure is performed inside the patient's vagina.

Fibroids Develop In Three Prime Areas

1. **Submucosal fibroids** reside just underneath the lining of the uterus and are responsible for the often-heavy period women with fibroids have. Women will often report having to change pads (typically > 8/day) less than every couple of hours and report episodes of blood "gushing" or "flooding" out with the passage of clots (sometimes as big as her fist).

2. **Intramural fibroids** are found in the muscular wall of the uterus. These tumors can grow in either direction (toward the lining or the outer surface or both) and therefore have the potential to cause heavy bleeding (submucosal fibroids) or bulk-related symptoms (sub-serosal fibroids) or both.

3. **Sub-serosal fibroids** are located just beneath the outer surface of the uterus and are responsible for the primary symptoms that women with fibroids may experience. These benign tumors grow away from the uterus and will press on adjacent structures in the pelvis and contribute to these symptoms.

On average, it took 9.28 years for women to receive a correct diagnosis of endometriosis. The study also revealed that the earlier the onset of symptoms, the greater the length of time before diagnosis, and the wider the variety of symptoms young women experienced. Those with symptoms as teenagers were more likely to suffer disability from the disease—a significant fact, considering that 66% reported having initial symptoms before age twenty. The data suggest that more girls may be experiencing more severe symptoms at younger ages. There is growing concern that hormonally active chemicals, such as dioxins and other chemicals that mimic hormones or cause other dysfunctions in the endocrine and immune systems, are accelerating the onset of puberty.

Above on the previous page are photos and illustrations of fibroids that have grown out of control.

Asian Medical Characteristics of Fibroids

1. Do you have abdominal pain? - Damp-Heat in the Large Intestines
2. Limbs/extremities tired? - Damp Heat In the Large Intestines
3. Anorexia? - Spleen Qi Deficiency.
4. Abdominal bloating and epigastric distention after eating?
5. Shortness of breath? Spleen Qi and Blood Deficiency
6. Sudden Anger and Mood Changes? - Liver and Spleen Disharmony
7. Nausea - Spleen Qi and Blood Deficiency
8. Irregular menses - Liver and Spleen Disharmony
9. Dysmenorrhea - Liver Qi Stagnation
10. Depression - Liver Qi Stagnation

According to a recent study in the Journal of Pediatrics, girls in the United States are reaching puberty earlier than ever. Nearly half of African American girls and 15% of White American girls are beginning to develop sexually at the age of eight. Development of breasts and pubic hair were two of the characteristics occurring at significantly younger ages than previously. The authors of the study called for more investigation into whether hormonally active chemicals (which are more prevalent in communities of color due to wealth disparity) are responsible for these findings.

Endometriosis epidemic is due to the exposure of industrial and technological xenoestrogens (synthetic estrogens) derived from petrochemicals. Again, these petrochemicals are the ingredient base of insecticides, pesticides, plastics bottles, meat packaging, canned goods, hair glues, adhesives, and more. So, this new age epidemic of fibroids and endometriosis among the masses of women is associated with an estrogen imbalance caused by synthetic estrogens or xenoestrogens.

Important Areas of the Female Reproductive System

Ovaries

The ovaries are a pair of small glands about the size and shape of almonds, located on the left and right sides of the pelvic body cavity lateral to the superior portion of the uterus. Ovaries produce sex hormones such as estrogen and progesterone as well as ova (commonly called "eggs"), the gametes. Ova are produced from oocyte cells that slowly develop throughout a woman's early life and reach maturity after puberty. Each month during ovulation, a mature ovum is released. The ovum travels from the ovary to the fallopian tube, where it may be fertilized before reaching the uterus.

Fallopian Tubes

The fallopian tubes are a pair of muscular tubes that extend from the left and right superior corners of the uterus to the edge of the ovaries. The fallopian tubes end in a funnel-shaped structure called the infundibulum, which is covered with small finger-like projections called fimbriae. The fimbriae swipe over the outside of the ovaries to pick up released ova and carry them into the infundibulum for transport to the uterus. The inside of each fallopian tube is covered in cilia that work with the smooth muscle of the tube to carry the ovum to the uterus.

Uterus

The uterus is a hollow, muscular, pear-shaped organ located posterior and superior to the urinary bladder. Connected to the two fallopian tubes on its superior end and the vagina (via the cervix) on its inferior end, the uterus is also known as the womb, as it surrounds and supports the developing fetus during pregnancy. The inner lining of the uterus, known as the endometrium, provides support to the embryo during early development. Visceral muscles of the uterus contract during childbirth and push the fetus through the birth canal.

Menstruation

While the ovum matures and travels through the fallopian tube, the endometrium grows and develops in preparation for the embryo. If the ovum is not fertilized in time or if it fails to implant into the endometrium, the arteries of the uterus constrict to cut off blood flow to the endometrium. The lack of blood flow causes cell death in the endometrium and the eventual shedding of tissue in a process known as menstruation. In a normal menstrual cycle, this shedding begins around day 28 and continues into the first few days of the new reproductive cycle.

Some complications that women have with their periods

Women can have a range of problems with their periods, including pain, heavy bleeding, and skipped periods.

Amenorrhea (uh-men-uh-REE-uh) – is the lack of a menstrual period. This term is used to describe the absence of a period in: • Young women who haven't started menstruating by age 15.
•Women and young girls who haven't had a period for 90 days, even if they haven't been menstruating for long lengths of time can include:

Pregnancy.
Breastfeeding
Extreme weight loss
Eating disorders
Excessive exercising• Stress

Serious medical conditions in need of treatment

As above, when your menstrual cycles come regularly, this means that important parts of your body are working normally. In some cases, not having menstrual periods can mean that your ovaries have stopped producing normal amounts of estrogen. Missing these hormones can have important effects on your overall health. Hormonal problems, such as those caused by polycystic ovary syndrome (PCOS) or serious problems with the reproductive organs, may be involved. It's important to talk to a doctor if you have this problem.

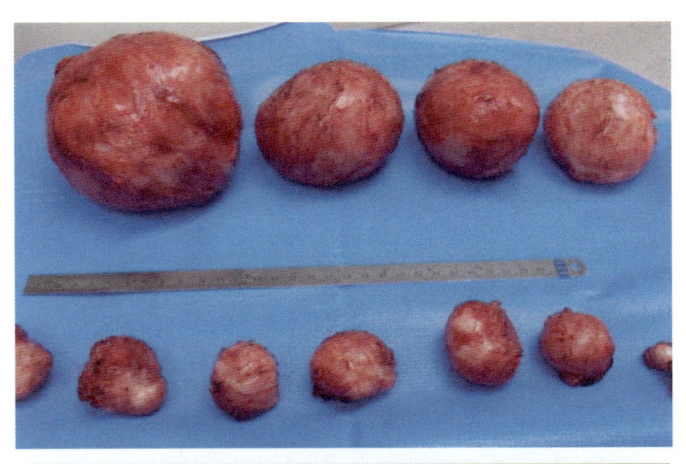

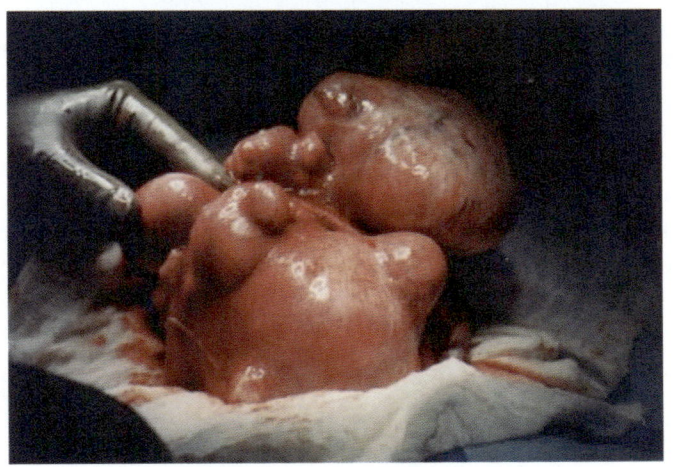

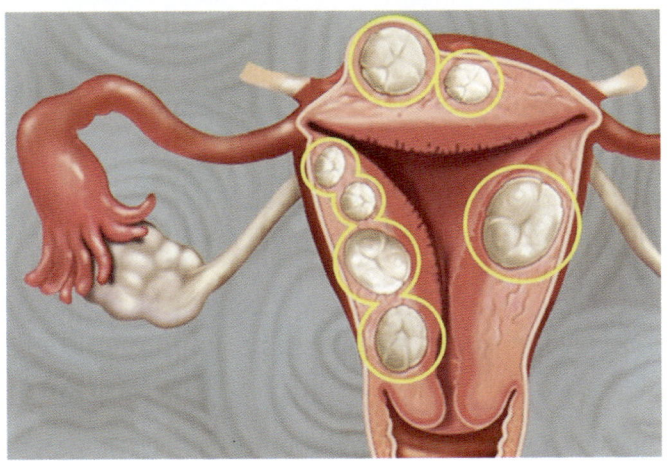

Dysmenorrhea (dis-men-oh-REE-uh) – is painful periods, including severe cramps. Menstrual cramps in teens are caused by too much of a chemical called prostaglandin **(pros-tuh-GLAN-duhn)**. Most that menstruate and experience dysmenorrhea do not have a serious disease, even though the cramps can be severe. For those who are older, the pain is sometimes caused by a disease or condition such as uterine fibroids or endometriosis.

Menstruation would often present an array of abnormal symptoms.

Disclaimer: *Before using any of these examples, please seek the advice of a medical profession. This information is not intended to diagnose or treat any medical or physical condition.*

Premenstrual syndrome (PMS) encompasses the most common issues, such as abdominal cramping, anemia, fatigue, headache, and even nausea. However, other complications may occur, like a very heavy, light, or even a skipped cycle, which is often signs of abnormalities. To seek relief for the former symptoms, one would select standard over the counter non-steroidal, anti-inflammatory drugs, or seek a prescription for them. Though Allopathic (Western medicine) drugs have shown to offer significant relief for an irritating menstrual cycle, side effects do occur. Hence, more focus has been on more natural "home remedies" and alternative formulas with less adverse effects.

Abnormal uterine bleeding – vaginal bleeding that is different from the normal menstrual periods. It includes:

Bleeding between periods
Bleeding after sex
Spotting anytime in the menstrual cycle
Bleeding heavier or for more days than normal.
Bleeding after menopause

Abnormal bleeding can have many causes. Your OBGYN may start by checking for problems that are most common in your age group. Some of them are not serious and are easy to treat. Others can be more serious. Treatment for abnormal bleeding depends on the cause. In teens and women nearing menopause, hormonal changes can cause long periods along with irregular cycles. Even if the cause is hormonal changes, you may be able to get treatment. You should keep in mind that these changes can occur with other serious health problems, such as uterine fibroids, polyps, or even cancer. See your doctor if you have any abnormal bleeding.

A natural process of the menstrual cycle

Menstruation is a natural process linked to the reproductive cycle of women and girls. It is not a sickness, but if not properly managed, it can result in health problems, which can be compounded by social, cultural, and religious practices.

Menstrual hygiene – the basics

Menstruation typically starts ('the time of menarche') during puberty or adolescence, typically between the ages of 10 and 14. At this time, they experience physical changes (e.g., growing breasts, wider hips, and body hair) and emotional changes due to hormones. Menstruation continues until they reach menopause, when menstruation ends, usually between their late forties and mid-fifties. Menstruation is also sometimes known as 'menses' or described as a 'menstrual period.'

The Internal Reproductive system

The menstrual cycle is usually around 28 days but can vary from 21 to 35 days. Each cycle involves the release of an egg (ovulation), which moves into the uterus through the fallopian tubes. The bleeding generally lasts between two and seven days, with some lighter flow and some heavier flow days. The cycle is often irregular for the first year or two after menstruation begins. Most women and girls experience some blood stagnation and hormonal fluctuation resulting in period pains such as abdominal cramps, nausea, fatigue, feeling faint, headaches, backaches, and general discomfort. They can also experience emotional and psychological changes (e.g., heightened feelings of sadness, irritability, or anger) due to the natural increase of testosterone during this time. Congestive cramping causes the body to retain fluids and salt. To counter congestive cramping, avoid wheat and dairy products, alcohol, caffeine, and refined sugar.

As many women grow and develop, they become more exposed to many estrogen-mimicking products through foods, household products, clothing, body care, cosmetics, shampoos, and menstrual products. Therefore, it begins to become as much of a business of ill-health as much as the crisis. Though it appears the be a mystery, women in America are challenged by this malady more than women in Africa, Asia, and other Eastern continents. This could be based on the fact that women from these countries indulge in a much less commercialized diet and personal care, but a more natural base consumer product. Fibroids exist in women of all lifestyles, ethnicities, professions, and income classes.

Natural options to alleviate cramping:

• Increased exercise, this will improve blood and oxygen circulation throughout the body, including the pelvis.

• Try not using tampons. Many women find tampons increase cramping. Don't select an IUD (intrauterine device) as your birth control method.

• Avoid red meat, refined carbohydrates, sugary foods, dairy, and foods with unhealthy fats. (Healthy fats are from avocados, coconut, etc.)

• Eat lots of fresh vegetables, whole grains (especially if you experience constipation or indigestion), nuts, seeds, and fruit

• Have an Orgasm with a partner that you are in spiritual harmony with.

• Avoid caffeine. It constricts blood vessels and increases tension.

• Drink Ginger and Ginseng tea (especially if you experience fatigue).

• Put cayenne pepper on food. It is a vasodilator and improves circulation.

• Breathe deeply, relax, notice where you hold tension in your body and let it go.

ASIAN FORMULAS THAT ARE TRADITIONALLY USED FOR WOMEN WITH ORGAN AND DIGESTIVE COMPLICATIONS

GUI ZHI FU LING WAN used in Traditional Chinese medicine to "activate blood circulation, to remove blood stasis and mass in the abdomen".[1] It is sweet in taste. It is used where there are symptoms such as "masses in the abdomen of women, amenorrhea due to blood stasis, menses with bellyache, or persistent lochia after delivery". Honey is used as the binding agent.

GUI PI TANG to "invigorate the spleen function, nourish blood and cause sedation". It has a slight odor, and tastes sweet, and then slightly bitter and pungent. It is used where there is "*deficiency syndrome* of both the heart and the spleen marked by shortness of breath, cardiac palpitation, insomnia, dream-disturbed sleep, dizziness, lassitude, anorexia, excessive menstrual discharge or hematochezia".[1]

Tan Kwe Gin A Classic Chinese tonic, it helps symptoms of dizziness, palpitations, poor memory. Good for irregular menstruation or postpartum weakness due to loss of blood. Made with a combination of: Angelica dang gui root, rehmannia root, licorice root, codonopsis root, poria fungus, astragalus root, white peony root, ligusticum root, honey, distilled water. **Tan Kwe Gin** is often used along with Women's Precious Pills, **Nu Ke Ba Zhen Wan.**

Nu Ke Ba Zhen Wan is used for women who suffer from a lack of energy, or qi, on a regular basis relating to their menstrual cycles. Nu Ke Ba Zhen Wan, also known as "Women's Precious " or "Eight Treasure ", is a unique Chinese herbal formula created especially for women to help bring back qi, boost energy and restore vitality. It's especially helpful for women feeling run-down from menstruation, premenstrual syndrome (PMS) and recent childbirth. It is referred to as "Women's Precious " due to its longstanding reputation as an effective herbal formula created just for women. Millions of Chinese women have used this ancient herbal formula regularly to tonify the blood and replenish qi/energy.

Disclaimer: The information within this section is based on case studies and interviews with several women who have experienced the above modalities and techniques.

Always seek the advice of a medical professional.

Anecdotal information suggests eliminating "Artificial Sweeteners" from the diet will significantly relieve menstrual cramps. If you drink sugar-free sodas or other forms of synthetic sweeteners, try eliminating them completely for two months and see what happens.

Lifestyle
The hormones in our bodies are especially sensitive to diet and nutrition. PMS and menstrual cramping are not diseases, but rather, symptoms of poor nutrition.

Premenstrual Syndrome or PMS
Women have known PMS for many years. However, within the past 30 or so years, pharmaceutical companies have targeted and created a market to treat this normal part of a woman's cycle as a disease. These companies then benefit from the sale of drugs and treatments.

Premenstrual syndrome refers to the collection of symptoms or sensations women experience as a result of high hormone levels before, and sometimes during, their periods. One type of PMS is characterized by anxiety, irritability and mood swings. These feelings are usually relieved with the onset of bleeding. Most likely, this type relates to the balance between estrogen and progesterone. If estrogen predominates, anxiety occurs. If there's more progesterone, depression may be a complaint.

Sugar craving, fatigue, and headaches signify a different type of PMS. In addition to sugar, people may crave chocolate, white bread, white rice, pastries, noodles, and other starchy foods. These food cravings may be caused by the increased responsiveness to insulin related to increased hormone levels before menstruation. In this circumstance, women may experience symptoms of low blood sugar; their brains are signaling a need for fuel. A consistent diet that includes complex carbohydrates will provide a steady flow of energy to the brain and counter the ups and downs of blood sugar variations.

Menstrual Myths:

Every woman's cycle is or should be 28 days long.
Every woman will or should bleed every month.

Every woman will or should ovulate every cycle.
If a woman bleeds, she is not pregnant.
A woman cannot ovulate or get pregnant while she is menstruating.

The above statements are myths because every woman has a different physical constitution.

It's true that most women will have cycles that are around 28 days. But, a woman can be healthy and normal and have just 3 or 4 cycles a year. [However, while variations might be healthy and normal, there could also be a sign of a serious problem. For example, a recent news article suggested that irregular menstrual cycles might predict Type 2 Diabetes.

Ovulation occurs about 14-16 days before women have their period (not 14 days after the start of their period). The second half of the cycle, ovulation to menstruation, is fairly consistently the same length, but the first part changes from person to person and from cycle to cycle. In rare cases, a woman may ovulate twice in a month, once from each ovary.

Conception/Fertilization of an egg can only occur after ovulation. The egg stays alive for about 24 hours once released from the ovary. Sperm can stay alive inside the body for 3-4 days, but possibly as long as 6-7 days. If someone has had intercourse before or after ovulation occurs, they can get pregnant, since the live sperm are already inside the woman's body when ovulation occurs. Thus, a woman can become pregnant from intercourse within about 7-10 days in the middle of the cycle.

Fertility Awareness is a birth control method where women monitor their cycles daily to identify ovulation. They are learning to predict ovulation to prevent or encourage pregnancy. It requires training and diligent record-keeping.

From our work providing abortion services, we know that some women can be pregnant and continue to have periods at the same time. We also know of cases where women have gotten pregnant during their menstrual cycle.

Here is a list of non-toxic brands of sanitary napkins to choose from:

• **Genial Day Organic Sanitary Napkins** and Cup The newest revolution sanitary napkin featuring the Anion strip (certified as a vegan)

Here is a list of other sanitary napkins that you may find at the Natural Product Store.

Nature care
Diva Cup
Organyc 100% Cotton Pads and Tampons
Glad Rags Organic reusable pads
Emerita Brand
Seventh Generation (listed as Chlorine-free organic cotton Tampons)

It is highly recommended that once you make this natural transition, keep an extra supply so that you or your daughters won't have to be compelled to purchase a non-organic substitute during the unexpected time of your cycle.

There are over 100 Medicinal plants that are in clinical use as a relief for dysmenorrhea or Amenorrhea. Some common herbs are Basil (Leaf), Cinnamon (bark), Fennel, (seeds), Feverfew, (Leaf), Parsley, Ginger (Root), Parsley, (Leaf), and Valerian, (Leaves) while several nutritional supplements like magnesium, vitamin A, and Omega-6 essential fatty acids (EFAs) have also been given credit for natural relief.

Source: Journal of Pharmaceutical, Chemical, and Biological Sciences, Department of Pharmaceutical Sciences, Dibrugarh University, Assam, India.

CHAPTER 8
WHY THE YOUNG WILL BE MORE VULNERABLE TO DIS-EASES

According to research, environmental toxicity from industrial chemicals is the absolute underlying cause of most health problems among women, men, children, and domestic animals in America. While adults are positively affected, it is the offspring who are internally injured the most during their growth and development.

According to Dr. Leo Trasande, "We are in an epidemic of environmentally mediated disease among American children today. Rates of asthma, childhood cancers, birth defects, and developmental disorders have exponentially increased, and changes in the human genome cannot explain it. According to an investigative report called "Body Burden" in July 2005, which was conducted by the Environmental Working Group regarding revealed that two hundred eighty-seven chemicals, one hundred eighty of which are known carcinogens, two hundred seventeen of which are known neurotoxins, and two hundred eight of which have been shown to cause birth defects or abnormal development in animals were discovered in the cord blood of newborn babies.

All people and mammals are vulnerable to the effects of environmental toxicity, but those most susceptible are the unborn and the very young. During pregnancy, chemical toxicity can affect the propensity of developing fetus, thus proliferate any number of chronic illnesses, especially neurologic ones. The concept, known as "transgenerational epigenetics," and which has been proven in numerous studies, says that exposure to a toxin can cause illness to future generations even if the individual is never exposed to the toxin again.

Thanks to the Breast Cancer Fund and the Campaign for Safe Cosmetics, a non-profit organization that provides bona fide reports on the toxic side effects of commercial cosmetics and body care products. Discerning parents can now use this resource to help them make a better choice when shopping for body care and hygiene products for young girls. This level of awareness can reduce the risk of the physical disparities that young and mature women face today.

According to the Campaign for Safe Cosmetics
Under Existing Law:

• Companies can use virtually any raw material in a finished cosmetic product—including chemicals linked to long-term adverse health effects like cancer, birth defects, hormone disruption, learning disabilities, and more.

• The ingredients in cosmetic products sold via the internet—a primary source of shopping for tweens, teenagers, and their busy parents—don't have to be labeled.

• The secret, often toxic ingredients in fragrance don't have to be labeled—a serious problem, because 40% of the cosmetics and personal care products on the market today contain fragrance. Although, it's just one little word on the ingredient label, "fragrance" can contain dozens, even hundreds, of chemicals—including known carcinogens, hormone/endocrine-disruptors, and other toxic offenders.

• Unlike food and drugs, the FDA cannot require recalls of cosmetic products that are harming consumers—even kids—without going to court to argue the need to remove those products from the market.

• Currently, the FDA cannot require manufacturers to register their cosmetic establishments, file data on ingredients, or report cosmetic related injuries. Instead, the FDA relies on voluntary reporting of ingredients, injuries, and establishments. Companies can use virtually any raw material in a finished cosmetic product, even those linked to cancer, birth defects, or learning difficulties.

• Protecting your children's health and well-being requires careful inspection of makeup, toys, paints, and even clothing sold in stores and online. Kids' face paints can be contaminated by heavy metals, including lead and cadmium. Lead causes altered brain development and learning difficulties, while cadmium disrupts the body's hormones.

• In addition to urging demand for manufacture reform, take you little girls to the local health food stores; educate them in addition to buying products that are organic-based and safe for them and the environment. This lifestyle movement will stimulate a natural mindset, ideology, and even improve their growth and development, which will create a new paradigm of health-conscious people and consumers.

What the **Campaign for Safe Cosmetics** found is the widespread presence of toxic chemicals in cosmetic products marketed to kids, which every parent must be made aware of so they can identify the difference between the good and bad products of the industry. More reports are coming out about products of American's use daily and potential hazards. Lead paint, lead lipstick, and children's toys are the most commonly known. Harsh chemicals in cleaning products also lead to some concerns. As their research goes further, one begins to understand exactly how deep that rabbit hole goes – almost everything American's use has potentially hazardous materials in them. The laws protecting people against these chemicals have not been properly carried out.

The CSC looked at the labels and found ingredients of concern, like parabens and formaldehyde-releasing chemicals. The presence of these chemicals marketed to children is a serious matter. Through lab testing, they found heavy metals such as lead, a neurotoxicant, and cadmium (a hormone disruptor), in face paints. In lip balms, nail products, and more, we found volatile organic compounds (VOCs) linked to a wide variety of cancers.

Here is what the CSC did. They researched the labels of 187 products marketed to kids. Then they tested 51 of these products through third-party laboratories to see what toxic chemicals they contained.

LABEL READING RESULTS:

Labels revealed a wide range of toxic chemicals in children's cosmetic and personal care products. Some chemicals of concern include "fragrance" (often a composite of dozens of undisclosed chemicals); and propylparaben in almost half of the products we examined.

TALK ABOUT SCARY LABORATORY TESTING RESULTS:

The Campaign for Safe Cosmetics tested 48 Halloween face paints for the presence of heavy metals such as arsenic, cadmium, chromium, lead, and mercury. Almost half of these—21 items—had trace amounts of at least one heavy metal. Some products contained as many as four metals. Heavy metal concentrations were higher and more common in darkly pigmented paints.

Working with 14 partners in 14 states, we collected 39 makeup products marketed to children, including lip balm, nail, and makeup kits found in toy aisles, shampoos and lotions, and party favors. There are many educational resources along with google to use to protect girls and boys from dangerous estrogen-mimicking and toxic chemicals, along with health food stores around the country. Please invest in the health and wellbeing of children so that they will become a healthier generation in the future. It will not only be a benefit for future generations but our wildlife and our planet.

Xenoestrogens Contributes to Puberty Issues

Girls are reaching puberty faster than usual because of the massive influence of estrogen in many types of foods, personal care, and environmental chemicals.

Hormone signals initiate puberty from the brain to the gonads (the ovaries and testes). In response, the gonads produce a variety of hormones that stimulate the growth, function, or transformation of the brain, bones, muscle, blood, skin, hair, breasts, and sex organs. Growth accelerates in the first half of puberty and stops after puberty. Before puberty, body differences between boys and girls are restricted to the genitalia. During puberty, significant differences of size, shape, composition, and function develop in many body structures and systems. The most obvious of these are referred to as "secondary sex characteristics."

In a normal puberty process, the brain makes a gonadotropin-releasing hormone (Gn-RH) Gn-RH causes the pituitary gland to release luteinizing hormone (LH) and follicle-stimulating hormone (FSH). LH and FSH cause the ovaries and testicles to produce hormones, and the body will also begin to make estrogen, testosterone, and produce hormones involved in the growth and development of female sexual characteristics (estrogen) soon physical changes occur. Of course, the production of estrogen and testosterone causes the physical changes of puberty.

There is an above-average physical change in children called "Precocious puberty" is when the growing body begins the change from a child into a physical adult state too soon. The process of changing from a child into an adult is known as puberty, and puberty that begins before age 8 for girls and before age 9 for boys is considered precocious puberty.

This happens to children who are exposed to growth hormones in food and estrogen-mimicking chemicals (xenoestrogens) in some commercial soaps, lotions, shampoos, and cosmetics. Personal care, household, environmental estrogens, are endocrine disruptors, structurally similar to estrogens. Xenoestrogens are clinically significant because they can mimic the effects of endogenous estrogen and thus have been implicated in precocious puberty and other disorders of the reproductive system. Exogenous estrogens can be found in pesticides, flexible plastics, flame retardants, the interior lining of canned foods, various cosmetics, and numerous other products. Exogenous estrogens are thought to cause many detrimental health effects, such as precocious puberty in girls.

Xenoestrogens may temporarily or permanently alter the feedback loops in the brain, pituitary, gonads, and thyroid by mimicking the effects of estrogen and triggering their specific receptors, or they may bind to hormone receptors and block the action of natural hormones. Thus, it is plausible that environmental estrogens can accelerate sexual development if present in a sufficient concentration or with chronic exposure. The similarity in the structure of exogenous estrogens and the estrogens has changed the hormone balance within the body and resulted in various reproductive problems in females. The overall mechanism of action is binding of the exogenous compounds that mimic estrogen to the estrogen binding receptors and cause the determined action in the target organs.

Precocious puberty has numerous significant physical, psychological, and social implications for a young girl. Unfortunately, premature pubertal growth spurt and accelerated bone maturation will result in premature closure of distal epiphysis, which causes reduced adult height and short stature. Precocious puberty has also been implicated in pediatric and adult obesity. Some studies have suggested precocious puberty places girls at a higher risk of breast cancer later in life; this certainly appears to be associated with the growth and development in. Precocious puberty is linked with other gynecologic disorders such as endometriosis, adenomyosis, polycystic ovarian syndrome, and infertility.

Precocious puberty can lead to psychosocial distress, a poor self-image, and poor self-esteem. Girls with secondary sex characteristics at such a young age are more likely to be bullied and suffer from sexual abuse Studies indicate that girls who become sexually mature at earlier ages are also more likely to engage in risk-taking behaviors such as smoking, alcohol or drug use, and engage in unprotected sex.

The people in America should not wait for a congressional bill to pass to force manufacturers to exercise more integrity and fairness for the consumer's safety. People need to step up to the plate of responsibility and hit directly on the issues of foul play. In order to put the manufactures in check, people have to become consumer conscious, which means if a product contains a list of ingredients that they do not comprehend, research it. If it is associated when any form of toxicity, then stop buying the product and find a natural alternative. This book practically lists every alternative to commercialized products that can keep the children out of harm's way regarding chemical exposure from body care, cosmetics, hygiene, and foods. Start protecting the children's health by investing in organic and chemical-free products, and it is as simple as that.

The ancestors were healthier internally and externally before the advent of the industrial revolution. Start using what is in harmony with nature to maintain the natural beauty of skin, nails, and hair. Some many women and men use the same oils that they cook or prepare food with on their bodies and hair such as extra virgin olive oil, borage oil, hemp seed oil, coconut oil, Shea Butter, Almond oil, and Argon Oil. These oils from nature have not only the capability to rejuvenate the skin but support the health of the scalp and protect from accelerated aging, plus it is non-toxic. Remember, if not natural, do not use it! Most natural and organic products are found in the natural products stores, buy only products that have ingredients that are found in nature.

This new lifestyle of "organic living" will improve your little girl's natural growth and development and set the stage for a more conscious generation of women. Also, do not forget to replace your child's fluoridated toothpaste with a natural fluoride-free brand that you will also find at your local natural product store. Please note that

Fluoride has been banned in at least 90% of the countries around the world.

GROWTH HORMONES CONTRIBUTING TO ACCELERATED PUBERTY?

In the late 1970s, there were concerns about the consumption of beef and poultry contaminated with stilbene and growth hormone residues in school meals, causing breast enlargement in very young children in Italy. However, the result of the investigation was inconclusive because the suspected beef and poultry samples were not available for testing.

In the 1980s, there was an increasing percentage of girls in Puerto Rico reaching puberty at the age of eight or earlier led to an investigation on stilbene residues in meat and poultry. Although a poultry sample obtained from the domestic market was shown to have a higher than average level of estrogen, the result could not be verified by further laboratory testing. After considering all available evidence, the investigating authority eliminated hormones in meat as the likely cause.

According to Cornell University's Report Early puberty in girls has been found to be associated with a higher risk for breast cancer. Height, weight, diet, exercise, and family history have all been found to influence age of puberty (see BCERF Fact Sheet #8, *Childhood Life Events and the Risk of Breast Cancer*). Steroid hormones in food were suspected to cause early puberty in girls in some reports. However, exposure to higher than natural levels of steroid hormones through hormone-treated meat or poultry has never been documented. Large epidemiological studies have not been done to see whether or not early puberty in developing girls is associated with having eaten growth hormone-treated foods.

A concern about an increase in cases of girls reaching puberty or menarche early (at age eight or younger) in Puerto Rico, led to an investigation in the early 1980s by the Centers for Disease Control (CDC). Samples of meat and chicken from Puerto Rico were tested for steroid hormone residues. One laboratory found a chicken sample from a local market to have higher than normal level of estrogen. Also, residues of zeranol were reported in the blood of some of the girls who had reached puberty early. However, these results could not be verified by other laboratories. Following CDC's investigation, USDA tested 150 to 200 beef, poultry and milk samples from Puerto Rico in 1985, and found no residues of DES, zeranol or estrogen in these samples.

In another study in Italy, steroid hormone residues in beef and poultry in school meals were suspected as the cause of breast enlargement in very young girls and boys. However, the suspect beef and poultry samples were not available to test for the presence of hormones. Without proof that exposure to higher levels of steroid hormones occurred through food, it is not possible to conclude whether or not eating hormone-treated meat or poultry caused the breast enlargement in these cases. Without proof that exposure to higher levels of steroid hormones occurred through food, it is not possible to conclude whether or not eating hormone-treated meat or poultry caused the breast enlargement in these cases.

HOW PLASTIC TOYS PUT YOUR CHILD AT RISK

For years, many toys created in indigenous tribes from around the world were made from natural earth material such as clay, linen, and cotton fabric before the advent of the plastic. Plastic base toys have also contributed to this modern-day "horror" of estrogen dominance. When a child plays with or puts their mouth on the base of plastic toys, it marginally wreaks havoc within the growing and developing body of the offspring. So, we highly suggest selecting a biodegradable, non-toxic chemical grade of material carefully. So read the labels for the child's sake!

This new study expands on a wealth of previous research in animals showing that exposure in the womb to chemicals known as phthalates was associated with lower testosterone production and subsequently impaired genital development. (This phenomenon, known as the phthalate syndrome, has also been shown to influence sexual development in animals later in life.

Don't even kiss the Rubber duckie's goodbye because it is laced with flame retardants. Rubik's Cubes are leaking electronic waste. Chalk it up to weak regulation-the U.S. isn't party to the Stockholm Convention, which handles this sort of thing-or corporate greed, but a whole lot of children's toys are contaminated with industrial chemicals, and the source is not mysterious at all. The proliferation of toxins like OctaBDE and DecaBDE (components of electronic waste), HBCD (found in building insulation), and SCCPs (metalworking chemicals) comes courtesy of the plastic recycling process. Today's chewed-up toys are yesterday's obsolete office equipment, which sounds good in principle, but may prove disastrous in practice.

Prenatal exposure to common chemicals used to soften plastics may impact boys' play behavior later in life, according to new research published in the International Journal of Andrology. "From a chemical manufacturing perspective, it's a cheap stream of plastics and, on the surface, recycling sounds like a good thing," Pamela Miller, co-chair of the International Persistent Organic Pollutants Elimination Network, explains. "But if you have toxic chemicals in the recycling stream and you're putting them in children's products…. I don't want parents to be alarmed unnecessarily, but I believe they have a right to know."

"In the vast majority of cases, the plastic used to manufacture new toys is, at least in part, recycled," Antonella Guzzonato of Birmingham University in the UK, and authors of the most recent flame-retardant study, told Fatherly. "This means that if contaminated items unintentionally end up in the recycling mix, those contaminants will be found again in the new toy." Countries that rely on cheap plastic exports lean heavily on recycled products. China, for instance, produced 3.2 billion tons of industrial solid waste in 2014. Two billion tons were subsequently recycled, which would be an environmental coup if chemicals weren't being recycled into jump ropes.

Still, there aren't very many robust studies on toddlers who have been exposed to these chemical contaminants, and what little literature exists remains inconclusive. Industry advocates maintain (correctly) that most of the research that has shown that these chemicals impact brain development and reproductive health has been based on animal studies, which may not translate to humans. And in 1999, the UK Department for Trade and Industry released a report that concluded that such fears were unfounded in humans, and merely "chemical paranoia."

Regulation, however, is only one piece of the puzzle. Experts like Buser maintain that these pollutants "need to be eliminated from the recycling streams as quickly as possible to avoid them from being in circulation for an extended period." In a global economy, where electronics are manufactured in one country, recycled in another country, and sold as plastic children's toys in yet another country, no intervention can have a meaningful effect unless all nations sign-on. That hasn't happened, and the U.S. lacks anything resembling those regulations embraced elsewhere. There are no signs that will change anytime soon.

Until it does, Miller advises parents to avoid plastic toys that young children are likely to put in their mouths (so, basically everything), especially when those products are made from polyvinyl chloride plastics (again, basically everything). "We found chemical pollutants in many different types of plastic toys and articles of clothing, like boots and sandals made for toddlers," she says. "We found them in plastic animal toys, balls, rubber duckies, jump ropes, and swim toys."

Growth Hormones in Food

According to a Live Strong article published in 2011, although a Cornell University study showed that research findings were mixed and limited, it did show that growth hormones used in meat and dairy products may be linked to early puberty. Cornell University's study stated the Centers for Disease Control (CDC) investigated Puerto Rico, which found higher than normal levels of estrogen in chicken and beef, which has been linked to early puberty in girls.

A University of Ottawa study also showed that "accelerated sexual development is plausible in individuals exposed to high concentrations of estrogenic substances." In the '80s, the use of growth hormones in cattle was banned throughout much of Europe. After an Italian study showed that the hormones were linked to early puberty, the European Union banned the import of beef from the United States and Canada in the 1990s because of the prevalent use of growth hormones in cattle.

There is also a possible link between elevated hormone levels and obesity. According to a study by Vanderbilt University School of Medicine; the body weight showed to be "significantly correlated" with elevated levels of testosterone, estradiol, and estrone. . A National Heart and Lung Institute study found that high levels of hormones called androgens, which include male sex hormone testosterone, can be found in individuals who are obese.

The Mayo Clinic suggests keeping children away from external sources of estrogen and testosterone as a way to possibly prevent early puberty, also known as "precocious puberty." Estradiol and testosterone are two of the hormones banned by the European Union but are used on cattle in the United States. Whether hormones in the American food supply can be directly linked to early puberty, or if obesity is the culprit is still in question among many in the medical community. The number of studies showing the possibility of a direct or indirect link in the case of obesity cannot be denied, however.

The CDC study showed a correlation between early puberty in girls and a higher risk for breast cancer. A Breast Cancer Fund report also shows a link between early puberty and a higher incidence of breast cancer, along with an increased chance of developing depression and anxiety disorders. According to an Environmental Health Monthly report, a University of North Carolina study has also found that early puberty may be linked to an increased risk of breast cancer, along with prostate cancer, infertility, and, potentially, birth defects.

Source:
http://www.digitaljournal.com/article/335214#ixzz623Xk4PON

According to the official Chinese Daily newspaper, medical tests performed on the babies found levels of estrogens circulating in their bloodstreams that are as high as those found in most adult women. These babies are between four and 15 months old. The evidence is overwhelming that the milk formula they have given to them is the problem.

Chinese dairy association says the hormones could have entered the food chain when farmers reared the cows. "Since a regulation forbidding the use of hormones to cultivate livestock has yet to be drawn up in China," says Wang Dingman, the former chairman of the dairy association in the southern province of Guangdong, "it would be lying to say nobody uses it." Bovine growth hormones are used in China, as they are in the U.S., to promote higher milk production.

After reading books The Food Revolution and Diet For a New America, written by nationally renowned health food advocate John Robbins this is not the first time something like this has happened. In the 1980s, doctors in Puerto Rico began encountering cases of precocious puberty. There were four-year-old girls with fully developed breasts. There were three-year-old girls with pubic hair and vaginal bleeding. Some one-year-old girls had not yet begun to walk but whose breasts were growing. It was not just the females; the young boys were also affected. Many had to have surgery to deal with breasts that had become grossly swollen. Writing a few years later in the Journal of the Puerto Rico Medical Association, Dr. Carmen A. Saenz explained the cause. "It was observed in 97 percent of the cases that the appearance of abnormal breast tissue was...related to local whole milk in the infants."

The problem was traced and found to stem from the misuse of hormones in dairy cows. When Dr. Saenz was asked how she could be sure the babies and children were contaminated with hormones from milk rather than from some other source, she replied: "When we take our young patients off... fresh milk, their symptoms usually regress."

Along with China, the U.S. is today one of the few countries in the world that still allows bovine growth hormones to be injected into dairy cows. Though banned in Canada, Japan, Australia, New Zealand, and most of Europe, the use of these hormones in U.S. dairy is not only legal; it is routine in all 50 states.

The U.S. dairy industry assures us that this is not a problem; however, there is a problem, and it's called Insulin-like Growth Factor-1 (IGF-1). It was discovered by the corporation's research, a 10-fold increase in IGF-1 levels in the milk of cows who have been injected with bovine growth hormone (BGH). (Google)

Why is that a problem? A report by the European Commission's official international 16-member scientific committee not only confirmed that excessive levels of IGF-1 are found in the milk of "factory farmed" cows injected with BGH. It also concluded that excess levels of IGF-1 pose severe risks of breast, colon, and prostate cancer.

How serious is the increased risk? According to an article in the May 9, 1998 issue of the medical journal The Lancet, women with even a relatively small increase in blood levels of IGF-1 are up to seven times more likely to develop breast cancer than women with lower levels.

IGF-1 that is consumed by human beings in dairy products is immediately absorbed into the bloodstream; therefore, it is not destroyed by human digestion. So, pasteurization does not help; the pasteurization process only increases IGF-1 levels in milk.

Unfermented Soy Products Will Put The Young At Risk

A full 91 percent of the soy planted in the U.S. is "is genetically bioengineered to survive heavy application of the Roundup herbicide. Organic soy is not genetically bioengineered, however, in order to receive any health benefit from soy, it must be in fermented form.

"Factory Farmers" use nearly double the amount of this herbicide on genetically bioengineered soy compared to non-GM soy, creating a much higher risk of residues in the finished product.

Even organically grown soybeans -- naturally contain "antinutrients" such as saponins, soyatoxin, phytates, trypsin inhibitors, goitrogens and phytoestrogens. Traditional fermentation destroys these antinutrients, which allows your body to enjoy soy's nutritional benefits. Unfortunately, some vegans and vegetarians may unconsciously consume *unfermented soy*, mostly in the form of soymilk, tofu, TVP, and soy infant formula.

When the Asian people in China discovered soy, it was acknowledged that is was not fit for consumption. Going back as far as 1100 BC the possible toxic effects of soy was recognized, which is why they were extremely careful in how they consumed it. In fact, today soy remains a food product that the Chinese and Japanese consume in small amounts mainly as a condiment. It was later found that the by fermenting soy it could be used for food consumption.

A study published back in the April 2000 issue of the Journal of the American College of Nutrition found that soy may speed the aging of brain cells. The brains of elderly people who ate tofu twice a week for 30 years were found to be aging much faster than normal. Another major worry in particular for women is the estrogen like molecules found in soy which are called Isoflavones. These isoflavones are known to have an effect on thyroid function, and menopausal women are at particular risk when it comes to soy induced hypothyroidism. Isoflavones are also known as phyto-endocrine disrupters. At dietary levels they can cause disruptions in female ovulation as well as stimulate the growth of cancer cells. Another problem with soy is that it can cause deficiencies in calcium, magnesium and vitamin D.

Soy consumption has also been shown to amplify hair growth in middle aged men which is a possible indication of lowered testosterone levels. There is also a wealth of information and studies which show that soy given to infants and young children is extremely unhealthy and quite possibly dangerous.

Unfermented soy contains antinutrients include potent enzyme inhibitors that block the action of trypsin, an enzyme needed for protein digestion. When soy is fermented, these compounds are deactivated, so they're not a concern.

Soybeans contain high levels of phytic acid, a substance that blocks the uptake of minerals in the intestines. Fermentation for a long period is beneficial and is the only process that will reduce these phytates in soy. Examples of this include soy sauce and miso soup. For example, people who drink soymilk every day run the risk of increased cavities and infection due to calcium loss, anemia due to iron loss, thyroid dysfunction due to iodine loss, and sexual and brain dysfunction due to zinc loss. Soy usage is particularly dangerous for children and pregnant mothers.

Here is a list of reasons why unfermented soy should be avoided

• **Soy contains hemagglutinin that promotes unwanted blood clotting.** Soybeans contain this potentially harmful substance that promotes clotting in your blood. With too high of levels of hemagglutinin, your red blood cells can clump together and inhibit oxygen uptake and growth. Hemagglutinin is deactivated during is soy fermented.

• **Soy contains phytates that lead to a mineral deficiency, especially if you are a vegetarian.** Phytates are substances that prevent the absorption of certain minerals, including calcium, magnesium, zinc, and iron. Soy has one of the highest phytate level of any grain or legume studied. When you also include meat in your diet, it helps reduce these mineral-blocking effects, leaving vegetarians who eat unfermented soy at serious risk of severe malabsorption of minerals.

• **Soy also contain Goitrogens** are substances that block the synthesis of your thyroid hormones and interfere with iodine metabolism, thereby lowering your thyroid function. When your thyroid becomes underactive, you can experience anxiety, mood swings, insomnia, weight gain, food allergies, and digestive problems.

Fermented soy products are healthy protein foods. But what exactly is fermented soy? It's a form of soy that has gone through a lengthy fermentation process that makes it digestion-friendly. The top three fermented soy foods are:

Natto - Fermented soybeans. **Nattokinase** which is derived from fermented is a very popular supplement that naturally dissolves blood clots.

Tempeh - A fermented soybean cake with a firm texture and nutty, mushroom-like flavor.

Miso - A fermented soybean paste with a salty, buttery texture that's commonly used in making miso soup.

Beware of These Soy Additives

Potassium chloride • Xanthan gum. Caution, ingredients may Soy protein concentrate • Maltodextrin • Natural flavors including "smoke" • Hydrolyzed corn or soy protein • Caramel color • Pea protein isolate • Leghemoglobin (soy) • Gum Arabic • Cellulose • Soy protein isolate • Carrageenan • Autolyzed yeast extract • Oleoresin paprika (color) • be derived from genetic engineering.

Glyphosates Is In Almost Everything Your Children Eat!

From a Media Article:

Common weed killer glyphosate increases cancer risk by 41%, study says, and found that higher levels of the mutant **Weed Killer are in children.**

SACRAMENTO (CBS13) — As the EPA decides whether to re-approve the weed-killing ingredient in Roundup for another 15 years, <u>a new report finds 90% of the families tested have that chemical in their bodies</u>, and most kids had much more than their parents.

The Center for Environmental Health (CEH), a non-profit that is focused on protecting people from toxins, reached out to parents who have researched or reported on chemicals in kids in the past to ask if they wanted to participate in the bio-monitoring study.

CBS13 investigator Julie Watts and her daughter were among the volunteers who submitted samples for testing. CEH used an independent lab to test a dozen parent-child pairs who all reported consciously trying to avoid pesticide exposure.

The lab found nine of the children had higher concentrations of the weed killer in their body than their parents. Half of the children had twice the amount of glyphosate in their body as their parents, and one had nearly 100 times more weed killer in their body.

It was not the first bio-monitoring study to find the weed killer in people's bodies, but it was the first to compare the amount in kids to their parents.

Sue Chaing, the Pollution Prevention Director at the CEH, also participated in the study. She recently worked on a different CEH report that found the Roundup chemical glyphosate in nearly 70% of oat-based food items on school menus. "Because I work on this issue, I was not necessarily surprised (by the bio-monitoring results), but I'm definitely concerned and disturbed," Chaing said.
Chaing says she is careful about the food her son Gabe eats and chooses organic food and cereal whenever they can. However, despite her best efforts, the lab found the weed-killing chemical used in Monsanto's Roundup in Gabe's body at much higher levels than his mom.

"That doesn't surprise me and that's true actually for a lot of environmental contaminants." said Environmental Health Scientist Asa Bradman, Associate Director of the Center for Environmental Research and Children's Health at UC Berkeley.

Bradman has studied pesticide exposures for decades. "Kids often have higher levels," Bradman said, "simply because they eat more, they drink more, and they breathe more per unit of body weight than adults." Bradman was not associated with the study but explained, while glyphosate residue in food is likely the primary source of exposure, kids are also more likely to come in contact with the chemicals at schools or parks. "It's important for us to understand exposures and measure them and be aware of them and then to follow up from there on ways to reduce exposures where we can," Bradman said.

According to (CNN) A story by Emily Dixon, Updated 2:45 PM ET, Fri February 15, 2019

Glyphosate, an herbicide that remains the world's most ubiquitous weed killer, raises the cancer risk of those exposed to it by 41%, a new analysis says.

Researchers from the University of Washington evaluated existing studies into the chemical -- found in weed killers including Monsanto's popular Roundup -- and concluded that it significantly increases the risk of non-Hodgkin lymphoma (NHL), a cancer of the immune system.

"All of the meta-analyses conducted to date, including our own, consistently report the same key finding: exposure to GBHs (glyphosate-based herbicides) are associated with an increased risk of NHL," the authors wrote in a study published in the journal Mutation Research.

In 2015, however, the World Health Organization's International Agency for Research on Cancer classified glyphosate as "probably carcinogenic to humans." Moreover, the chemical has triggered multiple lawsuits from people who believe that exposure to the herbicide caused their non-Hodgkin's lymphoma. In 2017, CNN reported that more than 800 people were suing Monsanto; by the following year, that figure was in the thousands.

The authors of the University of Washington report analyzed all published studies on the impact of glyphosate on humans. Co-author and doctoral student Rachel Shaffer said in a statement: "This research provides the most up-to-date analysis of glyphosate and its link with Non-Hodgkin Lymphoma, incorporating a 2018 study of more than 54,000 people who work as licensed pesticide applicators." The scientists also assessed studies on animals.

What we are now beginning to understand is how our actions today affect the lives and health of children who will be born twenty to fifty years from now. They will become susceptible to any number of chronic disorders before taking their first breath of life.
The next most vulnerable groups are those who are about to be born, neonates, and infants. Studies on one family of toxins called

phthalates, which is discussed more in chapter five, how plastics that contain Bisphenol-A can affect gonadal development, impair socialization, and cause endocrine disruption. Science is still in the early stages of a better understanding of how a child's growth and development are affected by environmental toxins.

Organic and Is the Only Solution?

When shopping for any food or body care products, consider buying them from a health food store, a health cooperative, or a grocery store that sales natural products and organic foods. "Grass-Fed" or Organic milk products from Cows or Goats by law cannot be produced with bovine growth hormone (BGH). Alternatively, look for dairy products that specifically say they are produced without BGH (also called recombinant bovine somatotropin, or **rBST**). Starbucks only uses dairy products that have not been produced with the hormone. There are many ice cream brands in the health food store that uses only milk and cream from dairy farms that have pledged not to use **rBGH.**

If you are going to eat cheese, remember that American-made cheeses are likely to be contaminated with BGH and excess levels of IGF-1 unless they are organic or labeled BGH-free. Most cheeses that are imported from Europe are safe, though, since much of Europe has banned the hormone.

Most people still overlook the fact that if a dairy company does not list that their cows are not treated with **rBGH**, then the dairy products purchased may still contain rBGH. Have you ever wondered why dairy products made from cows injected with the hormone are not labeled? It is because the original manufacturer of BGH (research on

Google), has aggressively and successfully lobbied state governments in the past to make sure that no legislation is passed that would require such labeling.

In addition to labeling scheme, the corporation had also insistently sought to make it illegal for dairy companies to list that their products are BGH-free. Fortunately, that is not the case today; more companies are now listing that their dairy products are rBGH free. Let us hope that there is integrity behind these consumer listings because this chemical agent is responsible for untold damage to human health.

The millions of babies in the American, Puerto Rico, and China who have been or will be adversely affected by the abuse of hormones in dairy production deserve a nutritional reform and a food structure that was intended by nature.

A great source of information can be acquired from this website, www.johnrobbins.info.

What Are the Organic Alternatives for Breakfast?

It is important that whatever choice you make regarding natural nutrition, it would be wise to choose only bona fide, certified organic foods – when you can and can afford to – this is the best choice you can make for your children's growth and development.

It has been proven that children who are fed an organic diet have much lower levels of metabolites from high-risk insecticides in their bodies. We also know that choosing organic food reduces the risk of toxicity from pesticides and insecticides. The 2008-09 President's Panel on Cancer report stated, "The entire U.S. population is exposed on a daily basis to numerous agricultural chemicals." Many of these chemicals are known or suspected to cause cancer or disrupt our hormones, mimicking testosterone or estrogen, its authors continued. "Nearly 1,400 pesticides ... registered by the Environmental Protection Agency for agricultural and nonagricultural uses ... have been linked to brain/central nervous system, breast, colon, lung, ovarian cancers ... as well as Hodgkin's and non-Hodgkin's lymphoma" and more.

In 2012, The American Academy of Pediatrics cautioned the public about the exposure to pesticides. "Children encounter pesticides daily and have unique susceptibilities to their potential toxicity," and "chronic health implications from both acute and chronic exposure are emerging."

The chemicals that are released in the environment exposed everyone toxins, however, we can limit the children's exposure to these chemicals through an organic diet. Even though no food source is 100% residue-free, but several University studies have found that organic food has significantly lower pesticide residues than conventional food.

For the families that consume animal protein, choosing organic meat and dairy is the best way to ensure that one is not exposed to endocrine-disrupting chemicals like the synthetic hormones given to nonorganic livestock to speed growth and alter reproductive cycles. Also, by choosing organic meat and dairy ensures that the children are not fed meat that was raised on the daily doses of antibiotics which is used to accelerate growth and leads to dangerous antibiotic-resistant bacteria.

Three studies conducted by scientists at the University of California, Berkeley, Columbia University, and Mount Sinai Hospital tracked women exposed to higher amounts of organophosphate pesticides while pregnant and found that once those children reached elementary-school age, had lower IQ performance. We know, for instance, that children born to women exposed to pesticides in agricultural fields or communities have lower IQs and other troubling health outcomes.

According to other studies, the cognitive performance of children can be limited due to other chemicals such as excitotoxins like MSG (monosodium glutamate), and Aspartame, and toxic food dyes.

1. Breakfast on the go: When you hit the snooze button one too many times before heading out for the work day, try any one of these items from Nature's Path, Stonyfield, Happy Family or Annie's. From yogurts to breakfast biscuits you won't be sacrificing your health in your rush out the door.

2. Breakfast toast: Avocado toast is a favorite around here along with turning an old classic into something new with a twist. Try <u>chia jam</u> or <u>eggs on toast with avocado.</u>

3. Breakfast cakes aka muffins: The closest thing to having cake in the morning is having a delicious fresh-baked muffin. Don't worry, we have healthy organic muffin recipes in mind for your mornings. Check out these delicious recipes from <u>Organic Valley</u>, <u>Annie's</u>, <u>Happy Family</u> and <u>Nature's Path</u>.

6. Breakfast bowls, superfood lattes and smoothies: Do you love smoothies, coffee and acai bowls? Get inspiring and healthy ideas from our friends at <u>Nature's Path</u>, <u>Annie's</u>, <u>Stonyfield</u>, <u>Back To The Roots</u>, and <u>Orgain</u>.

7. Eggs: Organic Eggs is a way to start the day. Get inspired with these healthy egg recipes from our partners: <u>strata</u>, <u>scramble</u>, <u>benedict</u>, and <u>frittata</u>.

8. Cereal from around the world: From Congee to Muesli, get inspired with some worldly fare from our friends at <u>Nature's Path</u>.

9. Homemade and frozen: We love to make large batches of homemade food and freeze them, especially during harvest seasons. Making large batches of breakfast favorites like waffles and fruit is just one way to make your mornings easier. <u>Buckwheat waffles are perfect for making in advance and freezing</u>. Another healthy and delicious recipe to make in a big batch and freeze is Orgain's peanut butter and jelly protein bars.

10. Breakfast in a jar: Breakfasts in a jar can be anything from chia pudding, to parfaits, to smoothies to overnight oats.

11. Pancake Protein mix from Bob'd Red Mill's and Kodiak

12. Seasonal favorites: One of the keys to eating healthy is to start by choosing fresh, in-season, organic and local ingredients. Look for seasonal additions to classic recipes from Dr. Jafari **"The Kitchen Physician."**

Food Additives to Avoid

While FDA generally recognizes most additives on this list as 'safe,' there are growing concerns about the safety of many common food additives if consumed in large quantities.

Sodium nitrate: Is used to processed meats and stop bacterial growth, it is linked to cancer in humans. (Worst Offender)

Sulfites: Are used to keep prepared foods fresh. It can cause breathing difficulties in those sensitive to the ingredient.

Azodicarbonamide: Are used in bagels and buns. It can cause asthma.

Potassium bromate: Added to bread to increase volume. Linked to cancer

Propyl gallate: Added to fat-containing products. Linked to cancer in humans

BHA/BHT: A fat preservative, used in foods to extend shelf life. Linked to cancerous tumor growth.

Propylene glycol: Also known as antifreeze. It thickens dairy products and salad dressing. It is deemed 'generally' safe by FDA.

Butane: Put in chicken nuggets to keep them tasting fresh – a known carcinogen.

Monosodium glutamate (MSG): Flavor enhancer that can cause headaches. Linked in animal studies to nerve damage, heart problems, and seizures.

Disodium inosinate: In snack foods.

Disodium guanylate: Also used in snack foods, and contains MSG.

Enriched flour: Used in many snack foods. Refined starch is made from toxic ingredients.

Recombinant Bovine Growth Hormone (rBGH): Genetically-engineered version of natural growth hormone in cows. It is used to increase milk production in cows. It contains high levels of IGF-1, which is thought to cause various types of cancer.

Refined vegetable oil: Includes soybean oil, corn oil, safflower oil, canola oil, and peanut oil, high in omega-6 fats, which are thought to cause heart disease and cancer.

Sodium benzoate: Used as a preservative in salad dressing and carbonated beverages. A known carcinogen and may cause damage to our DNA.

Brominated vegetable oil: Keeps flavor oils in soft drinks suspended. Bromate is a poison and can cause organ damage and birth defects. It is not required to be listed on food labels.

Propyl gallate: Found in meats, popcorn, soup mixes, and frozen dinners. Shown to cause cancer in rats and banned in some countries, deemed safe by the FDA.

Olestra: Fat-like substance that is unabsorbed by the body. They are used in place of natural fats in some snack foods, causes digestive problems and unhealthy heart function.

Carrageenan: Stabilizer and thickening agent used in many prepared foods. It can cause ulcers and cancer.

Polysorbate 60: A thickener used in baked goods, causes cancer in laboratory animals.

Carnauba wax: Used in chewing gums and to glaze certain foods. It can cause cancer.

Magnesium sulfate: Used in tofu and can cause cancer in laboratory animals.

Chlorine dioxide: Used in bleaching flour. It can cause tumors and hyperactivity in children.

Paraben: Used to stop mold and yeast forming in foods. It can disrupt hormones in the body and could be linked to breast cancer.

Sodium carboxymethyl cellulose: Used as a thickener in salad dressings. Could cause cancer in high quantities.

Aluminum: A preservative in some packaged foods that can cause cancer.

Artificial Sweeteners to Avoid

FDA regulates artificial sweeteners, just as food additives are, but this does not apply to products 'generally recognized as safe.

Saccharin: Carcinogen found to cause bladder cancer in rats. (Worst Offender)

Aspartame: An excitotoxin and thought to be a carcinogen. It can cause dizziness, headaches, blurred vision, and stomach problems.

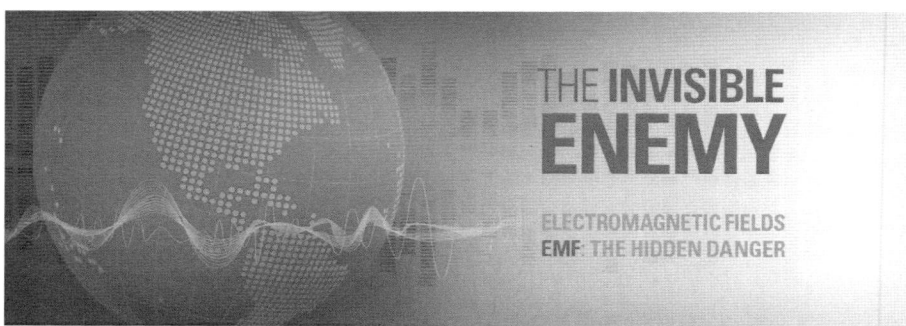

Near-Field Plume Penetration Comparison

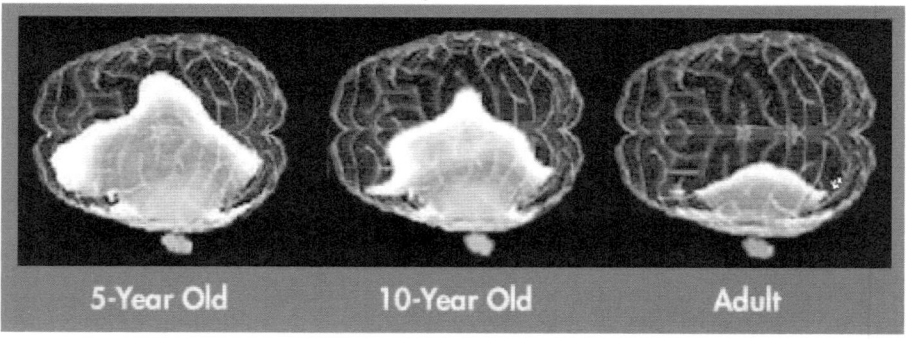

CHAPTER 9
THE DANGERS OF
ENDOCRINE DISRUPTORS AND EMF'S

The endocrine system consists of a series of glands that are distributed through- out the body Each gland produces one or more hormones. Hormones are natural chemicals that are produced in cells within a gland and released into the circulatory system, where they travel through the bloodstream until they reach a target tissue or organ. There, they bind to specific receptors, triggering a response such as production of another hormone, a change in metabolism, a behavioral response, or other responses, depending upon the specific hormone and its target. Some endocrine glands produce a single hormone, while others produce multiple endocrine hormones. For example, the parathyroid gland produces a single known hormone (parathyroid hormone), whereas the pituitary gland makes eight or more hormones, including prolactin and growth hormone. Prolactin is involved in making breast milk, and it is only synthesized and released from the pituitary glands of women who are breast feed.

Endocrine Disruptors (EDCs) often disrupt endocrine systems by mimicking or blocking a natural hormone. In the case of hormone mimics, an EDC can "trick" that hormone's receptor into thinking that the EDC is the hormone, and this can inappropriately activate the receptor and trigger processes normally activated only by a natural hormone. In the case of hormone blockers, an EDC can bind to a hormone's receptor, but in this case, the receptor is blocked and cannot be activated, even if the natural hormone is present.

Endocrine disruption of estrogenic hormones, act upon the body's estrogen receptors (ERs). In both males and females, ERs are present in many cells in the brain, in bone, in vascular tissues, and in reproductive tissues. While estrogens are best understood for their roles in female reproduction, they are important for male reproduction, and are also involved in neurobiological functions, bone development and maintenance, cardiovascular functions, and many other functions. Natural estrogens exert these actions, after being released from the gonad (ovary-female or testis-male), by binding to ERs in the target tis- sues. EDc's includes BPA-Phalates, Triclosan in Hand Sanitizers and soaps, Chemtrails, lead, arsenic, cadmium, aerosol sprays, Cleaning chemicals, Clothing Textiles, Laundry chemicals, etc.

Estrogen receptors are not the only receptors that are attacked in this manner by EDCs, although they are the best studied. Receptors for androgens (testosterone), progesterone, thyroid hormones, and even neurotransmitters by EDCs. Because EDCs are not natural hormones, a single EDC may have the ability to affect multiple hormonal signaling pathways. Thus, it is quite likely that one type of EDC can disrupt two, three, or more endocrine functions, with widespread consequences on the biological processes that are con- trolled by those vulnerable endocrine glands.

EDCs are a global and ubiquitous problem. Exposure occurs at home, in the office, on the farm, in the air we breathe, the food we eat, and the water we drink. Of the hundreds of thousands of manufactured chemicals, it is estimated that about 1000 may have endocrine-acting properties. Biomonitoring (measurement of chemicals in body fluids and tissues) show nearly 100% of humans have a chemical body burden. In addition to the known EDCs, there are countless suspected EDCs or chemicals that have never been tested.

Exposure to EDCs may indeed be in the form of pesticides, algicides, and other chemicals designed to kill unwanted organisms. Spraying of homes, agricultural crops, and ponds releases airborne and sedimented chemicals that are inhaled, get on skin, and are ingested from sprayed food.

EDCs are found in many common-use, household, and personal products that come into contact with the body or are around us in our home and work environments. For example, children's products, electronics, food contact materials, personal care products, textile/clothing, and building products are regular parts of daily life around the world (www.ipen.org/site/toxics-products-overview).

Consumers have little to no choice in whether or not they are exposed to chemicals in these products, because there is generally not full disclosure about these items' chemical constituents. Some of these chemicals are released into the air and remain in the indoor environment, particularly in poorly ventilated buildings. From the air, some chemicals can settle out into carpets and dust. This is of great concern with infants and children who often pick up and put items from the floor into their mouths or eat food that has fallen on the floor. Personal care products are applied to skin, and there are also chemicals in toothpastes and antimicrobial soaps that are absorbed or even ingested in small amounts.

EMF's And Cell Phone

We live within a wave of radiofrequency radiation never before seen in the history of human existence. All cell phones emit a type of radiation called an electromagnetic field (EMF), composed of waves of electric and magnetic energy moving together through space. Electromagnetic energy is measured by wavelengths and frequencies and comprises the electromagnetic "spectrum." The RF part of the electromagnetic spectrum consists of frequencies in the range of about 3 kilohertz (3 kHz) to 300 gigahertz (300 GHz). RF energy is used in telecommunications services, including radio and television broadcasting, mobile communication, GPS devices, radio communications for police and fire departments, and satellite communications. Non-communication sources of RF energy include microwave ovens, radar, and industrial uses.

Russian and Eastern European scientists issued the earliest reports that low-level exposure to RF radiation could cause a wide range of health effects, including behavioral changes, effects on the immunological system, reproductive effects, changes in hormone levels, headaches, irritability, fatigue, and cardiovascular effects.

The frequent use of cell phones is an unimaginable threat to human health. As known to many, it has been proven that talking on a cell phone for as little as 500 to 1000 minutes per month can increase the probability of brain cancer by 300%. Not only that, it also causes disturbance in sleep, difficulty in concentration, fatigue, headache, infertility, and hyperactivity in newborn children. Chances of Alzheimer's disease, leukemia, ear defects, and blurring of vision are too noticed to be higher in cell phone users. In addition, cell phones damage key brain cells as well as the DNA.

Since the first reports appeared in the literature, scientists have recognized the near-ubiquitous use and exposure to cell phones and other radiofrequency technologies in the last decade and have launched and completed many studies. As the science has matured, researchers and government officials have become increasingly concerned about exposures that affect pregnant women – and their fetuses . Their concern is also for children whose brains and organs do not fully mature until age 21.

We can expect in the future that our health will only continue to become more and more compromised, the bad effects manifesting in myriad ways. EMF sensitivity is cumulative, building up in our bodies over time and causing individuals to have great difficulty in warding off a simple flu while showing ill health in countless forms.

Most Common Symptoms From Cell Phone Use

According to Epidemiological studies - Sleep disruption, Headache , Depression, discomfort, irritability, nausea, dizziness, appetite loss, muscle spasms, numbness, tingling, altered reflexes Cognitive functions -Concentration, memory, behavior, etc. Other Subjects reported buzzing in the head, palpitations of the heart, light-headedness, heat, visual disorders, cardiovascular problems, respiratory problems, nervousness, agitation. More severe reactions include seizures, paralysis, psychosis and stroke.

EMF And Cell Phone History

In 1865, James Clerk Maxwell proposed and published the theory of electromagnetic radiation (Columbia Encyclopedia, 2008).

Electromagnetic radiation is "energy radiated in the form of a wave as a result of the motion of electric charges" (2008). If the motion of a magnetic field changes or accelerates, the magnetic field can provide an electric field (2008). The produced electromagnetic wave is both a transverse and a polarized wave (2008). More importantly, "electromagnetic radiation does not require a material medium and can travel through a vacuum" (2008).

Mobile phones produce EMR. Mobile phone use has greatly expanded both domestically and internationally in recent years. According to the U.S. Census Bureau's latest Statistical Abstract Report in 2004, cell phone use in the United States has increased by 300 percent since 1995. In 1995, only 34 million Americans had a cell phone subscription (2004). However, in 2004, the number of Americans that had a cell phone subscription approached 159 million (2004). According to Portio Research, a business of "Worldwide Cellular Markets Subscriber Data" that forecasts industry growth, "50% of the world's population will be using a cell phone by the end of 2009" (2006). The report predicts that Africa will have the highest rate of growth and will add "265 million new mobile subscribers over the next 6 years" (2006). The cell phone industry is substantial and continues to grow.

Debate regarding EMR and health started in the 1930s, when scientist began to postulate that high-frequency electromagnetic fields (EMFs) may cause health problems (Kundi, 2009, p. 316). Previously, the only health problem associated with EMFs was "tissue heating" (p. 316). Kundi writes, "Because of the enormous increase in mobile phone use starting in the mid-1990s and reaching almost 100% prevalence in many countries worldwide by now, concerns have been raised that even small risks for developing chronic diseases such as cancer from mobile phone use may have substantial impact on public health" (p. 316). Kundi continues, "In fact, never before in history has any device of comparative prevalent use been associated with such high exposure to high-frequency electromagnetic fields (EMFs)" (p. 316).

The first recorded study of a correlation between wireless technology, EMR, and health problems was published in 1975 in the journal *Annals of the New York Academy of Sciences* by Allan Frey. Since that study, scientists, doctors, and other professionals have issued dozens of reports and peer-reviewed journal articles that prove either a correlation between cell phones and cancer exists or does not prove that correlation exists. These reports are paid for privately, through a university or hospital, or by grants. These grants are paid for by individuals, hospitals, universities, NGOs, governments, and mobile phone companies. One must be cognizant of the source of funding when reviewing the results of such studies.

Dr. Martin Cooper, known as the father of the cell phone, set up a base station in New York with the first working prototype of a cellular telephone in 1973. Mr. Cooper and Motorola took the phone technology of the Motorola Dyna-Tac to New York to show the public.

Here are some of the shocking details of the disconnect between current science and our nation's actions:

Studies conducted outside of the cell phone industry consistently show **cell phone use. damages brain cell DNA. Children's brains are growing at much faster rates and are especially vulnerable.**

Dr. Franz Adlkofer, a professor of internal medicine who specializes in diseases with environmental and behavioral causes **conclusively proved that cell phone radiation unravels DNA.** Adlkofer's team found that 3G phones were much worse than 2G phones.

Independent studies of cell phone radiation dangers find problems at more than twice the rate than industry-funded studies find problems. Science journals are publishing papers on this gaping disparity.

A study found that **men who do not use cell phones have far more healthy sperm than those who used a cell phone between 2 and 4 hours a day.** Those who used a cell for more than 4 hours had the lowest and sickliest sperm counts of all.

In another experiment, **rats that have mastered getting out of a tank without drowning, once exposed to cell phone radiation for an hour, get lost and swim in circles.**

Other nations are beginning to act. France is banning the sale of phones for children. Russia, the UK, Canada, Belgium, Israel, Finland, Germany, and India have discouraged the use of cell phones by children. Lloyds of London, the oldest continuously active insurance marketplace in the world, now refuses to insure cell phone manufacturers against health-related claims, as do a number of other firms.

The cell phone industry has followed the playbook of the tobacco industry in dealing with any suggestion that phones could be problematic. Davis saw **serious scientists, raising questions about the long-term impact of cell phones on health, who were defunded and sometimes drummed out of re- search altogether.**

Bringing together research and interviews with scientists, government officials and industry leaders in the U.S. and around the globe, scientist **Dr. Devra Davis** pulls back the curtain on the dangers and how this trillion-dollar industry has tried to cover it up, potentially harming us all.

Children under the age of 10, in particular, are a lot more vulnerable to microwave radiation because their immune system is weak, their skulls are thin, and their nervous system is still developing. The dire health effects mentioned earlier are even more severe on children because of increased absorption.

For well over 50 years, scientists and industry insiders have known that microwave radio-frequency radiations, pulse-modulated day in and day out, are very toxic, particularly to pregnant women and children, and yet our leaders allow the telecom industry to continue its expansion in a completely unbridled manner, eviscerating the very protections that prevented the industry from steamrolling us in the first place.

Cell Phone and Brain Damage: Protecting Children from RF, EMF, and EMR

Few parents know that radio-frequency signals reach much more deeply into children's thinner and smaller heads than ours -- a fact established through the pioneering work of professor Om P. Gandhi, the leader of the University of Utah's electrical engineering department.

Keep your phone on Airplane Mode when you're not using the Internet. (You can find this by pressing the 'Settings Icon.'

Super Model and TSS Survivor Lauren Wasser

CHAPTER 10
A SUPER MODEL LIFE SHOCKED BY TSS

This chapter is about a woman whose career and life were almost utterly destroyed by the use of commercial tampons. This is a true tragedy and could have been prevented if Lauren Wasser was more informed by the manufacturer and had known about the natural and chemical-free alternatives. People and especially women in the US are not thoroughly educated on the toxic potential of commercial tampons. The synthetic materials from the tampon are released into the bloodstream, potentially causing extreme blood stagnation and organ failure. A toxic bacterium is known as Staphylococcus Aureus or staph infection causes Toxic Shock Syndrome.

Lauren Wasser became an unfortunate victim who faced the dangers of TSS from the use of commercial tampons. Like most that use tampons, during the beginning of their cycle, they find it necessary to buy a tampon from the nearest retailer. Lauren did not have a supply at that time and found it convenient to purchase from the nearby store which happened to be below her residence. Like anyone else, she would follow that standard procedure, but this time she would experience an episode that would alter her life.

She began experiencing flu-like symptoms the morning before heading out to a birthday party she was expected to attend. As the story goes, after she changed the tampon, Lauren began to feel worse. She stated that she felt like she had been hit by a truck, afterward began experiencing a high fever and went straight to bed. Lauren's mother communicated with her every day, and when she did not get a response after several attempted calls, her mother contacted the police. When they arrived and checked up on Lauren, they acknowledged that she appeared to be sick, and agreed to follow up with her. The next time when they arrived, Lauren was found face down on the floor with a fever of a 108 and was covered in her vomit and feces. The paramedics were contacted, and Lauren was rushed to the hospital.

The nurses and doctors were confused as to why a healthy woman at 24 years of age appeared to be so ill. Due to this, a doctor who specializes in infectious diseases was called and he was aware that she came to the ER still wearing a tampon. The specialist sent her tampon to the lab for testing. After three days, the results came back with signs of TSS-1. Lauren was placed in an induced coma, at this time all of her organs were failing along with abnormal blood pressure, which led to an episode of a heart attack and out of range fever. At this time, Lauren was fighting for her life as she went on life support. After being in a coma for over a week, she stated that she had no recollection of what previously happened.

Her weight elevated to 200lbs due to pressures and fluids that were administered to stabilize her blood pressure, but the pressure can also put the body in harm's way; the objective was to rescue the vital organs and prevent them from completely failing, even with this procedure, your extremities don't always receive the blood flow that is needed.

Lauren was eventually transferred to UCLA for Hyperbaric treatments. A Hyperbaric chamber is a closed chamber that patients are put in to receive the oxygen that is needed to increase blood flow. But the fight was not just focused on the blood flow, but to save Lauren's legs. Unfortunately, gangrene had already manifested in her right leg which then had to be removed immediately. Lauren's left side was also severely damaged along with all five toes. Although the doctors suggested that both legs be amputated, Lauren wanted to at least make an effort to save one of her legs.

Like most people, we trust the products we consume. Whether it is food, body or personal care, we feel that the regulations in place would simply have our backs and protect us from dishonest products that may contain ingredients that would promote harm. Warning labels on product packaging can be easily ignored because of the very fine print. Though the manufacturer should increase the print size to make warning statements more obvious so that the consumer may at least acknowledge safety precautions, Western Medicine would make less money if this were to happen. This is not the fault of the consumer.

Lauren finally read the fine print buried on the bottom of the tampon box and gave her a disheartening reality check. "TSS - Toxic Shock Syndrome: a potentially fatal complication of certain types of bacterial infections."

Because the vaginal area is the most absorbent area of the internal reproductive anatomy, once the tampon is placed within the vaginal canal, chemical toxins are immediately released and create a series of unidentified side effects, which are usually ignored due to lack of knowledge. Like many who have traveled through this dark tunnel of sudden ill health because of the disregard of the manufacturers and the lack of knowledge, they potentially end up experiencing a similar episode of what Lauren experienced. Lauren eventually became afflicted with PTSD (Post-Traumatic Stress Disorder) due to the trauma of this event.

The Reality of Crisis

Lauren's friend Jennifer Revero happened to be a photographer and created a play-by-play photo journal of her amputation recovery. Lauren stated in her story that photography became a therapy for her as she began to gain strength and beauty within herself. As they created the photos, they would ask young girls if they ever heard of Toxic Shock Syndrome, or if they believed it to exist? The majority of the girls said no.

Lauren eventually had her left leg amputated and is now referred to as the "Girl with the Golden Legs". Lauren went on to share with women from all walks of life that they are still worthy of existing no matter how trying a certain moment of life may be; because if you can find the will to live and love, then you have the potential to progress, love yourself, and succeed.

WHY ARE TAMPONS SO TOXIC ANYWAY?

If there's one place on the body where only the purest of materials are introduced-- it should be your genitals; therefore, harmful chemicals should be forbidden! The vulva and vaginal tissues are more permeable than the rest of your skin, becoming especially vulnerable to harmful chemicals and other irritants. With mucous membranes and a high concentration of lymphatic and blood vessels, the vaginal area provides a direct entryway for chemicals to circulate throughout the rest of your body. When tampons are left inside the vaginal canal for hours at a time, several days each month, this is increasing a great deal of toxicity, thus increasing the risk of TSS.

Research has shown that not only the chemicals from commercial tampons rapidly absorbed and circulated through the rest of your body via your vagina, some chemicals, like hormone-mimicking substances may lead to "higher exposures" chemicals like dioxin within the rest of your body.

Studies show that dioxin, a byproduct of chlorine-bleaching, collects in your fatty tissues, and according to a draft report by the US Environmental Protection Agency (EPA), dioxin is a serious public health threat that has no "safe" level of exposure! Published reports show that even low trace levels of dioxins may be linked to various cancers.

Another factor is contamination with bacteria and molds. Products may come pre-contaminated by their manufacturing process, but have you also noticed that most menstrual products are not completely sealed? Once you open the outside packet the individual wrappers have openings to the external air, they can then become contaminated with bacteria and mold spores in the air. There is a potential risk of infection.

Cervical cancer is also a serious reality; it is among the most life-threatening diseases around the world due to chemical toxicity. It has been discovered that one of the direct causes is from using the chemically treated menstrual products regularly each month. After years of using commercial menstrual products, the risk of cancer is much higher. It is very important to select a line of chemical-free menstrual hygiene products that are made only from 100% hypoallergenic organic cotton.

Young women may be more likely to get TSS from using any kind of tampon, which puts them at greater risk for TSS rather than using sanitary pads. Recommendations to help avoid the adverse effects of tampon use:

Follow package directions for insertion
Choose the lowest absorbency for your flow
Change your tampon at least every 3 to 5 hours
Know the warning signs of TSS
Don't use tampons between periods
Consider switching from tampons to pads

Maybe if the Robin Danielson Act proposed bill had passed, we would have more consumer protection from stronger regulations towards the manufacturing process of commercial tampons. This could protect the young who begin their cycles as early as 8 years old, thus preventing the same horrific episodes of fibroids, endometriosis, and TSS in the future generations. Robin Danielson was another woman who unfortunately died from TSS in 1988.

While using tampons, if you notice these symptoms such as Sudden high fever (over 101 degrees), Muscle aches, Diarrhea, Vomiting, Dizziness and/or fainting, Sunburn-like rash, Sore throat, or Bloodshot eyes take the tampon out and contact your doctor right away. Immediately find a natural alternative, starting with a non-insertable menstrual product as this area will still be sensitive and susceptible to infection.

Hormone-Disrupting Carcinogenic Chemicals may lurk in tampons aside from pesticides, traces of dioxin, and GMOs. If you're using "scented" tampons be aware that such products may contain any one of the nearly 3,000 fragrance chemicals. But, again, they probably won't be listed on the label. An analysis by Women's Voices for the Earth (WVE) which acquired public patented documents held by Proctor and Gamble (the maker of Tampax and Always), showed the following chemicals might be also in your tampons:

Creped cellulose wadding melt-blown polymers chemically stiffened fibers, polyester fibers, peat moss, foam Tissue wraps, laminate superabsorbent gels, open-celled foams Myreth-3-myristate (as a lubricant) (US Patent #5,591,123) Natural and synthetic zeolites (as odor-absorbing particles) Alcohol ethoxylates, Glycerol esters, polysorbate-20 (as surfactants to disperse fragrance).

Unidentified antibacterial agents (US Patent #8, 585, 668) Cancer-causing chemicals such as styrene, pyridine, methyleugenol and butylated hydroxyanisole (scented products) Phthalates of concern (DEP and DINP) Synthetic musk (potential hormone disruptor; natural musk is a fatty pheromone-filled substance secreted from a gland in Musk Deer). This type of chemical accumulation leads to Immune System suppression, hormonal and endocrine system disruption. Many of today's menstrual hygiene products are made primarily from rayon, viscose, and cellulose wood fluff pulp... not cotton- let alone organic cotton. Rayon and viscose present a potential danger in part of their highly absorbent fibers. These fibers can stick to your vaginal wall, and when you remove the tampon, the loosened fibers stay behind inside your body, thereby raising your risk of TSS. Though the FDA notes that tampons containing rayon do not appear to have a higher risk of TSS than cotton tampons of similar absorbency, it is the absorbency level that appears to have the greatest association linked to increased TSS risk. Fortunately, there are safer alternatives, and since the FDA regulates tampon absorbency, all tampons on the market must meet the same absorption guidelines.

If women were aware of safer alternative sanitary personal care products by companies such as Genial Day or the Diva Cup, the risk of acquiring a dreadful condition such as TSS would be very rare because of the zero exposure to the toxic composition of commercial tampons.

There are several factors that contribute to abnormal menstrual complications in addition to tampon toxicity, such as consumption of unbeneficial foods and high *EMF* radiation (*See Chapter 21*) via repeated cell phone use, computers, hi-tech watches, and other electronics.

These frequencies emitted from electronics disrupt the body's natural Electromagnetic Field, which has its Frequency; while the effects may not be easily perceived by individuals; constant exposure to such frequencies puts the body in a state of disharmony. Energy depletion and high blood toxicity are two of the most common effects of a very long list of symptoms.

It was discovered in some papyrus such as the Ebers Papyrus that contained holistic prescriptions for the menstrual cycle and the use of menstrual blood as an ingredient for medicinal recipes for beauty mixtures and specific illnesses. For example, it was suggested that menstrual blood should cover the chest, belly, and thighs to remedy sagging breasts. Kemetic/Egyptian women from Hout Ka-Ptah or Kemet the original name for Egypt would use particular throw-away tampons that are assumed to be made from papyrus or another type of grass indigenous to the land. Below is an O.B. tampons ad taken from the German Burda magazine from the year 1989. Today, tampons are highly toxic because of the chemical composition within the material.

Other Materials That Proliferate Danger

Rayon is the main ingredient in generic tampons. It's a material that is made from cellulose fibers. Cellulose is a natural fiber found in plants, but to produce Rayon, chemicals such as carbon disulfide, sulphuric acid, chlorine, and caustic soda are required. Side effects from exposure to too much Rayon can include nausea, vomiting, chest pain, headaches, and many others. Tampons are also bleached using chlorine, which results in the production of dioxin, and is linked to breast cancer, endometriosis, immune system suppression, and other various ailments.

• **Tampons can cause infections** – Tampon use causes micro lacerations (tiny wounds) every time you insert one and pull it out, leaving your vaginal wall more exposed to the potential for infection or disease.

• **Tampons disturb PH-Balance** –Tampons absorb your flow, but they also absorb all the moisture that is very important to keep PH balanced and to maintain health.

• **Tampons contribute to odor** – Remember, there is nothing toxic, dirty, or smelly about menstrual blood. Genitals are not meant to smell like fruit or flowers, during or between menstruations. But as soon as the tampon is inserted, the process of oxidation starts and bacteria develops, which can explain abnormal odors.

• **Tampons leave chemical residue** in your vaginal area.
Loose fibers are left behind in your vagina, which the body does eventually flush out but until then, there are chemicals stored in your body and these can cause bladder, vaginal infections, and TSS. Some of the fibers might also get stuck in the cervix, which might cause uterine infection. If you want to test this, take a tampon and jiggle it in a glass of water and see what happens to the fibers!

The Origin of TSS

In 1978, Toxic shock syndrome was identified and named by Dr. James K. Todd, a pediatrician based in Denver. His discovery found staphylococcal illness in three boys and four girls between 8-17 years. Even though S. aureus was isolated from mucosal sites in patients, bacteria could not be isolated from the blood, cerebrospinal fluid, or urine, raising speculation that a foreign toxin was involved. It was also revealed from reports that similar staphylococcal illnesses had occasionally occurred as far back as 1927, but the research at the time failed to consider the possibility of a connection between toxic shock syndrome and tampon use, as the three girls who were menstruating at the time symptoms developed while using tampons. Many cases of TSS occurred after tampons were left inside those using them.

After a controversial test period of marketing in Rochester, New York, and Fort Wayne, Indiana, in August 1978 Procter & Gamble introduced superabsorbent Rely tampons to the United States market in response to women's demands for tampons that could contain an entire menstrual flow without leaking or replacement. Rely used carboxymethylcellulose (CMC) and compressed beads of polyester for absorption. This product design could absorb nearly 20 times its weight in fluid. Further, the tampon would "blossom" into a cup shape to hold menstrual fluids without leakage.

In January 1980, epidemiologists in Wisconsin and Minnesota reported the appearance of TSS, mostly in menstruating women, to the CDC, S. aureus was successfully cultured from most of the women. A CDC task force investigated the epidemic as the number of reported cases rose throughout the summer of 1980, accompanied by widespread publicity. In September 1980, the CDC reported that users of Rely were at increased risk for developing TSS.

On September 22, 1980, Procter and Gamble recalled Rely following the release of the CDC report. As part of the voluntary recall, Procter and Gamble entered into a consent agreement with the FDA "providing for a program for notification to consumers and retrieval of the product from the market." However, it was clear to other investigators that Rely was not the only culprit. Other regions of the US saw increases in menstrual TSS before Rely was introduced. It was shown later that higher absorbency of tampons was associated with an increased risk for TSS, regardless of the chemical composition or the brand of the tampon. The sole exception was Rely, for which the risk for TSS was still higher when corrected for its absorbency. The ability of carboxymethylcellulose to filter the S. aureus toxin that causes TSS may account for the increased risk associated with Rely.

Toxic shock syndrome (TSS) is a very rare but potentially fatal illness caused by a bacterial toxin. Different bacterial toxins may cause toxic shock syndrome, depending on the situation. The causative bacteria include Staphylococcus aureus and Streptococcus pyogenes. Streptococcal TSS is sometimes referred to as toxic shock-like syndrome (TSLS) or Streptococcal Toxic Shock Syndrome (STSS). Symptoms vary depending on the underlying cause. Adverse effects of TSS are a result of an infection in connection with Staphylococcus aureus which typically manifests in healthy individuals with high fever, followed by low blood pressure, malaise, and confusion, which can rapidly progress to stupor, coma, and multi-organ failure. The characteristic rash, often seen early in the course of illness, resembles sunburn and can involve any region of the body.

According to clinical data, TSS is caused by Staphylococcus Pyogenes or TSLS, which become present in people with pre-existing skin infections associated with bacteria. These people often experience severe pain at the site of the skin infection, followed by rapid progression of symptoms as described above for TSS. In contrast to TSS caused by Staphylococcus, Streptococcal TSS less often involves a sunburn rash.

According to Epidemiology, Staphylococcal Toxic Shock Syndrome is rare, and it has been reported that the number of reported cases has declined significantly since the 1980s. Patrick Schlievert, who published a study on it in 2004, determined incidence at 3 to 4 out of 100,000 of those who use tampons per year; the information supplied by manufacturers of sanitary products such as Tampax and Stayfree puts it at 1 to 17 of every 100,000 menstruating women per year.

According to a reported case, there was a rise in TSS in the early 2000s: eight deaths from the syndrome in California in 2002 after three successive years of four deaths per year. Based on Schlievert's studies, cases within the State of Minnesota more than tripled from 2000 to 2003. Schlievert considers the earlier onset of menstruation to be a cause of the rise; others, such as Philip M. Tierno and Bruce A. Hanna, indicated that a new high-absorbency tampon product introduced in 1999 contributed to the rise because the manufacturers discontinuing warnings of not leaving tampons inside the vagina overnight.

According to pathophysiology, TSS is caused by Staph, aureus and TSLS caused by Strep. Pyogenes. Disease progression stems from a super antigen toxin that allows the non-specific binding of MHC II with T cell receptors, resulting in polyclonal T cell activation. In typical T cell recognition, an antigen is taken up by an antigen-presenting cell, processed, expressed on the cell surface in complex with class II major histocompatibility complex (MHC) in a groove formed by the alpha and beta chains of class II MHC, and recognized by an antigen-specific T cell receptor.

By contrast, super-antigens do not require processing by antigen-presenting cells but instead interact directly with the invariant region of the class II MHC molecule. In patients with TSS, up to 20% of the body's T cells can be activated at one time. This polyclonal T-cell population causes a cytokine storm, followed by a multisystem disease. The toxin in S. aureus infections is Toxic Shock Syndrome Toxin-1 or TSST.

Tampons leave chemical residue in your vaginal area.

Loose fibers are left behind in your vagina, which your body eventually flushes out but until then you have chemicals stored in your body and these can cause bladder, vaginal infections, and TSS. Some of the fibers might also get stuck in the cervix, which might cause uterine infection. If you want to test this, take a tampon and jiggle it in a glass of water and see what happens to the fibers!

After a controversial test period of marketing in Rochester, New York, and Fort Wayne, Indiana, in August 1978 Proctor & Gamble introduced superabsorbent Rely tampons to the United States market in response to women's demands for tampons that could contain an entire menstrual flow without leaking or replacement. Rely used carboxymethylcellulose (CMC) and compressed beads of polyester for absorption. This product design could absorb nearly 20 times its weight in fluid. Further, the tampon would "blossom" into a cup shape to hold menstrual fluids without leakage.

By the end of 1980, the number of TSS cases reported to the CDC began to decline. The number of reduced episodes was attributed not only to the removal of Rely on retail but also to the reduced use of all tampon brands. According to the Boston Women's Health Book Collective, 942 women were diagnosed with tampon-related TSS in the USA from March 1980 to March 1981, 40 of who died.

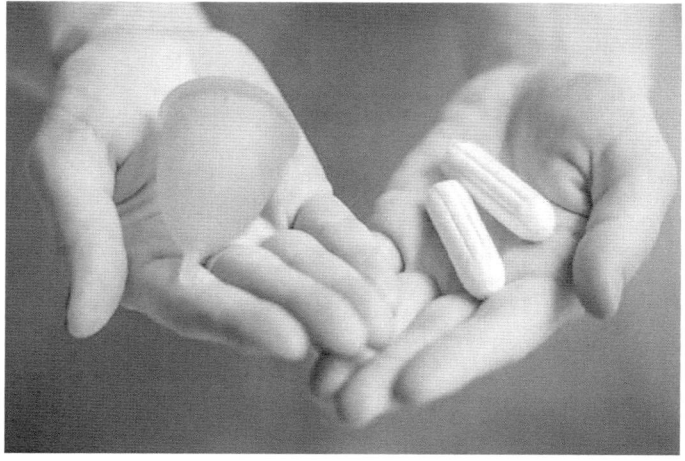

Toxic shock syndrome (TSS) is a very rare but potentially fatal illness caused by a bacterial toxin. Different bacterial toxins may cause toxic shock syndrome, depending on the situation. The causative bacteria include Staphylococcus aureus and Streptococcus pyogenes. Streptococcal TSS is sometimes referred to as toxic shock-like syndrome (TSLS) or Streptococcal Toxic Shock Syndrome (STSS). Symptoms vary depending on the underlying cause.

Adverse effects of TSS are a result of an infection in connection with Staphylococcus aureus which typically manifests in healthy individuals with high fever, followed by low blood pressure, malaise, and confusion, which can rapidly progress to stupor, coma, and multi-organ failure. The characteristic rash, often seen early in the course of illness, resembles a sunburn and can involve any region of the body.

According to a clinical data report, TSS is caused by Staphylococcus Pyogenes or TSLS, which become present in people with pre-existing skin infections associated with bacteria. These people often experience severe pain at the site of the skin infection, followed by rapid progression of symptoms as described above for TSS. In contrast to TSS caused by Staphylococcus, Streptococcal TSS less often involves a sunburn rash.

According to Epidemiology report, Staphylococcal Toxic Shock Syndrome is rare, and it has been reported that the number of reported cases has declined significantly since the 1980s. Patrick Schlievert, who published a study on it in 2004, determined incidence at 3 to 4 out of 100,000 tampon-using females per year; the information supplied by manufacturers of sanitary products such as Tampax and Stayfree puts it at 1 to 17 of every 100,000 menstruating females per year.

According to an investigative report, there was a rise in TSS in the early 2000s: eight deaths from the syndrome in California in 2002 after three successive years of four deaths per year. Based on

Schlievert's studies, cases within the State of Minnesota more than tripled from 2000 to 2003. Schlievert considers the earlier onset of menstruation to be a cause of the rise; others, such as Philip M. Tierno and Bruce A. Hanna, indicated that a new high-absorbency tampon product introduced in 1999 contributed to the rise because the manufacturers discontinuing warnings of not to leaving tampons inside the vagina overnight.

According to pathophysiology report, TSS is caused by Staph. aureus and TSLS caused by Strep. Pyogenes. Disease progression stems from a super-antigen toxin that allows the non-specific binding of MHC II with T cell receptors, resulting in polyclonal T cell activation. In typical T cell recognition, an antigen is taken up by an antigen-presenting cell, processed, expressed on the cell surface in complex with class II major histocompatibility complex (MHC) in a groove formed by the alpha and beta chains of class II MHC, and recognized by an antigen-specific T cell receptor.

CHAPTER 11
THE STORY OF Ann Anderson
PERSEVERING THROUGH THE MEDICAL DISPARITIES AND HORMONE HYSTERIA

Ann Anderson who decided not to allow the medical methodologies of western medicine compromise the will to love and live even published a book so that the all women may maintain a powerful esteem

I am an African-American woman and thought my menstrual cycle pain *("period")* was going to be the death of me. The pain was debilitating, uncontrollable cramps, heavy bleeding leading to anemia, and lasted for 12 consecutive days. I came to realize that something had to be done when the period lasted longer than expected, starting as a young girl, and tended to come twice a month, strapped with pains.

Over the years, my periods made it difficult for me to maintain any semblance of a normal lifestyle during this cycle. *I would miss school or work at least 3-4 days per month.* Finally, I was put on birth control pills as an adolescent to control the length of my periods. I was told that the use of the pills for this purpose would reduce the length of the period to less than 4 or 5 days without a new occurrence. My cramps were so painful that I often balled up in a fetal position while crying out to relieve the pain. Every over the counter medication failed me. The Tylenol stopped working, Advil, and even the Ibuprofen gave me no relief. Eventually, as an adult, I was prescribed a narcotic called Percocet to relieve my pain. I marveled at the possibility of getting some relief, so I tried this drug without hesitation, but it only masked the problem.

Over time, I went to the hospital for various doctors' visits. *By 2004, I was 43 years old when I visited a local OB-GYN*, who gave me a glimpse of hope by suggesting surgery. I didn't realize at that time that my health was spiraling out of control. I was referred to a specialist who diagnosed me with a fibroid tumor the size of a melon along with some smaller ones and also an advanced case of endometriosis. After my consultation, I was told that the use of a narcotic drug for menstrual pain is an indication that my reproductive organs must be removed. Heeding the doctor's advice, I scheduled a total hysterectomy believing the problem would be solved.

I became curious about the subject of fibroids, so I went on a search for knowledge. It was then that I learned that fibroids are benign tumors found within or on the uterus. They can grow as large as melons or the size of the one that caused me problems. Symptoms include excessive menstrual bleeding, painful cramping, pelvis, and lower back pain. With that answer, I then searched to find the cause of endometriosis. My research revealed that *"Endometriosis"* is often a painful disorder in which tissue that usually lines the uterus grows outside the womb. Also, most often with endometriosis, the tissue can be commonly found on the ovaries, fallopian tubes, or the intestines. Even in other cases of endometriosis, displaced endometrial tissue continues to act as it normally would – it thickens, breaks down and bleeds with each menstrual cycle. Because this displaced tissue has no way to exit the body, it becomes trapped. When endometriosis involves the ovaries, and the fallopian tubes as in my case, cysts called *endometriomas* may form, and surrounding tissue can become irritated and eventually developing scar tissue and adhesions – abnormal bands of fibrous tissue that can cause pelvic tissue and organs to stick to each other.

The silence and stigma of menstrual pain, namely fibroids, and endometriosis, can destroy a woman's life. For years I suffered in silence while holding onto the shame. My quality of life had shrunk to the point of non-existent. It was a nightmare that consisted of continued episodes of constipation, chronic fatigue, excessive bleeding, and the most unbearable pain.

The new battle cry to demand women's voices not only to be heard but also taken seriously faces a challenge within the healthcare community that can, to this day, erode a woman's trust in herself. Because those with whom our health is entrusted are not always knowledgeable about complex GYN conditions that cause menstrual pain and are often dismissive towards female patients. This unacceptable behavior can result in delays in treating complex GYN conditions like endometriosis or fibroids that put a woman's health at risk.

Research shows that 50 percent of women with endometriosis see at least five health care professionals before receiving a diagnosis and referral for treatment. It is estimated that a woman with endometriosis will have to wait 7-9 years for proper diagnosis of the disease, if not longer, as it is not visible on any diagnostic imaging. During that time, the inflammation caused each month can lead to scarring in the pelvic cavity, which can lead to fertility, chronic pain, or difficulty going to the bathroom.

Fibroids affect approximately 80 percent of women by age 50, yet the common practice by OBGYNs and Primary Care Physicians is to watch them and wait on treatment. However, waiting to remove a small fibroid can lead too much more complicated removal procedures down the line, as in my case since one of them grew to the size of a melon. Unfortunately, waiting to remove a large fibroid can result in irreversible damage to the uterus, putting fertility at risk.

Beyond hysterectomies, there are medical treatments that can alleviate fibroid symptoms. Now my condition has improved immensely. Thanks for getting the help I needed, which was the correct choice for me. Since I didn't want any more children, in addition to IUDs option, when treating fibroids, "there are options for therapy, including birth control and other hormonal agents which are generally first-line before surgical interventions."

If a surgical has been recommended, and the woman desires to have children in the future, myomectomy may be a viable, less intrusive option. Do your research. Unlike a hysterectomy, fibroids are removed from the uterus, leaving it intact during the myomectomy. Also, relief may be as simple as a trip to your health food store, comparing conventional procedures or researching recent articles on women's health. There's been a lot of research looking at the role that vitamin D plays in fibroid disease development and growth. Vitamin D has been proven to reduce the presence of fibroids.

Overall, it can be comforting – even liberating – for women from all walks of life, but especially African American/Brown-Tone women to remember that they're not alone, whether they join an online support group or share offline with their friends. Studies reveal that while approximately 70 percent of white women will have uterine fibroids by age 50, "that number is greater than 80 percent for African-American women." In addition to this, research shows that Brown-Tone women are more likely to report severe or very severe symptoms. Regardless of unknown determinants, African-American/Brown-Tonewomen should be aware that something as innocuous as our hair could play a role in our bodies' connection with fibroids. Most importantly, women as a whole should use our voices to demand the proper help that we need and insist on getting it before any further damage can occur and not have to wait and see.

These days, in the aftermath of my treatment, I am thankful to share my experience. I think the best part of it all is that I'm not afraid to talk about what I've been through in terms of everything, and still be hopeful – reflecting on my experience by my being open and talking about the fibroids, endometriosis, and the pain. I'm learning that other women have similar journeys, and they need to hear my story because it does not belong to me. I also realize that I went through this situation to help other women. This experience has taught me the importance of self-care, which is the same as self-love. The choice of self-care is not selfish but necessary.

On top of that, self-care has caused me to become proactive about my health. I am determined to feed my body foods that nourish it and to discover what deficiencies I might have and start to supplement my body with whatever it might be missing from the foods that I eat. What I love most about my journey is that it has made me the advocate for women and for women's health that I am today.

CHAPTER 12
CHEMICALS AND LIFESTYLE CAN CONTRIBUTE TO BREAST CANCER

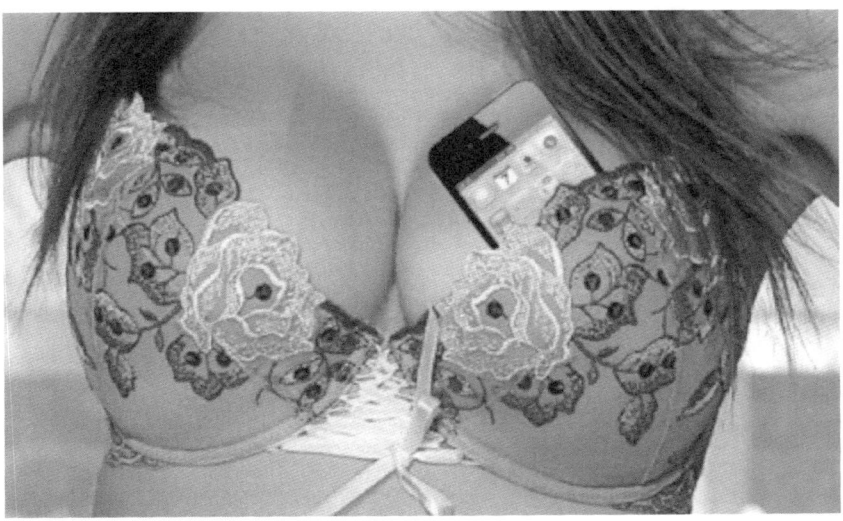

Disclaimer:

The Information Provided In this report is not presented with intention of diagnosing or prescribing but is offered only as Information for the use in maintaining and promoting health in cooperation with a physician. In the event that the information presented in this program is used without a physician's approval, the individual will be diagnosing for him/herself. No responsibility is assumed by the author, publisher, or distributors of this information should anyone use the information contained herein in lieu of a doctor's services. No guarantees of any kind are made for the performance or effectiveness of the products mentioned. The following information is presented to help give you more ammunition in your fight with the war with cancer. Some of the information in this report may be a little technical, but we feel that you should know about it and discuss it with your doctor, health care provider or holistic practitioner. Many of the products discussed in this report are presented with the scientific studies, which can be found on www.PubMed.gov.

According to the World Health Organization (WHO), Breast cancer is the most prevalent form of cancer among women, affecting 2.1 million women each year, and contributing to the greatest number of deaths among women. In 2018, it was estimated that 627,000 women succumb to breast cancer - that is approximately 15% of all cancer deaths among women. Though breast cancer appears more prevalent in the western develop regions, the statistics are revealing increasing numbers globally.

Two prime factors that contribute to breast cancer:
• General External factors of cancer development: aerosols, tobacco, perfumes, radiation, Petro-chemicals, and Infections.
• General Internal factors of cancer development—include inherited mutations, estrogen dominance, progesterone deficiency, immune system deficiencies, mutations resulting from metabolizing, refined foods, sugar, non-organic Caffeine-containing stimulants (coffee and Tea), and meat, dairy, adulterated and irradiated food intake.

Women around the world are at risk of cancer, especially in America due to the combination of the Standard American Diet (SAD), chemicals, Synthetic hormones, and stress. Because of toxic synergy, the DNA gene structure, along with tumor genes, T-helper cells, and other molecules that keep the tumors and cancer cells in check. Detrimental factors such as stress accelerated aging starting at pre-puberty and the daily exposure to dangerous environmental estrogen-mimicking compounds that will affect a woman's breast cellular structure through a compromised immune response.

Breast cancer and other similar diseases invariably begin at the DNA and cellular level. The earlier the body is exposed to toxic molecular structures in food, water, body care, cosmetics, household products, radiation and stress, the earlier the DNA malfunctions begin. As anti-life chemicals are consumed daily, both the DNA and the "normal" gene will develop a glitch or malfunction, thus triggering a more malignant activity. The tumor suppressor gene becomes (the genes that keep cancer cells in check) becomes dormant, like a sleeping usher in a theatre unconsciously allows non-ticket payers to sneak in the movie theatre, the unregulated cell replication begins to mutate, this is referred to as a tumor promoter gene, which becomes active. Therefore, anything that you internally or externally consume outside the natural boundaries of nature's molecular structure of life will make your cellular defense system dormant and more susceptible to malignancy.

Study Suggests Link between Exposure to Chemicals Early in Life and Breast Cancer Risk

Depending on where you live and work, you're likely to be exposed to many chemicals every day. Plastics, food and beverage containers, personal care products, sunscreen, cleaning products, and lawn and garden products all contain chemicals. Chemical pesticides are used in many commercially grown fruit, vegetable, and grain crops to protect them from insects, weeds, diseases, and other pests.

A study suggests that exposure to certain chemicals in the environment, especially early in life, is linked to a higher risk of breast cancer. The study was published online on Oct. 6, 2017, in the journal Environmental Research. **Read "Environmental chemicals and breast cancer**: An updated review of epidemiological literature informed by biological mechanisms."

The highest incidence of breast cancer occurs when women are in their mid-thirties to their mid-forties. The peak time is about 5 years before menopause. This is a time when the level of estrogen is still high in the body, but a time where progesterone has already started its declining production. Studies have shown that by the time a lump is discovered in the breast, the tumor has been there already for about 7 years and according to research, the cancer cell production is up to about 4 trillion! Non-Genetically linked cancer is one that starts in women early, usually in her thirties and not a cancer of estrogen deficiency.

This is the time when many women in industrialized nations have anovulatory cycles (a cycle characterized by the absence of ovulation, thus creating an inability for pregnancy). As explained earlier, anovulation can be due to a variety of causes, the most important being stress and excessive xenoestrogen exposure during prenatal life. Women suffering from anovulation have reduced progesterone in their bodies and resulting in unopposed estrogen and estrogen dominance.

There are many forms of breast cancer. Some grow slowly, while others are much more aggressive. 90% of breast cancers start in the milk glands or milk ducts, and 10% in the fatty or connective tissue. The size of the tumor alone is not an accurate marker for virulence. About 15% of all breast cancer is called in situ carcinoma. This cancer is contained entirely within a milk duct with no invasion into the surrounding tissue. 92% of breast cancer-stricken women aged 30 to 39 and 43% of all breast cancers in women aged 40 to 49 have what is called ductal carcinoma in situ (DCIS). This is considered a precursor to invasive cancer. It is localized but can be invasive. The diagnosis of DCIS has risen dramatically with the advent of the mammogram since it often presents as small calcifications on this test.

In 2007, the researchers that did this study published a review paper on the link between environmental chemicals and breast cancer. The review identified 216 chemicals that are linked to mammary tumors in animals and offered guidelines for studying the chemicals in people. To do the study reviewed here, the same researchers searched through studies on the 216 chemicals linked to mammary tumors in animals published between 2006 and 2016. The researchers reviewed 158 of the studies in light of new information on the biology of breast cancer, including the influence of genetic variations and hormones on the development of the disease.

The results of the studies reviewed suggest that exposure to certain chemicals early in life -- in the womb, during puberty, and pregnancy -- increases the risk of developing breast cancer later in life. The chemicals included: DDT, a pesticide banned by the U.S. Environmental Protection Agency in 1972; still, the chemical persists for long periods in the environment and some residues remain dioxins, which are formed when fuels such as wood, coal, or oil are burned; like DDT, dioxins persist for long periods in the environment, air pollution, gasoline organic solvents used in industry, including benzene and dimethylformamide (DMF) Differences in people's genetic make-up also can affect how they respond to certain chemicals.

One study reviewed found that among women exposed to polycyclic aromatic hydrocarbons (PAHs), a chemical in vehicle exhaust, women with certain genetic variants had a higher risk of developing breast cancer. "During these so-called windows of susceptibility, the body is changing, breast cells are dividing quickly, and the breast tissue becomes vulnerable to damage from chemicals," said lead author Kathryn Rodgers, a research scientist at the Silent Spring Institute, a nonprofit organization dedicated to studying links between environmental chemicals and women's health, especially breast cancer. "Every day, we come into contact with many different chemicals, and new ones are constantly being introduced to the market," she added. "Unfortunately, it's hard to measure exposures to multiple chemicals at multiple times in a person's life."

It's important to know that the hazards of chemical exposures depend on a lot of things, including the amount of exposure, the frequency of exposure, the duration of exposure, and your age when exposed. Chemicals considered carcinogens usually require regular exposures over long periods to contribute to the cause of cancer. It can be regular, low exposure overtime or a large exposure for brief periods. Most of the information we have comes from laboratory animals, not people.

The chemicals that are in gasoline, diesel and other vehicle exhaust, flame retardants, stain-resistant textiles, paint removers, and disinfection byproducts in drinking water. Gasoline and chemicals formed by combustion (for example, benzene and butadiene) are among the largest sources of mammary carcinogens in the environment, according to the researchers. Exposure comes from vehicles, lawn equipment, tobacco smoke, and charred or burned food.

Other mammary carcinogens include solvents, such as methylene chloride and other halogenated organic solvents used in spot removers, specialty cleaners, and industrial degreasers; pharmaceutical hormones such as hormone replacement therapy; certain flame retardants; a chemical used in stain-resistant textiles and nonstick coatings; and styrene, which is in tobacco smoke and is also used to make Styrofoam, drinking water from Styrofoam is potentially dangerous.

Bad Nutrition Increases the Risk of Breast Cancer

Women who consume animal fat on a regular basis will increase their risk of breast cancer by over 300 percent. Multiple observations have discovered that there is a tight link between animal-based diets and breast cancer. According to research and report by the Breast

Cancer Fund synthetic hormones routinely injected into beef cattle in the US are a contributory factor to the development of breast cancer. There is also an association between higher consumptions of grilled meats and fish that increased the risk postmenopausal breast cancer.

Burning meat or cooking over a grill or at high heat, creates powerful **cancer-causing** compounds called **heterocyclic amines**. Likewise, eating foods containing **nitrates** (a food preservative) also increases breast cancer risk. In the stomach, **nitrites** form carcinogenic compounds called **nitrosamines**. Eating a combination of healthful green and yellow vegetables with meals neutralizes these compounds significantly. Women with **DNA repair problems** (that is those with a strong family history) are also much more susceptible to the cancer-causing effects of bad nutrition as well. For example, they are even more likely to develop breast cancer should they eat pan cooked or grilled red meats every day or drink alcohol every day.

Studies have shown that a diet high in meats dramatically increases the risk of many types of cancer. There are several reasons for this, besides the carcinogens mentioned above. Iron promotes cancer development as well as the growth and spread of existing cancers. Meats have one of the highest absorbable forms of iron, with about 80 percent to 90 percent is absorbed. Vegetables, such as spinach and kale, can have high iron levels, but the flavonoids in the vegetables prevent the iron from being absorbed and may explain why mixing vegetables with meats reduces risk. Likewise, studies have shown that omega-6 fats strongly promote the growth and spread of tumors. These are oils such as corn, canola, safflower, sunflower, peanut, and soybean. Americans generally consume about 50 times more of these oils than are needed for health. Such high levels are strong promoters of cancer.

Deficiencies in many nutrients, either alone or in combination, have been shown to dramatically increase the risk of breast cancer in women, especially deficiencies in vitamin E and selenium. When taken together, studies involving large numbers of women have shown a 60 percent reduction in breast cancer. When they are combined with a proper diet, results are even better. There is at least theoretical evidence that fluoride can promote breast cancer growth since studies have shown that fluoride in drinking water promotes the growth of many cancers. Therefore, it should be avoided.
Mercury from dental amalgam fillings, vaccines containing mercury, and air pollution can also promote the growth of cancers and interfere with immunity.

Genetic Risk of Breast Cancer
Several mutated genes have been associated with an increased risk of breast cancer (**BRACA-1, BRACA-2, ATM genes**). Women who possess these genes to have an increased risk of developing breast cancer, have a poorer prognosis and are more sensitive to breast radiation exposure.

One of the many functions of these genes when normal is to repair damaged DNA. Our DNA is under a constant barrage of free radicals, which are increased by **chronic inflammatory diseases (diabetes, autoimmune diseases, heart disease, etc.), heavy metals (mercury,** lead, cadmium, aluminum, fluoride, etc.), rBGH (Growth Hormones) Glysophate, and industrial chemicals and pesticides/herbicides.

In most of us, DNA repair enzymes repair 98 percent of the damage. People with mutated repair genes have difficulty performing this vital function, and as a result, they have significantly higher cancer rates. Mutated genes, passed on from generation to generation, explain high-risk cancer families.

Even modest alcohol consumption dramatically increases a woman's risk of developing breast cancer by as much as 292 percent. Folate, at a dose of 800 micrograms a day, significantly reduces this risk. Unknown to most people as well as many doctors is the fact that fats can act as powerful pharmacological drugs. We now know that the type of fat that you eat is more important than the amount of fat you eat. The most dangerous fat of all is omega-6 oil. Omega fats promote chronic inflammation and stimulate the growth, spread, and invasion of cancers. Omega-6 fats can convert some cancers into very fast-growing, aggressive cancers.

The Influences of **Alcohol on Estrogen and Cancer Development Alcohol increases levels of estrogen.** High levels of estrogen can cause a cancer cell to multiply out of control" it is important to understand drinking alcohol doesn't just increase the risk of developing breast cancer; it is also linked to six other types of cancer (drinkaware.co.uk) The use of Tobacco in any form (Hookah, cigarettes, cigars) is also a factor in many types of cancers.

This article is republished by of Dr. John R. Lee, M.D.
A Recipe for Beating (and Preventing) Breast Cancer

The latest research on natural progesterone and breast cancer clearly indicates how important it is for women to maintain healthy, normal levels of progesterone that are in proper balance with estrogen. Doing so could not only increase many women's' chances of recovering from breast cancer – as the latest research indicates – but could also help them to avoid getting breast cancer in the first place.

As Dr. John Lee and Dr. David Zava point out in their book, hormonal imbalances have reached epidemic proportions in most developed countries over the last several decades. Due to poor diets, lack of exercise, a rise in obesity levels, the widespread use of hormone-altering chemicals, and other factors, many women suffer from chronically higher than normal estrogen levels and much lower than normal progesterone levels. In other words, many women are in chronic states of **estrogen dominance** This is one of the key reasons why breast cancer rates are as high as they are.

Considering the epidemic levels of hormonal imbalance, we are experiencing, how can a woman know if her progesterone and estrogen levels are in proper balance? If they are out of balance, how can she return them to proper balance and maintain them in that all-important state? Dr. Lee and Dr. Zava answered these questions in their landmark book. "**What Your Doctor May Not Tell You About Cancer**" While it is not possible here to cover everything they wrote, here is a short summary of their recommendations.

- **Check yourself for symptoms of estrogen dominance.** While being estrogen dominant is bad news, the good news is that it usually leaves a clear trail of symptoms. To find out if you may be estrogen dominant, read Dr. Lee's list of estrogen dominance symptoms. If you find that you have a number of the symptoms on this list, chances are good that you are suffering from this syndrome.

- **Get your hormone levels tested.** While symptoms are good indicators of hormonal imbalances, the most decisive tool for identifying imbalances is a hormone test. As a general rule, Dr. Lee and Dr. Zava recommended that women who are concerned about breast cancer test at least five hormones. These are estradiol (the most potent estrogen in the human body and the one most frequently linked to breast cancer), progesterone, testosterone, cortisol, and DHEA-S.

- **Work with doctors who are trained in the use of natural hormones.** Beating breast cancer is a team effort, so build a team that will support rather than thwart your quest for hormone balance. While growing numbers of doctors are becoming aware of the value of natural hormones, many have not kept up with the latest research and may resist your suggestions.

- **When needed, take physiological doses of bioidentical progesterone and other bioidentical hormones to restore proper balance.** When it comes to taking natural hormone supplements, it is critical to remember that *more is not better*. The goal is to return hormone levels to what would be considered normal for a healthy person. In most cases, this means taking relatively small amounts of bioidentical hormones and regularly reevaluating hormone levels through saliva testing. Many women find after testing their hormones that all they need is some bioidentical progesterone to establish proper balances between the major hormones. Others, however, find that they may need to add other natural hormone supplements to achieve balance and get adequate symptom relief. A good doctor who understands and is trained in the use and prescribing of natural hormones can advise you on your supplement strategy and help you consider your options.

- **Eliminate hormone-altering chemicals and xenohormones from your life.** Every day, our bodies are exposed to toxic chemicals that did not exist just a decade or two ago. There are synthetic hormones in the foods we eat, pesticides in our air and water, and estrogen-like compounds in many of the products we use every day. Many of these chemicals and xenohormones are known cancer-causing agents. Fortunately, we can sharply reduce our exposure to these substances and dramatically reduce their presence in our bodies. What Your Doctor May Not Tell You About Breast Cancer identifies the sources of these chemicals and offers concrete advice for avoiding them.

- **Use diet and exercise to support hormone balance.** Our modern diets are heavily tilted towards foods that promote obesity and estrogen dominance. Our sedentary lifestyles only reinforce this problem. Both women and men can benefit from reducing their intake of sugars, refined carbohydrates, and foods that are high in trans-fatty acids while increasing their intake of organic, cruciferous (e.g. cauliflower, broccoli, Brussel sprouts) vegetables, fruits, and fiber. They can also benefit from regular, moderate exercise, which helps metabolize and eliminate excess estrogens.

- **Keep educating yourself, for you are your best health advocate.** When it comes to preventing or fighting breast cancer in your body, you have every right to be the leading decision maker. Dr. Lee and Dr. Zava firmly believed this and wrote What Your Doctor May Not Tell You About Breast Cancer for patients as well as their doctors. The book contains a wealth of information that can help you make important decisions with your doctor. For instance, if your doctor is recommending you take an estrogen inhibitor such as Tamoxifen, the book can help you weigh the pros and cons of using such drugs as well as chemotherapy, radiation, and other treatment options.
- So, we encourage you to read it carefully and discuss it with your doctor. In addition, we encourage you to read the free articles about breast cancer on The Official Website of John R. Lee, M.D. as well as the references listed at the end of this article.
-

Thanks to the latest research, we have further proof that Dr. Lee and Dr. Zava were ahead of their time when they said that natural hormone balance could help prevent and treat breast cancer. We support you in learning from them, putting what you learn into practice, and sharing what you learn with your family, friends, and doctors.

The Revolutionary New Science and the Possible Key to Cancer Prevention

A science called epigenetics has received recognition as a new revolutionary technology that reveals some facts about our ability to control or become more vulnerable to the development of cancer. The science of epigenetics is the study of long-lasting modifications in gene function or activity, which does not involve changes in gene structure. This "new science" demonstrates how nutrients can stimulate or deactivate our genes, like an "on and off switch."

For example; if a gene is an active tumor suppressor gene (a gene that prevents mutant cell replication), or one that triggers termination of defective cells (like pre-existing malignant cells through a natural biological apoptotic elimination process) these epigenetic regulatory processes maintains its natural intelligence, thus blocks the proliferation of a cancer cell. (Epigenetics for Breast cancer Prevention, November 2012, Harvard university college of Medicine, Washington, DC 20059, USA)

This new science finally articulates how nutrients and certain drugs can alter the way breast cancer cells age and reproduces. Make no mistake nature will always be ahead of the game of health or disease development because it was already hidden in the blueprint of creation.

Breast cancer is caused by a complex interaction of multiple dietary, environmental, stress, and genetic factors. There has been a great magnitude research and facts that clearly show the standard commercial, body care, hygiene, shampoo, cosmetics, hydrogenated oils, irradiated foods, adulterated food, plastics containers, plastic liners, alcohol, dairy, and commercial meats without a shadow of a doubt contribute to the rising statistics of cancer among all adult women. However, if one were to conform to a more holistic lifestyle and diet, science also shows that the chances of developing fibrocystic breast disease and breast cancer can greatly reduce the risk. Research has shown that an organic plant-based chemical-free diet can give the body greater resistance.

Since most cancers are estrogen-driven, based on research, it is important to become familiar with two significant metabolites that estrogen is broken down into the body. Scientists have identified these two hormonal components; as the good 2-hydroxy estrone, and the bad, 16-alpha-hydroxy estrone, along with indole-3-carbinol (13C) that can change the mutated course of estrogen to work in favor of the female body.

As mentioned throughout the book the exposure to and the consumption of Xenoestrogens – chemical estrogens must be avoided as much as possible. We must remove as many brands as possible to prevent estrogen dominant conditions, such as breast cysts and malignant (cancer) development.

Scientists and cancer researchers have proven that estrogen dominance can destroy your good health—and shorten your life span by years. As you age, estrogen and testosterone can easily get out of balance. Industrial pollution—including pesticides, plastics, car exhaust, soaps, carpeting, scratched Teflon pans and even furniture material—contributes to rising estrogen levels. Over time, environmental exposure and dietary toxicants lead to estrogen dominance. This can cause debilitating health problems such as fluid retention, headaches, weight gain, brittle bones, and fatigue.

Such exposures are of particular concern in view of the virtual lifelong use of multiple carcinogenic ingredients in common cosmetics and personal care products; their application to large areas of skin; and the concomitant presence of strong detergents in these products, notably sodium lauryl sulfate, which facilitate the skin absorption of carcinogens. Also, the "Standard American Diets" are high in animals, dairy fats contaminated with carcinogenic, estrogenic and endocrine disruptive pollutants. Exposure to carcinogenic chemical pollutants from neighboring chemical plants or hazardous waste sites is increasing the risk of cancer.

Breast cancer is a rampant epidemic, striking 1 in 9 women in the U.S., up from 1 in 30 women in 1960, before estrogen replacement therapy was popularized. The greatest surge of breast cancer diagnoses was in the western hemisphere and now spreading globally to all industrialized countries. Among women between the ages of 18 to 54, it is the most common cause of death. Though cancer is a leading killer among women age 45 to 50, younger women are expected to be as great of a risk because of the chemicals in body care, produce, estrogen dominance.

Beware Estrogen Replacements

Though the FDA approves HRT drugs, these estrogen drugs have been documented to cause cancer. Published studies have shown that women taking estrogen and a synthetic progesterone drug had a 32 to 46% increases in their risk of breast cancer. This was based upon a large pool of data from the famous Nurses' Health Study conducted at Harvard Medical School. This study indicated that the carcinogenic risk of estrogen-progestin replacement therapy became most prevalent when used at least 10 years or more.

Recent data from the Breast Cancer Detection Demonstration Project suggest that relative risk is increased by 20% even after four years of use compared to no hormone treatment, and that surprisingly there was a 40% increased risk of breast cancer using both estrogen and synthetic progesterone (called progestin) combined, compared to only 20% increase for estrogen alone. Progestin's (such as Provera) that is supposed to counterbalance the estrogen is not what the body recognizes as good maybe because the molecular structure is not found in nature and is recognized as a foreign agent to the body.

In addition to breast cancer risk, it was also found that long-term estrogen replacement therapy increased the risk of fatal ovarian cancer. A large 7-year study included 240,073 pre- and post-menopausal women focus on this. After adjusting for other risk factors, women who used estrogen for 6 to 8 years had a 40% higher risk of deadly ovarian tumors, while women who used estrogen drugs for 11 or more years had a startling 70% higher risk of dying from cancer of the ovaries.

Clinicians have often reported seeing patients returning with breast lumps 6-12 months after starting on HRT. This "classic history" reflects the effect of HRT on breast cells. Researchers have shown that estradiol increased breast cell proliferation rate by 230%, while progesterone decreases it by more than 400 %. When estradiol is combined with progesterone, the normal proliferation rate is maintained. Unopposed estrogen (especially estradiol) is an important causative factor of breast cancer.

This is well documented by numerous scientific studies. Besides, studies also show estrogen stimulates breast cell (and breast cancer cell) hyperplasia and dysplasia, whereas progesterone inhibits it. Pathologically, estradiol has been shown to stimulate and up-regulate the oncogene, Bcl-2, leading to cancer cell proliferation. Progesterone, on the other hand, up-regulates the p53 gene that increases apoptosis and blocks the Bcl-2 carcinogenic effect. Estrogen stimulates breast cancer while progesterone has the opposing effect.

Breast cancer is proliferated by Non-organic, commercial manufacturers of cosmetics, toiletries, soaps, nail polish, hair glues, shampoos, and fragrances, contain a wide range of fractionally distilled Petrochemicals and carcinogenic ingredients, such as formaldehyde, phenyl-p-phenylenediamine, and diethanolamine.

Cancer Among Women In America:

- A woman's lifetime risk of breast cancer is 1 in 8.
- Breast cancer has the highest mortality rate of any cancer in women between the ages of 20 and 59.
- African American/Aboriginal Indigenous women have a 31% breast cancer mortality rate – the highest of any racial or ethnic group in America.
- Among women younger than 45, breast cancer incidence is higher among African American/Aboriginal Indigenous women than women of European Descent.

- Younger women in general, and younger African American/Indigenous women in particular, are more likely to incur the **triple-negative subtype** of cancer, a subtype that is both more aggressive and associated with a higher mortality.
- Over the past 20 years, despite the so-called "universal drop" in mortality rates, there is a rise in the incidence of breast cancer in African American/ Aboriginal Indigenous women. In particular, disparities between mortality rates for women of European descent and African American/Aboriginal Indigenous have grown significantly.
- The mortality rate for African American/Aboriginal Indigenous women diagnosed with breast cancer is 42% higher than the comparable rate for women of European descent. Triple-negative breast cancer is diagnosed more often in American women of African or American Aboriginal descent than in those of European descent in North America.

Other "hidden" carcinogens from precursors such as: diethanolamine, which apart from its own carcinogenicity following skin application to mice, interacts with nitrites to form the potent carcinogen nitroso diethanolamine; diazolidine urea and quadrennium 15, which break down to release formaldehyde; and polyethylene glycol, which is contaminated with two carcinogens, ethylene oxide and 1,4-dioxane.

EMF & CANCER

There is a connection between "electromagnetic frequency" (EMF) radiation from domestic appliances, cell phones, the proximity of residence to power lines, microwave, laptops, electrical and other occupations to a wide range of cancers. These include male and female breast cancers, over one million U.S. women who work in blue-collar industries are exposed to over 50 carcinogens, incriminated as causing breast cancer.

Studies after studies have now repeatedly shown that most breast cancers in adults are non-genetically linked, and upwards of 80% of breast cancer is caused by estrogen dominance. Therefore, breast cancer can be cured and reversed if the body's estrogen level is brought under control. It is not a coincidence that after menopause (reduced rate of estrogen production), the increasing rate in the risk of breast cancer declines dramatically; therefore, it may be wise that you find a physician or holistic practitioner who may be familiar with an Estrogen Reduction Protocol.

The cancer crisis is not exclusive to women. Since everyone is exposed to estrogen-mimicking toxins, men are losing testosterone production and gaining estrogen through xenoestrogens from the chemicals in practically all non-organic foods, produce, beverages, lawn chemicals, and body care. Breast cancer in men is even becoming prevalent due to the rising estrogen levels from hormonal weight gain and environmental pollutants, plus the loss of testosterone, which is putting men at risk for prostate, heart, and other serious health concerns.

It is important to acknowledge that there is an emerging advent of **"growing breast"** (**Man Boobs**) that is knocking at the doors of every growing boy and man in American because of the overconsumption and exposure to xenoestrogens. It is crucial to avoid the following: in-organic produce, estrogen-mimicking body care products, plastic containers, (even if listed as **Bisphenol-A-free**, and all non-organic, GMO soy products except for products that are made from **Organic, Non-GMO fermented soy**).

The best way to correct estrogen's influence on breast cancer is first to avoid all estrogen-mimicking products; supply the body with organic nutrient-dense foods, and organic raw juices. Please consult with your licensed health professional or holistic practitioner before deciding to shoot from the hip and freelance into the supplementation. This dietary and lifestyle paradigm will put the endocrine and hormonal system back in balance. Please note that natural progesterone also helps to protect the body from estrogen-linked cell damage.

"DANGEROUS CONSUMER PRODUCTS"

• Beef frankfurters, hotdogs, bologna, salami, head cheese, ham, and other types of processed meats may contain the following unlabeled toxic ingredients: benzene hexachloride, carcinogenic; Dectal, carcinogenic (can be contaminated with dioxin); dieldrin, carcinogenic; DDT, carcinogenic; heptachlor, carcinogenic; hexachlorobenzene, carcinogenic; lindane, carcinogenic; hormones, carcinogenic and feminizing; antibiotics, some are carcinogenic, e.g., sulfamethazine. Labeled toxic ingredients: nitrite, nitrates, that interacts with meat amines to form carcinogenic nitrosamines.

Special Notes: According to Nutrition Digest Published by The American Nutrition Association, Volume 38, No. 2 in Los Angeles, a study was conducted and stated that children who consume more than 12 hotdogs per month increase the risk of cancer six times to average rate. There is substantial evidence of proliferation to lymphoma, multiple myeloma, and other cancers. According to the Journal of Breast Cancer, 2015, Dec; 18(4): 313-322, there is an association between dairy intake and Breast Cancer in Western and Asian populations.

• Agricultural Chemicals/Commercial Dairy: including Whole Homogenized Milk with Recombinant Bovine Growth Hormone (rBGH) (Unlabeled toxic ingredients: Atrazine, DDT, dieldrin, heptachlor, hexachlorobenzene, antibiotics, some are carcinogenic; recombinant bovine growth hormone and IGF-1.

Become more educated on herbicides, insecticides, fungicides, pesticides, parathion, fungal estrogens, and industrial chemicals like (cadmium, lead, and mercury).
• BHS: Butylated Hydroxyanisole, a common food preservative.
• Birth Control pills warning contain a high concentration of synthetic estrogen
• Cosmetics and toiletries: Skin lotions, creams, and soaps still contain parabens and phenoxyethanol as preservatives.
• Talcum powder labeled toxic ingredients is talc (carcinogenic) Special Note: According to research, there is Substantial evidence of causal relation to ovarian cancer.
• Commercial Toothpaste Labeled toxic ingredients are: FD&C Blue #1, (carcinogenic); saccharin, (carcinogenic); sodium fluoride (carcinogenic).

- Commercial nail polish and nail polish removers
- Conditioners Labeled toxic ingredients are formaldehyde, (carcinogenic); polysorbate 80, can be contaminated with the carcinogen 1, 4-dioxane; FD&C Red #4, (carcinogenic).
- Disinfectant Spray Labeled or unlabeled toxic ingredients: orthophenylene (OPP), carcinogenic.
- Dryer Sheets, fabric softeners, and detergents will transfer petrochemicals directly through the skin and into the bloodstream.
- Hair color/Dyes Labeled toxic ingredients are: quaternium-15, formaldehyde releaser, carcinogenic; diethanolamine (DEA), interacts with nitrites to form a carcinogenic nitrosamine; phenylene-diamine, carcinogenic.
- Hormone education: Know more about DES, Premarin, and Primero.
- Household products unlabeled toxic ingredients: crystalline silica, carcinogenic, crystalline silica, carcinogenic.
- Lawn Weed Killers Labeled toxic ingredient is sodium 2,4-dichlorophenoxyacetic acid (2,4-D), carcinogenic. NOTE: Substantive evidence of causal relation to lymphoma, soft tissue sarcoma, and other cancers.
- Nail Polish: includes phthalates, benzophenone-3, homsalate, 4-methyl-benzylidene camphor (4-MBC), octyl-methoxycinnamate and octyl-dimethyl-PABA.
- Phthalates are commonly found in baby lotions and powders
- Pet Lovers beware of Cat & Dog flea collars Labeled toxic ingredient is: propoxur, carcinogenic. There are pet collars available in your local natural food markets with Organic Essential oils that will not cause Health risks (talk to your Holistic Veterinarian)

• Replenishing Natural Finish Make-Up (Foundation) Labeled toxic ingredients are: BHA, carcinogenic; talc, carcinogenic; titanium dioxide, carcinogenic; triethanolamine (TEA), interacts with nitrites to form carcinogenic nitrosamines; lanolin, often contaminated with DDT, and other carcinogenic pesticides.

One-way cancer cells spread is by secreting large amounts of a group of enzymes called metalloproteinases (MMP-2 and MMP-9) that dissolve protein. Studies have shown that women whose tumors secrete large amounts of these enzymes have very aggressive cancers, the highest recurrence rate, and shorter survival. Inhibiting these enzymes reduces the spread of cancer and improves the patient's prognosis. Several flavonoids inhibit these enzymes. For example, luteolin (artichoke extract and celery) inhibits MMP-2, and curcumin inhibits MMP-9.

Sugar, Especially Refined, White Can Be Dangerous

Because of cancer cells' unusual metabolism, they are extremely dependent on sugar for their growth and spread. Sugar is a cancer fertilizer. You should eat only complex carbohydrates, such as whole grains, and those only in moderation. Avoid starches like potatoes, since the body utilizes them as sugars. It is also important to avoid eating a lot of fruits. Even though they contain some useful flavonoids, they also contain high levels of sugar. Some sugarless fruit extracts, such as blueberry extract, can be used. Raspberries are of special value since they contain a very powerful anti-cancer flavonoid called ellagic acid (you can also buy this as a concentrated extract).

It is also important to avoid artificial sweeteners, such as aspartame and Splenda. Aspartame has been shown to increase cancer development in many studies dramatically. And aspartame is metabolized in the body into formaldehyde, which continues to damage DNA over a very long time.

Most people refuse to drink water because they say it tastes bad, but this is because of the high levels of chlorine that have been added. Drink only filtered or distilled water. To make it even healthier, you can add a small amount of magnesium to each glass – about 20 milligrams. Once you drink pure water, you will begin to prefer it.

Holistic Supplements That Are Use by Alternative Health Professionals and Some Medical Doctors:
Dindolylmethane (DIM)
This is a metabolic product of a compound found in broccoli (indole-3-carbinol). Studies in people have shown that it increases the level of the cancer-inhibiting 2-hydroxyestrone and lowers 16-alpha hydroxyestrone, which promotes breast cancer.

Calcium-D-glucarate
This compound occurs naturally in humans and animals. Its main action is to enhance the detoxification of carcinogenic compounds and to help the body eliminate them. In addition, calcium-D-glucarate inhibits the formation of cancers, especially breast cancers. Studies using human breast cancer have shown dramatic results.

IP-6 is a sugar-like substance that belongs to the water-soluble B vitamin complex. Being present in many plants, this compound can also be found in your body (liver, kidney, skeletal and heart muscle). Inositol hexaphosphate (IP-6 or phytate) is a naturally occurring substance, present in almost all mammalian cells in smaller amounts. Source IP-6 International. You may acquire through All Health Concerns, LLC at 1-888-453-5526.

Modified Citrus Pectin is pectin is found in the peel and pulp of citrus fruits (lemons, oranges, grapefruits) and apples. It is what we use to make jam set. The pectin in modified citrus pectin has been changed to make it easier for the body to take in through the gut.

According to researcher and Medical professional Dr. Issac Eliaz, MCP is an alternative therapy. Some websites claim that it can help to stop breast, prostate cancer, and melanoma skin cancer from spreading due to its ability to inhibit the Galactin-3 molecule. Excess levels of Galactin-3 are associated with heart failure, kidney disease, and cancer.[1-4]

Doctors have long recognized galectin-3 as a biomarker for degenerative disease.[5-10] *New research is revealing that galectin-3 is far more than an indicator of disease–it is purported to have a causative role in these conditions.*[11-14]

Drug companies have had little success in their attempts to fight the destructive actions of galectin-3. Fortunately, scientists have discovered a citrus extract that has potent *galectin-3 inhibitory* properties. Modified citrus pectin (MCP) has been shown to *inactivate* galectin-3, blocking its ability to send destructive molecular signals throughout the body.[4] Because of its ability to block galectin-3, modified citrus pectin is emerging as a key natural compound in the battle against heart failure, cancer, and kidney disease.[4,15,16]

Astragalus has immune-stimulating effects and may help to reduce side effects from chemotherapy. It has not been shown to treat or prevent **cancer**. Astragalus root belongs to a group of medicinal plants from the legume family.

THE BENEFITS OF VITAMIN C, PROLINE AND LYSINE

It has been generally assumed that vitamin C functions as an anti-cancer agent because of its antioxidant activity, that is, by quenching the reactive oxygen species (ROS). Now it is known that vitamin C exercises its effects in several other ways. According to **Dr. Matthias Rath's Orthomolecular research**, Vitamin C should be accommodated with the amino acids **Proline and Lysine**. To Find out more on this research, please call 1.888.453.5526.

AHCC

Consisting of a cultured extract of hybridized mushroom mycelia (roots), AHCC® (active hexose correlated compound) is a specialty immune supplement supported by over 20 clinical studies.[1-20] Studies on AHCC® have been conducted at some of the finest research institutions worldwide, including Ivy League universities and major health centers.

AHCC helps maintain, optimal NK cell activity, cytokine production, optimal T-cell activity, Optimal macrophage activity, and the activity and number of dendritic cells.

CHAPTER 13
THE HOLISTIC WAY TO REDUCE TO FIBROIDS AND HIP REPLACEMENTS

Osteoporosis is a major public health issue affecting more than 10 million Americans. It is usually diagnosed in later life, but the most important time to focus on building healthy bones is during the first 3 decades of life.

By Ellen Kamhi, PhD, RN

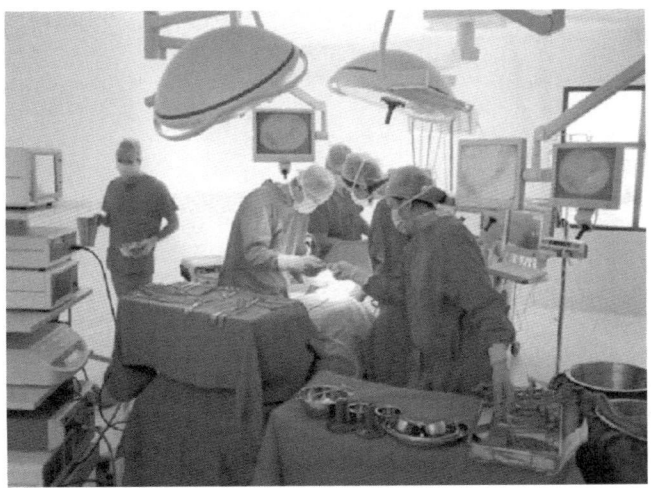

Hysterectomies and C-sections are two of the most overused surgeries. One in three women have a hysterectomy by age 60 and about half eventually have one. Approximately 600,000 women undergo hysterectomy annually, 50,000 to 60,000 of which are for a cancer diagnosis. In 2014, 70% of surgery's were outpatient— in ambulatory surgery centers or in hospitals with discharge in less than 24 hours. So, one could say that ~90% of the ~600,000 are unnecessary.

Fibroid masses and endometriosis can become such an unbearable crisis that women finally submit to the suggested surgery. As we mention earlier in the book, small uterine myomas are usually asymptomatic, but larger masses can cause excessive menstrual bleeding, and very large fibroids can contribute to miscarriage, abdominal pain, profuse bleeding (with resultant anemia) and other symptoms for which surgical removal of the fibroids is recommended, thus leading to hysterectomy in part or whole.

Modern forms of laser surgery and the new non-surgical method of fibroid embolization are distinct improvements over total hysterectomy or major abdominal surgery, but women may still seek natural approaches to resolving the masses. It is important to become familiar with fibroids and all the treatment options so that patients can be properly advised.

Why Statistics Are Higher In African American/Aboriginal Indigenous and Caucasian Women?

It is interesting that most of the women that we know or hear about regarding hysterectomies are the women of European/Caucasian or African-American/Indigenous decent. It is interesting that these groups of women grew up and still consume the Standard American Diet (Sad). Both groups of women use commercialized shampoos, cosmetics, body care, fluoridated toothpaste, have the nails manicured and polished. Regarding foods, both groups of women consume the same conventional produce that sprayed with pesticides, insecticides. Both groups of women indulge in chemically derived petrochemicals and estrogen mimicking chemicals. Both groups use the same commercialize sanitary napkins and tampons, which are also toxic in many ways. Both groups also consume fast foods, irradiated foods and microwave foods. Both groups are challenges with the rat race of society social chaos and stress.

So, would it be fair to say that the possible contributing factor to fibroids is the lifestyle, diet and the absence of an ancestral diet. Because, on the average we don't see Asian women, East Indian women, Iranian women in and out of the OBGYN's office or the surgery room. We also rarely see Hispanic/Latin women going through these medical procedures.

Could it be because the women from other ethnic group thrive on their ancestral diet instead of the commercialized, standard American diet that is comprised of hot dogs, fried chicken, hamburgers, French fries, vegetable oil, Monosodium Glutamate and microwaved foods? Could it be that the women from other cultures use natural henna instead of toxic dyes, or a more natural cosmetic of no cosmetic at all? Could it be that their ancient holistic modalities such as Traditional Chinese medicine, Macrobiotics Japanese women, Ayurveda Medicine for Eastern Indian women or Ancient Persian medicine for Iranian and other Eastern cultural women?

Example of Traditional Chinese medicine

Chinese doctors believe that uterine myomas up to the size of a goose egg can be successfully treated with herbs to reduce the size to a comfortable level and, in many cases, to eliminate them. Larger myomas are usually treated with surgery in China as they are elsewhere, though pre-treatment with Chinese herbs may reduce the complications of surgery.

The effectiveness of the Chinese herbal treatments for small to medium size fibroids has been demonstrated by clinical trials conducted in China and Japan. American practitioners of Chinese medicine have frequently reported success in treating fibroids, at least to the extent of alleviating common symptoms and thus avoiding surgery for their patients.

CHINESE THEORY OF ABDOMINAL MASSES, SUCH AS FIBROIDS

The first theory of uterine fibroids in the Chinese literature was in the *Ling Shu* (ca. 100 B.C.), which defined *shijia*, a stony tumor (*shi* = stone; *jia* = mass). From this text arose the general concept of abdominal masses as *zhengjia*, which denotes two types of masses: *zheng* refers to one in fixed position that is painful, and *jia* is a mass that can be moved, and only hurts when pressure is applied. These masses were described in the *Ling Shu* (1) scroll on water swellings, *zheng* corresponds to uterine masses and *jia* corresponding to intestinal masses (bracketed statements are inserted to aid explanation of the text):

Cold qi is a guest [that is, it takes residence there] in the outer [wall of the] intestines, and battles with the protective qi. The qi does not receive nourishment, and because cold qi and protective qi are tied together [in battle], indigestion comes from internal confusion. The sick qi then rises [e.g., upward flux of stomach qi], and sick flesh is born [below]. At the commencement of its birth, the mass is as large as a chicken's egg. Gradually, it increases its sized until it reaches the its conclusion with a shape like carrying a child.

For a long time, that is, with years intervening, if the hand is then used to press [on the abdomen], it will feel solid, but if it is pushed, it will move [hence, it is due to an accumulation of stagnated qi]. The menstrual period will be in accord with the tides [i.e., will be regular]. [These are the symptoms when the intestines are affected...alternatively,] the abdominal masses begin in the middle of the womb. Cold qi is a guest at the mouth of the womb. The mouth of the womb is blocked and obstructed.

Qi cannot penetrate. Sick blood should leak out but does not leak. The bleeding at times is detained and stops, day by day, [the womb] will increase in size so that the appearance will be like pregnancy. The menses do not respond to the tides [they are irregular].

Based on these concepts, one of the earliest methods of herb therapy for the uterine mass was to use the five-ingredient formulation called *Guizhi Fuling Wan* (Cinnamon and Hoelen Formula), first described in the *Jingui Yaolue* (ca. 220 A.D.).

The cold qi is dispelled by using cinnamon twig; the water stagnation is dispelled by hoelen (poria); the blockage and obstruction of blood flow is treated by the combination of persica, red peony, and moutan. In the *Jingui Yaolue* (2), the situation was described whereby menstrual bleeding would cease for three months, followed by incessant bleeding indicating that a mass had formed.

This scenario is consistent with the concept that the womb is blocked and obstructed (hence the lack of bleeding), but then it develops a mass, which causes the incessant bleeding. The condition was distinguished from pregnancy, where menstrual bleeding would stop, and a mass would begin to form in the abdomen, but incessant bleeding would not follow. *Gui zhi Fu ling Wan* halts the incessant bleeding by removing the mass.

In the modern text **Practical Therapeutics of Traditional Chinese Medicine** (3), the distinction of the two mass types as understood today is presented:

Zheng describes solid masses (concretions) with defined physical form and fixed location, accompanied by pain in a specific location. In these cases, pathological changes have taken place in the visceral organs; thus, these patterns usually involve the blood. *Jia*, on the other hand, describes masses without a distinct physical form (conglomerations), manifesting and dispersing without apparent pattern. Accompanying pain is not fixed in location. In these cases, pathological changes have taken place in the bowel organs. Hence, these patterns involve qi. Despite the differences between *zheng* and *jia*, the two are closely related in terms of pathogenesis and are difficult to differentiate, hence the use of the compound term *zhengjia*.

An extensive review of the theoretical basis for the etiology and treatment of abdominal masses, including fibroids, is found in the **Advanced Textbook of Traditional Chinese Medicine and Pharmacology** (4); it is reproduced here with only slight editing. Gynecological examinations were not a practice in China until the recent introduction of modern techniques, so fibroids could not be specifically identified and differentiated during the development of the theories outlined here. Fibroids are now frequently diagnosed before they reach a size that causes pain, which had been one of the first signs of a problem for people lacking modern routine examinations and an integral part of the ancient description of the masses.

For the more serious and advanced stage masses described here, symptoms described, such as pain and loss of appetite (and accompanying weakness and weight loss), may not be presented as significant symptoms by patients today because analgesics and other therapies already have been skillfully employed to minimize those effects. Further, some of the cases included in the description may be cancers of the reproductive or abdominal organs, which produce severe systemic effects as they progress. The masses are here divided into two broad groups: qi masses (called *ju*, these are like the ones referred to as *jia*) and blood stasis masses (called *ji*, like those referred to as *zheng*). Parenthetical statements are added for explanation of the original text.

Etiology and Pathogenesis

Among the causes of abdominal masses are mental depression, an improper diet, and attacks by pathogenic cold-dampness or toxin-heat. The (underlying) internal cause of abdominal masses is a deficiency in the body's anti-pathogenic qi (normal qi). Classics on traditional Chinese medicine hold that "People with strong resistance (those with strong qi) do not have abdominal masses, only weak people (those with weak qi) are likely to suffer from them." Abdominal masses gradually develop when the body's antipathogenic qi fails in its struggle against the attacking pathogenic factors. This disease is principally related to the liver and spleen. The stagnation of the qi and the blood and phlegm retention play a major role in the pathogenesis of abdominal masses.

According to Asian Medicine, The three basic causes are:

1. Mental Depression and Qi and Blood Stagnation. Mental depression causes the stagnation of liver qi, which produces *ju* lumps. This leads to blood stagnation, which over a long period forms masses, thus producing *ji* masses.
2. Improper Diet and Production of Turbid Phlegm. An improper diet refers to voracious eating or overindulgence in alcohol. This damages the spleen and stomach, producing turbid dampness whose accumulation forms phlegm; this further results in qi and blood stagnation. These combine with phlegm to cause abdominal masses.
3. Attack by and Retention of Pathogenic Factors. When pathogenic cold, dampness, heat, or toxins attack, they may remain for a long time. This impairs the functions of the affected *zang fu* organs, causing qi and blood stagnation and turbid phlegm. Over a long time, abdominal masses are produced.

Differentiation and Treatment

The pathological changes that occur with *ji* and *ju* are different. In the *ju* syndrome, the disease is located in the qi system and the basic principle of treatment is to soothe the liver, regulate and circulate qi, and disperse accumulation, with the major focus on regulating qi. In the *ji* syndrome, the blood system is affected, and treatment seeks to activate blood circulation and remove stasis, soften hardness and disperse the masses, with the major focuses on treating the blood.

Ju Syndromes (Qi Masses)

Ju usually involves liver qi stagnation and/or retention of food and accumulation of phlegm.

Liver Qi Stagnation: Qi accumulates and flows to the chest, hypochondrium, epigastrium, and lower abdomen, causing pain in these areas. This condition changes according to the patient's emotional state.

Retention of Food and Phlegm: Retained food in the intestinal tract impairs transportation and transformation, and thus produces phlegm-dampness, which, combined with retained food, blocks the qi circulation, thereby causing abdominal pain, constipation, and a poor appetite.

Ji Syndromes (Blood-Stasis Masses)

Ji syndromes are divided into three stages: qi and blood stagnation; retention of stagnant blood; and qi deficiency with accumulation of blood stasis.

Initial Stage: Qi and Blood Stagnation. Stagnant qi and blood form abdominal masses. At the initial stage, pathogenic factors move to the blood system from the qi system. The masses have only recently formed and so they are still soft to the touch. Distensive pain, a blue tongue, and a taut pulse are indications of stagnant blood caused by liver qi stagnation.

Middle Stage: Retention of Stagnant Blood. The protracted presence of abdominal masses and gradual aggravation of blood stagnation explain the hard-enlarged masses and fixed pain.

Late Stage: Anti-Pathogenic Qi Deficiency and Accumulation of Blood Stasis. Prolonged accumulation of blood stasis in the vessels gives rise to hard masses and violent pain. This also damages the spleen and stomach qi and impairs transport and transformation; thus the appetite is greatly reduced and emaciation results. Accumulation of blood stasis also prevents the production of new blood, leading to extreme deficiency of nutrient qi; its symptoms include sallow or dark-yellow complexion.

In a Japanese study of the mechanism of action of **Cinnamon and Hoelen Formula**, it was mentioned that shrinkage of uterine myoma occurred in 62% of the 110 cases treated, and that the treatments alleviated excessive menstrual bleeding and resulting anemia as well as dysmenorrhea (11). There were no significant changes in plasma levels of several hormones, including LH, FDH, PRL, and estradiol, indicating that the mechanism of action did not involve reduction of hormone stimulus to fibroid growth. It was noted that small myomas with smooth surface generating elevated levels of CA-125 appeared to be most responsive to treatment; elevated CA-125 often indicates adenomyosis, a fibroid-like condition with small masses of the uterine wall.

As indicated by these recommendations and studies, a wide range of formulas, most with qi and blood regulating properties, as well as herbs for warming the abdomen and herbs for resolving phlegm accumulation, have been used to accomplish reduction of fibroids. Complete resolution of fibroids has been reported several times, and substantial reduction of myoma size is apparently common in all but the largest or most aggressively growing fibroids. Treatment times are typically in the range of 1-8 months, with some lasting up to 10 months.

CLINICAL PRACTICE IN CHINA
Several reports about traditional Chinese medicine treatments for uterine myoma were published during the period 1980-1993, and relatively few have appeared since then, probably because of the widespread introduction into China of surgical methods for treating fibroids and a conclusion that the herb therapies had been adequately tested to reveal their level of effectiveness. A representative selection of herbal treatment strategies is presented in the following summary of descriptions found in books and journals.

A review of the early portion of this literature was presented by Dr. Hong-yen Hsu in 1984 (5). Herbal therapies involve qi-regulating herbs, herbs to vitalize blood and dispel stasis, and agents for removing food stagnation and resolving phlegm masses.

One of the most effective synergies for fibroids and body toxicity is Traditional Chinese Medicine, Persian Medicine, Ayurvedic Medicine and Homeopathic Medicine. These modalities are proactive professions that uses applications that are in harmony with nature, with very few side effects.

Osteoporosis and The Risk of Hip Surgery

Pharmaceutical agents can be effective in treating osteoporosis, but there is an increased interest in non-pharmacological prevention and treatment for the condition.

Osteoporosis is a disease of the skeletal system that is characterized by deterioration of bone tissue, along with a decrease in bone mass. It can strike anyone at any age, although it is most prevalent in Caucasian and Asian, small-boned women over 50. Osteoporosis is recognized as a major public health issue. More than 10 million Americans are afflicted, and 34 million more may already be exhibiting signs of low bone mass, which increases the risk of developing osteoporosis.

Bone mass can be determined by a bone mineral density test (BMD), such as a dual-energy x-ray absorptiometry (DXA). Low bone mass increases the risk of developing osteoporosis and fractures. Osteoporosis can affect any bone in the body, although the most common sites are the wrist, spine, and hips. It increases fracture risk, causing a huge amount of personal suffering and loss of quality of life.[1] Osteoporosis also has a high cost to society. The cumulative economic burden of care for fractures due to osteoporosis from 2008 to 2028 is estimated at $474 billion dollars in the United States alone.[2]

Bone is made up of minerals, mainly calcium salts, bound together by strong collagen fibers. Our bones have a thick, hard outer shell (called cortical or compact bone) which is easily seen on x-rays. Inside this, there's a softer, spongy mesh of bone (trabecular bone) which has a honeycomb-like structure. Bone is a living, active tissue that's constantly renewing itself. Old bone tissue is broken down by cells called osteoclasts and is replaced by new bone material produced by cells called osteoblasts. According to research osteoclast activity accelerates after a women has a total hysterectomy and the ovaries are removed.

Common Causes of Bone loss and Osteoporosis.

Lack of oestrogen in the body – If you have an early menopause (before the age of 45) or a hysterectomy where one or both ovaries are removed, this increases your risk of developing osteoporosis. This is because they cause your body's **oestrogen** production to reduce dramatically, so the process of bone loss will speed up. Removal of the ovaries only (ovariectomy or oophorectomy) is quite rare but is also linked with an increased risk of osteoporosis.

Lack of weight-bearing exercise – Exercise encourages bone development, and lack of exercise means you'll be more at risk of losing calcium from the bones and so developing osteoporosis. Muscle and bone health are linked so it's also important to keep up your muscle strength, which will also reduce your risk of falling. Also, women who **exercise too much** that their periods stop are also at a higher risk because their **oestrogen** levels will be reduced.

Poor and Toxic Diet - If your diet doesn't include enough calcium or vitamin D, or if you're very underweight, you'll be at greater risk of osteoporosis. Consuming adulterated, factory foods, white bread, white sugar, and excessive coffee drink may be contributing factors to bone degeneration.

Smoking - Tobacco is directly toxic to bones. In women it lowers the oestrogen level and may cause early menopause. In men, smoking lowers testosterone activity and this can also weaken the bones.

Heavy drinking - Drinking a lot of alcohol reduces the body's ability to make bone. It also increases the risk of breaking a bone as a result of a fall.

Natural Ways to Prevent Bone Degeneration

Osteoporosis is big business. 55% of people over fifty have osteoporosis and most of these are women, but 1 in 12 men in this age group also suffers from the same fate. In fact, osteoporosis and its close cousin arthritis affect 30% of the population in the developed countries. The following supplement information can possibly address the concerns regarding bone degeneration.

Boron is ubiquitous throughout the human body, with the highest concentrations found in the bones and dental enamel. Although there is currently no RDA for it, boron appears to be indispensable for healthy bone function, possibly because of its effects on reducing the excretion and absorption of calcium, , 27, and phosphorus.[57] It also affects signal transmissions across cell membranes by acting indirectly as a proton donor, which influences ion gradients that are involved with cell/cell communication.[58,59]

The story of Borax and how this arthritis and osteoporosis cure has been stopped.

In the 1960's **Rex Newnham, Ph.D., D.O., N.D**, developed arthritis. He was a plant scientist in WA, and he looked for the cause of his disease in the plant kingdom. He noticed that plants in the area where he lived were very mineral deficient and that plants need **Boron to thrive.** So, he started taking **30 mg of borax** per day and in three weeks all pain, swelling and stiffness had disappeared.

It was discovered that **Boron** supplementation made bones harder than normal and surgeons found them more difficult to saw through. With additional Boron bone fractures heal in about half the time in both humans and animals. Horses and dogs with broken legs or pelvises have fully recovered with extra boron. Though not recommended by the medical profession, **Borax** is effective with all forms of arthritis, be it rheumatoid arthritis, juvenile arthritis and Lupus.

Dr. Newnham wrote that commonly people can get rid of their pain, swelling and stiffness in about 1 to 3 months. After that they can reduce their boron from 3x 3mg per day to 1 mg per day to avoid future arthritis. **Disclaimer**: We are not suggesting the use of Borax, please consult with your physician, clinician. We take no responsibility for any supplement actions pertaining to this information.

Magnesium is the second most common mineral in the body, after calcium. Magnesium is important for many metabolic processes, including building bone, forming adenosine triphosphate, and absorbing calcium. Dietary sources of magnesium include nuts, whole grains, dark green vegetables, fish, meat, and legumes. Magnesium is often deficient in the standard American diet, due to low consumption of foods containing this nutrient, as well as soil depletion from commercial farming practices such as overcropping.[32]

Low levels of blood magnesium correlates with low bone density,[33] and several studies have supported the use of oral magnesium supplementation to increase bone density.[34,35,36,37] Even a moderate magnesium deficiency has been documented to cause bone loss in rats.[38] Magnesium deficiency may impair the production of parathyroid hormone and 1,25-dihydroxyvitamin D, which negatively affects bone mineralization.[39] Supplementing with 250-400 mg a day of magnesium is usually recommended. Magnesium glycinate and magnesium gluconate are preferable to magnesium oxide and are less likely to cause loose stools.

Adverse effects of magnesium usually occur at higher dosages and are most often associated with intravenous magnesium. Drug interactions include neuromuscular weakness and possible paralysis when combined with aminoglycoside antibiotics, decreased absorption of biphosphates, tetracycline antibiotics, and calcium channel blockers. Conversely, many drugs cause hypomagnesemia, including aldesleukin, aminoglycosides, and amphotericin-B (common).[40] Magnesium supplementation helps to balance a number of health issues in addition to osteoporosis, such as insomnia, headaches, chronic constipation, restless leg syndrome, anxiety, and irritability. It is often the first supplement we recommend in our clinical practice, after implementing a whole-foods based diet.

Calcium is the most abundant mineral in the human body. It is well recognized for its importance in the development of bones and teeth and has many other functions as well. The ability of calcium supplements to "maintain good bone health and reduce the high risk of osteoporosis later in life" is one of the few health label claims allowed by the U.S. Food and Drug Administration. The best food sources of calcium, other than dairy, include whole grains, beans, almonds and other nuts, and dark green leafy vegetables like kale.[18] Milk and dairy products contain a substantial amount of calcium; however, it is interesting to note that individuals who avoid dairy due to lactose intolerance do not experience a corresponding increase in osteoporosis.[19]

Calcium supplements have been shown in several studies to be effective at slowing bone loss in both perimenopausal and postmenopausal women.[20] A 2004 Cochrane Database Review Article states that "calcium supplements ... at 500 to 2,000 mg per day, are the simplest and least expensive way to prevent bone loss."[21] A comprehensive literature review published in the *British Medical Journal* (2010) questioned the commonly held belief in the benefits of using calcium supplements. In this meta-analysis the reviewers concluded that subjects who took a 500 mg/day calcium supplement (without vitamin D) experienced an increased risk of myocardial infarction when compared to those who did not take calcium supplements. These results will likely lead to further investigation of current recommendations.[22]

According to clinical human clinical studies, to maintain bone health, **500-1,500 mg/day of calcium** (including food sources and supplements) is recommended (varies with age, weight, sex, etc.) by the National Academy of Sciences.[23] **For people who are on dialysis or chronic kidney disease should see a physician before taking calcium supplements.** Sufficient calcium intake is important in preventing osteoporosis, because if the body's stores of calcium is low, calcium will be leached from bones, which can lead to decreased bone mass and the initiation or worsening of osteoporosis. While diet is the ideal source for all nutrients, calcium supplementation is often recommended to ensure that adequate amounts of this important mineral are ingested daily. This can be confusing due to the many forms of calcium on the market, the differences in dosage levels, absorption rates, delivery forms (i.e., tablets vs. liquids), cost, and other variables.

Several studies have shown that calcium citrate is absorbed better than tricalcium phosphate, calcium lactate, and calcium carbonate (the kind of calcium in antacid tablets).[24] Calcium citrate does not tend to cause gastric distress and has a pleasant taste. One study surmised that calcium format is better absorbed than either calcium citrate or calcium carbonate.[25] Microcrystalline hydroxyapetite (MH) is a form of calcium that was demonstrated to be more effective at slowing bone loss than calcium carbonate.[26] MH was also shown to support bone density in a randomized, double-blind 2007 control study.[27] Since calcium is so intimately involved in an array of metabolic reactions, it is not surprising that there is a long list of possible interactions with pharmaceutical drugs.

Vitamin D-3. is essential for the formation and maintenance of bone tissue, due to its involvement in several complex mechanisms, including the regulation of calcium and phosphorous absorption. If vitamin D-3 levels are low, parathyroid hormone (PTH) increases and triggers osteoclasts to release calcium into the blood via bone re-absorption. If this process continues over time, it weakens bone and leads to osteoporosis. In addition, vitamin D-3 stimulates intestinal epithelial cells to synthesize calcium-binding proteins that support the absorption of calcium in the blood.[41]

Vitamin D-3 is synthesized when sunlight hits the skin and transforms 7-dehydrocholesterol into vitamin D3 (cholecalciferol). D-3 is shuttled to the liver where it is converted to 25-hydroxycholecalciferol, which is then transformed into 1,25-dihydroxycholecalciferol (calcitriol). Calcitriol is 10 times more potent than vitamin D3. Magnesium and boron act as cofactors in this reaction. Food sources of vitamin D-3 include fish and fish oils.

Vitamin D-3 deficiency is now recognized as an epidemic in the United States[42] and is especially common in dark-skinned persons, the elderly, people living in northern areas, and anyone who has limited sun exposure. Deficiency can create secondary hyperparathyroidism, leading to a loss of collagen matrix and minerals, which increases the risk of osteoporosis and fractures. Poor bone remodeling due to higher osteoclast vs. osteoblast activity can occur with low levels of vitamin D-3, reduced synthesis of calcitriol in the kidneys, or a lack of calcitriol receptors in target organs.[43]

Vitamin D-3 is available as a supplement in several forms. Vitamin D-3 (cholecalciferol), vitamin D-2 (synthetic) (ergocalciferol), and alfacalcidol are 3 common forms. Studies have demonstrated that alfacalcidol prevents osteoporosis in women on high-dose corticosteroids[44] and increases muscle power and walking distance in the elderly.

Vitamin D3 is more effective than Vitamin D2 and is a better supplement choice for most individuals.[47] An exception would be vegans, who prefer not to use animal-sourced products, since the starting material for D3 is fish or lanolin. Mechanisms of action of vitamin D's role in building healthy bones includes increasing the number and activity of osteoblasts,[48] reducing the activity of osteoclasts,[49] and normalizing the turnover of bone in osteoporosis.[50]

Vitamin D-3 appears to be most effective as a therapy for osteoporosis when combined with calcium.[51] While 400 IUs of oral vitamin D-3 (cholecalciferol) is the current recommended daily allowance (RDA), this level of supplementation appears to be insufficient to prevent fractures; while 700-800 IU/day appears to reduce the risk of hip and any nonvertebral fractures in both institutionalized and ambulatory elderly persons.[52] Vitamin D-3 is well tolerated at doses of 400-800 IU/day.

Strontium. Is a powerful agent in the treatment and prevention of osteoporosis. Strontium is a naturally occurring mineral present in water and food. Trace amounts of strontium are found in the human skeleton, where it is adsorbed at the matrix crystal surface of bones. The Spinal Osteoporosis Therapeutic Intervention study is a double-blind, randomized, placebo-controlled trial that compared 2 groups of postmenopausal women who already had a diagnosis of osteoporosis. One group was given 2 grams daily of nonradioactive strontium ranelate, while another group received a placebo.

The strontium group illustrated a significant reduction (41%) in the relative risk of experiencing a new vertebral fracture.[66] Other promising studies showed reduced risks for nonvertebral fractures, including hip fractures, following the use of strontium.[67] In addition to reducing the risk of fracture, strontium ranelate increased bone mineral density throughout the study, peaking at 3 years, with augmented scores of 8.2% in the femoral neck and 9.8% in the hip.

Japanese pharmaceutical researchers have trade named the strontium salt PROTELOS™ and are in phase 2 drug trials. The mechanism of strontium's bone-strengthening effect is believed to be decreased bone resorption and increased bone formation, which increases bone mass, microarchitecture, and strength.[68]

Collagen. Seventy percent of our skin is made from collagen. Within the skin, collagen is the main component of the dermis: the layer that gives our skin elasticity and flexibility. Beginning at age 21, our body's production of new collagen begins to decline and existing collagen begins to break down. By the time we are around 60 years old, we have half as much collagen as we did at the age of twenty-one. In addition, collagen synthesis rates – our body's ability to create new collagen – have dropped by 75%[1]. Exposure to UV rays throughout our lifetime furthers this depletion, which can lead to wrinkles, dryness, and saggy skin. Research shows oral collagen protein supplementation may help in firming and hydrating skin, as well as help in reducing the appearance of deep wrinkles. Additionally, collagen may help protect against UV-induced skin damage. Learn about all the collagen anti-aging benefits below.

Everyone has a different physical constitution, therefore, there is no one size fits all protocol. There are several other supplements that can strengthen bone and reduce the risk of osteoporosis. **See a holistic practitioner or contact Dr. Jafari's or Dr. Botanica's at 1-888-453-5526 to acquire more details.**

CHAPTER 14
WHY WOMEN NEED ORGANIC SANITARY NAPKINS

One hundred years ago, the average woman started her menses between 13 and 16, today because of the growth hormones, antibiotics, xenoestrogens from BP-A and array of toxic chemicals, a young girl will start her cycle as early as nine years of age. Incessant menstruation has been associated with the increased occurrence of a myriad of pathological conditions, including infertility, cancer, fibroids, anemia, migraines, mood swings, abdominal pain, fluid retention, and endometriosis thanks to the industrial revolutions and fractionally distilled toxic chemicals.

It is estimated that the average woman uses 11,000 sanitary napkins and tampons in her lifetime. Each of those tampons, along with pads, can take centuries to break down in landfills because of the toxic composition of these materials, especially if they are covered in plastic before being thrown away. While many environmental advocates are promoting methods to discontinue use of plastic containers, plastic-laden feminine hygiene products which happen to contribute to about 180 billion bags to our waste stream", according to the resource Naturally Savvy, more people just have to be introduced to cleaner and safer alternatives that do not wreak havoc on the environment.

One of the main reason that causes women to have all of these health problems are the use of sanitary napkins (pads) and panty liners that contains the Dioxin (Toxin). From the beginning of her first period until around premenopausal stage, she would have used sanitary pads & tampons around 35 years of her life, if she has not met the unfortunate advent of the hysterectomy.

Generally, these industries (pad-making, diapers-making industry) are not governed or monitored (like food or electrical items). Before the pads & tampons are introduced to the market nowadays, twenty to thirty years ago, women used cloth made out of cotton and not recycled waste. However, the pads & tampons that women are using nowadays are made from recycled waste such as old newspapers and trash.

The recycled waste goes through a highly chemical bleaching process to make it white and soft. Also, chemicals produce highly toxic poison dioxin within the pads & tampons. International expert research on Cancer Research and the World Health Organization (WHO) states that the dioxin can cause cancer by attacking and weakening the immune system.

The commercial brands of sanitary products are not only bleached but contain traces of dioxin (organo-chlorine). Organo-Chlorine was used during the Vietnam War era to deforest trees in the villages and is still used as an industrial bleaching agent in the United States. The manufacturing of sanitary products maintains an overload of toxicity according to research.

Commercial sanitary napkins also contain other toxic chemicals that are made from recycled materials that require large amounts of chemicals such as bleaches, dioxins, deodorizers, and other toxins to process them. If cotton is used in the manufacturing process, the raw material could come from a GMO source of cotton. These toxins remain in the pads and are absorbed through the tissue membranes; an accumulation of these toxins can cause long term health problems.

Some pads also use an industrial adhesive that contains benzene (a known carcinogen), which may still be detected in your underwear even after several washes. The second possibility is the contamination of bacteria and molds. Pads may become pre-contaminated by their manufacturing process, and it is the fact that most pads are not completely sealed? By wearing them, you are creating a greater potential for infection.

CHEMICAL-FREE SANITARY NAPKINS IS A MUST
Though there have been many articles printed that articulates various cautions when using the commercial sanitary napkins. Women still have a limited alternative option to choose from in the mass retail market because merchants just don't receive the mass request for something natural and alternative, therefor women are compelled to buy the mainstream brands that are on the shelf.

Women can now seize the time for making a natural transition in personal care with a more organic and dioxin free sanitary napkin. There are several chemical-free brands of organic sanitary napkins like **Seventh Generation, Emerita, Organyc, Nature care.** Choosing an organic natural sanitary napkin has been shown to improve balance and reduce the risk of irritating symptoms such as inflammation, itching, and odor. Below is one the most revolutionary chemical-free napkins called Genial Day that also contains an "anion strip," which has been tested and proven to help create better balance during a women's menstrual cycle.

The primary advantages of a non-commercial sanitary napkin are that it is "free" of petrochemicals, dioxins, inorganic cotton, chlorine, and bleaches. Most commercial sanitary pads have a plastic base, which does not allow air to circulate, making the pad a breeding ground for bacteria. The commercial pads have radical chemical fibers on the surface, which usually nylon. Pads sold in the natural product industry have soft cotton layers minus the irritation and toxicity.

In 2009 a family-owned company from Lithuania launched a new type of sanitary napkin brand called **Genial Day**. The makers of this brand had a desire to produce a product that would improve the way a woman feels when on their cycle. This unique personal feminine product is made from non-irritating and organic cotton and also contains an anion that contains traces of a mineral called **Tourmaline**. The anion strip on the pad gives off negative ions and is proven to promote better PH balance, thus preventing irritation, inflammation, a build-up of bacteria, and exposure from wasting management materials and traces of dioxins.

The pads are air permeable; toxin-free and liners are also made from organic cotton. Women who have used this product line have experienced more comforts and balances. In 2016, **Genial Day** entered the American consumer market and was one of the few brands in the entire retail market that is dioxin, Petro chemical-free, organic, and even vegan certified. It is also the premier choice of most Europe and used by over one million women. The manufacturing partner of **Genial Day is backed by efficacy and certified with ISO 9001. ISO 14001, and GMP (Good Manufacturing Practice).**

According to 64 women who used the **Genial Day** sanitary pads, most said that they would continue using this brand instead of the standard commercial tampons and pads.

- **100% of the women noticed no irritation**
- **100% percent found it to be more economical**
- **100% reported that the pads were very comfortable**
- **Over 50% of the women noticed a changed in odor after the first month.**

Several brands are a better alternative than the non-organic sources of personal feminine care, so if Genial Day is not available in your area, at least find a natural product store or a store that stocks the alternative non-toxic organic sanitary napkins or tampon alternative.

Very Important Product Points to Remember when choosing a toxic-free sanitary napkin brand:
Chemical-free. No toxins, dioxins, or bleaches are used during their manufacturing process and contain only chemical-free cotton with plant derivatives.

Hypoallergenic: Provides Superior protection from bacteria, skin irritation, and odor.

Maximum Absorption. Genial Day pads have been proven to absorb five times more than any other organic pads on the market.

4.Safe for the environment. Genial Day is ECO Certified, unbleached, free of heavy metals, **BPA (Phthalate Free)**, and formaldehyde-free. Sanitary Napkins that contains Tourmaline Makes A Difference

Disclaimer: The research below that pertains to Tourmaline is for educational purposes only and not intended to treat or cure any diseases.
Tourmaline is a unique mineral combined with silver to reduce bad odor and the proliferation of irritating bacteria within the lining of the vagina. Tourmaline gives off negatives ion and is called the "**Air Vitamin.**"

Chemical Composition: Tourmaline is a complex silicate of boron and aluminum. Tourmaline crystals are hexagonal, prismatic crystals that commonly have a rounded triangular cross-section, striated lengthwise, also gives a radiant presence. Colors include blue, green, pink, red, yellow, brown, black, bi-colored, and tri-colored. Tourmaline may be found in Brazil, Russia, Burma, Afghanistan, Malagasy Republic, Maine, and California.

It is believed by many that the crystals are used to express purpose, guiding us into new dimensions of being. Although I believe that all crystals can help us in this way, I do have a special appreciation for members of the tourmaline family. The 1500 years ago, **Avicenna**, "**The Prince of Medicine of Persia**, used all form of crystals and metals as a tool for ridding some health conditions."

According to research, Tourmaline has been found to have powerful healing properties, linking spiritual energy with physical matter. It found that even a small dish of ground tourmaline can neutralize odor in your bathroom. (Caution: keep out of children and animal). Whether it is used in metaphysical works, or wearing it as jewelry, this gemstone is a unique and beneficial treasure for all who practice or are interested in the power of crystals.

WHY YOU REALLY NEED ORGANIC UNDERGARMENTS

Cotton is considered the world's '**dirtiest**' crop due to its heavy use of **insecticides**. If a consumer uses a non-organic source of cotton, they will also be adding additional toxicity to the body's system. This is one reason why organic cotton is better for clothing, especially concerning the use of tampons and sanitary napkins (pads) because it comes in direct contact with the most sensitive area of the body.

The commercial production of cotton contains heavy loads of hazardous insecticides, pesticides, and herbicides used in cotton farming. According to the **Organic Trade Association:** "Cotton covers 2.5% of the world's cultivated land yet uses 16% of the world's insecticides, more than any other single major crop. Aldicarb, parathion, and methamidophos, three of the most acutely hazardous insecticides to human health as determined by the World Health

Organization (WHO), ranks in the top ten most commonly used chemicals in cotton production.

Aldicarb, cotton second best-selling insecticide and most acutely poisonous to humans, can kill a man if one drop if absorbed through the skin, yet it is still used in 25 countries and the U.S., where 16 states have reported it in their "groundwater," not to mention, 91 percent of the cotton planted in the U.S. is genetically modified.

The 2002 introduction of the **Bt cotton**, which is genetically modified to produce a toxin from the bacteria Bacillus thuringiensis (Bt) that is deadly to the bollworm, was supposed to lead to a reduction in the use of insecticides on cotton crops for farmers in the developing world (where 99 percent of all cotton farmers reside.) Bt cotton requires more pesticide sprayings than indigenous cotton—MANY times more. Bt cotton has created new resistant to pests, and to control these, farmers must use 13 times more pesticides than they were using before its introduction. So, this promotes a higher risk to women who are exposed daily to GMO cotton material in addition to the chemically processed fabric.

The Indigenous people from every continent around the world did not endure these symptoms of ill health concerning chemical toxicity until the industrial revolution and after 1945. Thanks to the provocateurs of the chemical corporations, practically everything is saturated with chemicals in our walls, flooring, fabrics of our sheets, mattresses, and covers. This is why periodic detoxifying is necessary. If possible, replace your conventional bedding, sheets, and covers with untreated organic cotton replacements. These natural cotton fibers breathe better, and so do their workers.

The Simple Difference between Conventional and Organic

Conventional cotton is cultivated with pesticide chemicals/fertilizers in seeds: Anything (Genetically modified or conventional, etc.) during cultivation: usage of any pesticides, insecticides, or fertilizers – which are TOXIC (poisonous) in nature to human health.
Organic cotton from the organic cottonseed and the non-GMO process is allowed during cultivation. There is restricted use of chemical-based insecticides/pesticides/ fertilizers.

Organic cotton also requires 25% less water, which has less impact on the environment and maintains the fertility of soil production at a cost that is 13-20% lower than conventional cotton production, which could cut consumer cost. Naturally colored cotton comes from plant pigments, producing shades of color ranging from tan to green and brown. Consumers need natural and organic fibers because human skin is the largest organ in our body. It contributes to the metabolism and respiration of the body; It is also sensitive to heat and cold, humidity, and dryness. The choice of clothing has an essential influence on our wellbeing. Synthetic fibers, however, do not allow our skin the breathing freely, therefore, is not in vibrational harmony with our body. So '**organic**' is the better choice!

The following page illustrates the Genial Day line of organic sanitary napkins, cups which is completely organic alternative to the toxic person care that has been sold of the retail market. **Genial Day**

wants to also increase the demand in American for **organic cotton undergarments**. This would be a wise investment for the health-conscious women and her young daughters.

The use of inorganic cotton may compromise our histamine gene activity, thus leading to asthma, allergies, skin irritation, and the body's innate resistance to allergens. Because of the unpredictable adverse effects of commercial or GMO cotton with synthetic dyes and padding, women are better off by investing in chemical-free undergarments. Certified Organic cotton underwear does not contain GMO cotton, pesticides, chlorine, or toxic dyes, thus creating fewer allergy and respiratory problems. Non-GMO cotton also feels softer to the skin and has a pleasant smell. Naturally Colored Cotton is still relatively rare because it requires specialized harvest techniques, making it more expensive to harvest than white cotton.

Why Should There Be A Daily Need For Panty Liners

Most commercial underwear has cotton or rayon lining, but the material could be made from a harsh chemical source such as GMO cotton. Women who choose not to invest in organic underwear should undoubtedly consider a material that is free from chemicals-based material.

All-commercial non-organic underwear worn by both men and women is treated with chemicals and dyes, which can contribute to bacteria, inflammation, and yeast infection. For women, it is wise to use at least a natural panty liner, which can be found in a natural product store when wearing commercial underwear. What makes the **Genial**

Day's panty liners more unique is the anion strip, which inhibits irritation and maintains a better PH balance because of the negative ion activity within the anion strip.

The **Genial Day panty liners** are also manufactured from the same facility that produces the sanitary napkins. Though we suggest, women shop at the health food stores where they can have a higher chance of finding chemical-free and organic liners that are made from organic cotton, we have found that our customers are delighted with the feel of Genial Day sanitary liners and napkins. Their products are thoroughly tested and approved by **Oeko-Tex® 100 and are VEGAN certified.** The Bonus to this product is that it is not tested on animals and is Vegetarian Society approved.

Genial Day also manufactures an organic sanitary wipe so that women can avoid toxic chemicals found in commercialized hand sanitizers.

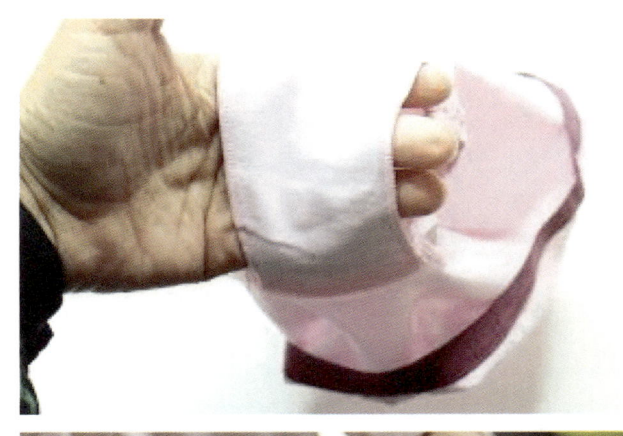
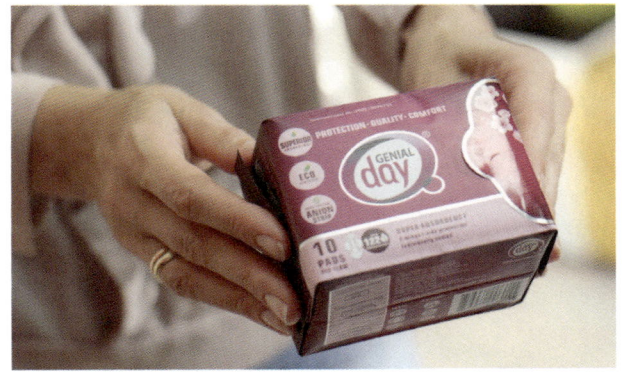

Symptom Checklist for WOMEN

Use each of the following checklists to determine signs & symptoms of hormone imbalance and help you choose the appropriate profile.

Category 1: Basic Hormone Imbalance
Mark which of the following factors/symptoms are present and/or persist over time.

___ Hot flashes	___ Mood swings (PMS)	___ Urinary incontinence	___ Night sweats
___ Heart palpitations	___ Cystic ovaries	___ Vaginal dryness	___ Acne
___ Heavy menses	___ Foggy thinking	___ Weight gain	___ Depressed mood
___ Fibrocystic breasts	___ Irritability	___ Increased body/facial hair	___ Headaches
___ Low libido/decreased sexual function	___ Uterine fibroids		___ Bone loss

Category 2: Adrenal Hormone Imbalance
Mark which of the following factors/symptoms are present and/or persist over time.

___ Aches and pains	___ Weight gain	___ Morning fatigue	___ Food cravings
___ Sleep disturbances	___ Depression	___ Anxiety	___ Susceptibility to infections
___ Chronic health problems	___ Evening fatigue	___ Allergies	___ Autoimmune diseases
___ Low blood sugar	___ History of steroid usage	___ Bone loss	___ Diabetes/prediabetes

Category 3: Thyroid Hormone Imbalance
Mark which of the following factors/symptoms are present and/or persist over time.

___ Aches and pains	___ Anxiety	___ Brittle nails	___ Depression
___ Dry skin	___ Cold hands and feet	___ Headaches	___ Infertility
___ Fatigue	___ Foggy thinking	___ Weight gain	___ Feeling cold all the time
___ Heart palpitations	___ Low libido	___ Inability to lose weight	___ Sleep disturbances
___ Constipation	___ Thinning hair	___ Menstrual irregularities	___ Elevated cholesterol

Category 4: Cardiometabolic Risk
Mark which of the following factors/symptoms are present and/or persist over time.

___ History of smoking	___ Weight gain	___ Heart disease or family history of heart disease
___ High blood sugar	___ Sugar cravings	___ Diabetes or family history of diabetes
___ High blood pressure	___ Fatigue	___ Waist size greater than 35 inches
	___ Low physical activity	___ Elevated triglycerides

If you checked symptoms in <u>all four categories</u>, the suggested test profiles are:
MINIMUM: Female Blood Profile II (Blood Spot)
PREFERRED: Comprehensive Female Profile I or II (Saliva/Blood Spot) and CardioMetabolic Profile (Blood Spot)

If you checked symptoms <u>ONLY in Category 1</u>, the suggested test profiles are:
MINIMUM: Female Blood Profile I (Blood Spot) or Female/Male Saliva Profile I (Saliva)
PREFERRED: Comprehensive Female Profile I or II (Saliva/Blood Spot)

If you checked symptoms <u>ONLY in Category 2</u>, the suggested test profiles are:
MINIMUM: Adrenal Stress Profile (Saliva)
PREFERRED: Comprehensive Female Profile I or II (Saliva/Blood Spot)

If you checked symptoms <u>ONLY in Category 3</u>, the suggested test profiles are:
MINIMUM: Essential Thyroid Profile (Blood Spot)
PREFERRED: Comprehensive Female Profile I or II (Saliva/Blood Spot); OR Comprehensive Elements Thyroid Profile (Blood Spot/Dried Urine) plus Female/Male Saliva Profile III (Saliva)

If you checked symptoms <u>ONLY in Category 4</u>, the suggested test profiles are:
MINIMUM: CardioMetabolic Profile (Blood Spot)
PREFERRED: CardioMetabolic Profile (Blood Spot) plus Female/Male Saliva Profile III (Saliva)

866.600.1636 | info@zrtlab.com | zrtlab.com

ZRT LABORATORY

CHAPTER 15
BIOIDENTICAL TESTING
HOW MAINTAIN HORMONE BALANCE

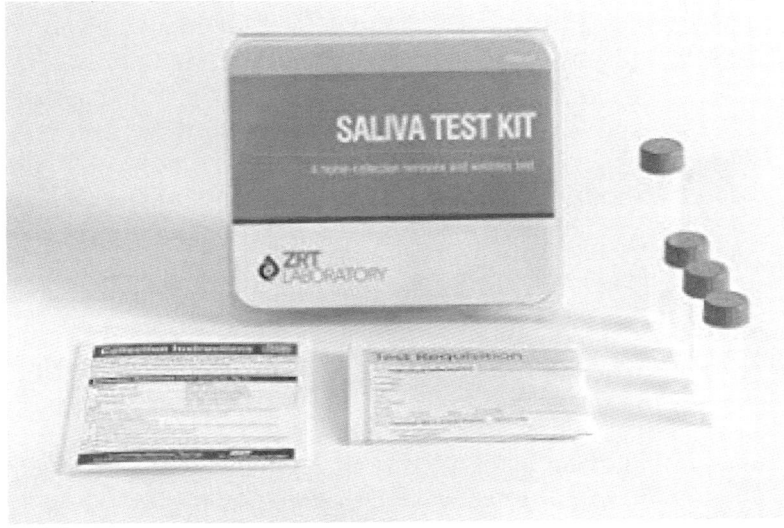

The Unpredictable Dangers of Hormone Imbalance

A media source, Birmingham News, reported in July 2002 that government scientists abruptly ended the nation's biggest study of a type of hormone replacement therapy. Why? They concluded that long-term use of estrogen and progestin hormone replacement therapy— commonly prescribed to menopausal women, significantly increase their risk of breast cancer, heart disease, and strokes! Remember, this stunning revelation came after more than 50 years of ERT prescriptions had been doled out to unsuspecting women! Although the Journal of the American Medical Association and other medical institutions admit that ERT grossly increases the risk of many types of cancers and heart attacks, leading gynecologists around the country are still prescribing synthetic estrogen. And many have said that they will continue to recommend ERT!

As stated in previous chapters, **estrogen dominance** is the cornerstone of the hormonal disparities that challenge women across America, which is why bio-identical testing is paramount.

We are all exposed to a "tidal wave" of industrial chemicals that mimic estrogens in such a broad spectrum that every woman, man, and child in the modern American society need some bio-identical hormone monitoring system. Estrogen is a beautiful hormonal which contributes many good physical attributes and should not be considered a villain in any case but should be better regulates through proper lifestyle and diet. However, xenoestrogens are the culprit through the various synthetics of the food, clothing, and body care industry.

By making bio-identical testing a part of one's lifestyle, along with conforming to a more organic vegetarian-based diet, would certainly allow the body to reach a healthy and healing platform. For those who still insist on consuming animal protein, please make a wise choice by selecting wild-caught salmon, ocean perch, cod, grass-fed, kosher, or Halal beef, lamb, or bison as forms of protein. While in this dietary and lifestyle transition, still consider bio-identical hormone testing. Below is a recap of the components of estrogen.

Estrone (E1) - This is found in both women and men (in small amounts). It is obtained from the adrenal gland and is also made, as well as stored in fatty (adipose) tissue.

Estradiol (E2) - The most active form of estrogen, the ovaries in women, and mainly produce it by the testes and adrenal glands in men.

Estriol (E3) - This is the dominant type of estrogen produced by women during pregnancy with large amounts produced in the placenta. The level of this hormone continues to rise until just before delivery.

Comprehensive baseline testing gives an in-depth scope of the hormone levels. This type of testing reveals the level of hormone production and identifies imbalances, and measures hormone ranges compared to healthy averages for specific age groups and gender.

Bio-identical test results, combined with the appropriate health assessment, can accurately help the health practitioner implement the appropriate changes for one's physical constitution.

Concerning Menopause in Women
When hormone levels begin dropping during menopause, a deficiency of one hormone can appear as a relative excess of another, resulting in symptoms of hormone imbalance. On the average, the start of menopause typically occurs around the age of 50, but it is not uncommon for women to experience symptoms as early as the mid to late '30s depending on the stress level, diet, lifestyle, amount of exercise, and even chemical exposure. Menopause can also be surgically induced through oophorectomy (removal of ovaries), radiation, and chemotherapy.

A woman's first symptoms may include:
• Anxiety • Changes to menstrual cycle length • Irregular cycle • Insomnia • Headaches • Mood swings Fatigue • Depression • Foggy Thinking • Weight gain • Night sweats •Decrease urinary flow

Testing and monitoring hormone levels enable women to work with their health care providers to find appropriate solutions that alleviate menopause symptoms and lead to hormonal wellness. A specialist or provider can provide a patient with saliva test kits to test hormone levels. Progesterone, pregnenolone, melatonin, estriol, T3, T4, DHEA, and testosterone can all deplete after menopause; therefore, all three primary estrogens and other hormones should be tested. Menopause is anything but a disease caused by low estrogen levels and cured by estradiol and estrone supplementation.

According to research, most women are tested for estradiol or estrone, and certainly not for **estriol, DHEA, testosterone, androstenedione, FSH, LH, prolactin, cortisol, progesterone, melatonin, pregnenolone**, thyroid hormones, or growth hormone. The many medical studies that have been done on women after menopause show that their levels of estrone and estradiol do fall somewhat, but just enough to prevent menstruation and fertilization.

After menopause, estrogen levels are intentionally high enough for all other necessary and needed bodily functions.

Nature understandably does not want women having children at this age. We can see the natural order stops childbearing at about age 40. Menopause is an essential and necessary part of the natural order of life. The postmenopausal levels of estrogens are sufficient for the normal functioning of the body, and it is unusual to find a deficiency of estradiol or estrone in Western women. It would do women immeasurable good by getting testing on levels of ALL their primary hormones and balancing them as much as possible. Fortunately, one can have an accurate bio-identical hormone test that is measured through saliva and blood, which is safe and non-invasive. Seek out a provider for **ZRT** near your area or call **1-888-453-5526, 314-600-1642**, or visit www.zrtlabs.com.

Symptoms of Estrogen Deficiency
Hot flashes • Night sweats • Sleep disturbances • Vaginal dryness/atrophy • Dry skin • Headache • Foggy thinking • Memory lapses • Heart palpitations • Yeast infections • Painful intercourse • Depression • Low libido • Bone loss

Symptoms of Estrogen In Excess
Water retention • Heavy, irregular menses • Breast swelling and tenderness • Fatigue • Craving for sweets • Weight gain • Fibrocystic breasts • Mood swings • Uterine fibroid • Low thyroid symptoms • Nervousness/anxiety/irritability • Progesterone Deficiency

Symptoms of Progesterone In Excess
Somnolence • gastrointestinal bloating • Mild depression • Breast swelling • Candida exacerbation • Exacerbates symptoms of estrogen deficiency

Symptoms of Testosterone Deficiency
Fatigue, prolonged • Mental fuzziness • Memory problems • Depression • Decreased libido   Blunted motivation • Muscle weakness • Diminished feeling of well-being • Heart palpitations • Thinning skin • Bone loss • Vaginal dryness • Incontinence • General aches/pains

Symptoms of Testosterone In Excess
Acne • Male-pattern hair growth • Deepening of voice • Clitoral enlargement• Irritability/moodiness • Insomnia • Loss of scalp hair

Symptoms of Low Cortisol
Fatigue • Allergies • Cravings for sweets • Irritability • Chemical sensitivities • Symptoms of hypothyroidism • Symptoms of low progesterone

Symptoms of High Cortisol
Same symptoms as low cortisol, including Bone loss • Anxiety • Sleep disturbances • Depression • Low libido • Hair loss • Anxiety• Elevated triglycerides

Low Thyroid Function
Fatigue (especially evening) • Low stamina • Cold extremities • Low body temperature low libido • Headaches • Dry skin • Intolerance to cold • General aches and pains • Weight gain • Depression • Anxiety • Scalp hair loss • Swollen, puffy eyes • Brittle nails

DAVID ZAVA, Ph.D., is a Biochemist, Research Scientist, and internationally known speaker on the subject of hormone imbalances, natural hormone replacement, saliva hormone testing, and breast cancer. After receiving his Ph.D. in Biochemistry from the University of Tennessee, Memphis, in 1974, he pursued his interests in cancer research. Working in the U.S. and Switzerland, he focused on hormonal control of breast cancer. Over the past 25 years, he has published extensively on basic and clinical research relating to the effects of estrogens (natural and plant estrogens and pollutant xenoestrogens) and progesterone on breast cancer.

Dr. Zava developed saliva testing as a simple non-invasive means to test hormones and as a means to evaluate hormonal risk factors for breast cancer. Because steroid hormones play such a vital role in the maintenance of health, knowledge of an imbalance in any one or more hormones can help to illuminate the cause of health problems and provide a basis for correcting the imbalance through diet, exercise, or hormone supplementation.

He is the Founder and Laboratory Director of ZRT Laboratory (CLIA certified) located in Beaverton, Oregon, using saliva for testing hormonal levels since 1998. His goal is to develop research projects with physicians and academic groups to understand the role of steroid hormones in health and disease, particularly breast cancer. ZRT Laboratory currently has several ongoing research projects.

Dr. Zava has co-authored 60 Scientific Publications and is a co-author with John Lee, M.D. of "**What Your Doctor May Not Tell You About Breast Cancer**": How Hormone Balance May Save Your Life that was published January 2002.

HORMONES AND WEIGHT MANAGEMENT

Most women are not aware that the prime source of weight management, weight loss, or even weight gain is directly associated with hormone balance. Our hormones influence the regulation of metabolism, glucose (blood sugar) insulin, weight, and where your body stores fat. The aging factor, choice of food we eat, level of stress that we endure, and the amount of exercise we get can create hormones in excess or deficiency, which is responsible for how well we maintain a good BMI Body Mass Index.

Bioidentical test results are supported by a holistic protocol that has the potential to promote better hormone balance. Overweight patients who experience hormones in excess or deficiencies can determine the reason their body cannot lose fat and weight. Here are several factors that have an impact on your once-perfect figure:

Belly fat around the waistline (some people refer to this as a tube around the waistline)

Increased appetite.
Thyroid metabolism
Vitamin D-3 Deficiency
Belly (Visceral) fat storage.
Hyperinsulinemia
Estrogen and Progesterone disharmony
Water retention and even edema
Low thyroid function
Weight gain at the hips and thighs (Some people refer this to Aging Thunder Thighs)
Fasting Insulin Elevated.

Insulin resistance and metabolic syndrome
TSH Elevated (Thyroid Stimulating Hormone)
Hypothyroidism (Sluggish Thyroid activity)
Testosterone and DHEA (Dehydroepiandrosterone, a natural youth steroid that our bodies produce)
HbA1c ranges are off

Women who are challenged with hormone imbalances find it difficult to lose weight as easily as they did in high school. But weight gain that is due to hormone imbalance can occur at any age. Younger premenopausal women between the ages of 20 and 30 tend to experience irregular cycles or lack of ovulation due to hormonal imbalance. As a result, women begin to retain more fluid and develop more sugar cravings.

If your cortisol levels are out of range, stress can be a contributing factor to a sluggish fat metabolism. Desperation causes some women to randomly invest in the latest weight-loss trend and experience disappointing results with only a minimum amount of weight loss the typical "yo-yo" diet. This disenchanting weight loss effort is more than due to hormonal imbalances and endocrine disruption from foods and consumer products that contains xenoestrogens, which takes the entire body out of balance. This is why bio-identical hormone testing in very important. Women between the 40 and 50 premenopausal aging range also experience the challenge of stubborn weight loss, increased belly fat, and unwanted sugar cravings.

Women who are beyond 50 years of age are also no exception to the rule of experiencing a roller-coaster of symptoms from because at this age her progesterone takes a dive, thus creating a surplus of estrogen – a state of estrogen dominance – that influences weight gain in thighs, hips and belly, and even an excess of water retention. Even when there is an imbalance of insulin and cortisol, thyroid metabolism also slows down and creates a condition known as "metabolic syndrome," indicating a diabetic condition.

The promotion of optimal health, prevention of diseases and illnesses, rehabilitation, and restoration of physical balance can not only be achieved through an organic diet and exercise but through the hormone balance. Bioidentical testing is the key to helping us all achieve and maintain hormonal, cardiometabolic, and neurotransmitter balance as we age.

Patients may contact all health concerns at 1-888-453-5526 or visit www.womanstreasure.com for additional information regarding ZRT's bio-identical hormone testing. **Dr. Botanica's All Health Concerns, LLC** is a provider for ZRT's bio-identical hormone testing. They also offer first-time discounts on testing and consultation. Visit **ZRT at www.zrtlab.com.**

Thyroid Function

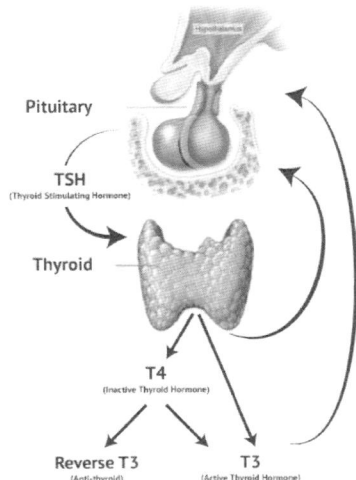

The thyroid is a small butterfly-shaped gland that sits behind and below Adam's apple. When it is working correctly, the body responds to it; however, a range of factors from hormone imbalances to mineral deficiencies and environmental pollutants can interfere with thyroid production, leading to health problems.

According to the research conducted by ZRT, Life Extension, other clinical studies, thyroid dysfunction is notoriously under-diagnosed. The American Thyroid Association estimates that as many as 60% of people with thyroid disease are not aware of it. Additionally, the landmark Colorado Thyroid Disease Prevalence Study found that almost 10% of subjects with abnormal thyroid test results were not being treated. Statistics show that women are seven times more likely than men to develop thyroid problems, facing as much as a one in five chance of developing a problem, particularly during the peri-menopause years when hormones start to fluctuate.

Thyroid hormones T3 and T4 are essential to total hormone balance. A patient can have levels tested by ZRT or Life Extension provider for certain test levels of free T3 and free T4 to see if the numbers are in mid-range, and just barely in range. After hysterectomy or menopause can determine bone health and be a key factor of joint inflammation.

Thyroid hormones act throughout the body, influencing metabolism, body temperature, and growth and development. Healthy thyroid function can be affected by interactions between thyroid hormones and other hormone systems. In particular, excess estrogens can effectively block the delivery of thyroid hormones to the cells that need them, as can imbalances of cortisol stress hormones. Thus, discovering how well our thyroid is working requires a big-picture assessment of all the hormone levels that matter and vital elements that, if too high or too low, can run interference on thyroid hormone production.

Our bodies produce several thyroid hormones, but two are essential: thyroxine or T4, the most abundant in the body, and triiodothyronine or T3, the most active of the two. The others are also important for optimal health. Thyroid health can also be undermined by nutritional deficiencies, particularly of iodine and selenium, or overexposure to bromine, arsenic, selenium, cadmium, and mercury. These elements are found all around us: in the food we eat, in the water we drink, in materials we touch, in the air, we breathe.

Dr. Botanica with Client who recovered from female complications following Bio identical and Holistic Testing.

The benefits of Bioidentical hormone testing are phenomenal. Dr. Botanica's client was suffering from hormonal complications and inflammation. After seeing two different OBGYN's, she decided to take the alternative path and was referred to All Health Concerns, LLC, owned by Dr. Botanica©. After the initial consultation, Dr. Botanica suggested that she have a bio-identical hormone test provided by ZRT labs to identify her hormone ranges, including estrogen, estradiol, estriol, progesterone, and cortisol. Because of the unique and accurate test results provided by ZRT, Dr. Botanica was able to implement a natural harmonious protocol that accelerated this patient's recovery, allowed her to go back to work in a much healthier state of mind, body, and confidence.

- **TSH** – Thyroid Stimulating Hormone Produced by the pituitary gland.

- **TSH** acts on the thyroid gland to stimulate the production of the thyroid hormones T4 and T3.

Free T4 - Thyroxine The predominant hormone produced by the thyroid gland

T4 is converted to its active form, T3, within cells.

Total T4 - Thyroxine Total T4 includes both free T4 and protein-bound T4 and is an indicator of the thyroid gland's ability to synthesize, process and release T4 into the bloodstream.

Free T3 - Triiodothyronine T3 is the active thyroid hormone that regulates the metabolic activity of cells.

TPO. - Thyroid Peroxidase An enzyme involved in thyroid hormone production.

The body produces antibodies, including **TPOab,** that attack the thyroid gland in autoimmune thyroiditis and Hashimoto's. Testing **TPOab** levels can diagnose these conditions.

Tgbn - Thyroglobulin A protein-rich in tyrosine, the residues of which when bound to iodine become the building blocks of T3 and T4. If iodine levels are low, thyroglobulin accumulates; thus, high levels indicate insufficient iodine for healthy thyroid function.

Symptoms of Thyroid Disorder

Weight gain or inability to lose weight despite exercise and diet • Feeling cold all the time (when others don't) • Low energy and • Memory lapses • Irregular bowel habits • Dry, thinning, itchy skin • Dry/brittle hair and nails • Menstrual irregularities • Water retention • Hair loss • Insomnia • Low libido • Infertility • Depression.

CHAPTER 16
WHY MEN NEED TO PLAY A ROLE IN WOMEN'S HEALTH CARE

Relationships are sometimes injured because of the unexpected crisis of female physical complications such as fibroids, endometriosis, cancer, and hormonal imbalances. Some men are familiar with the emotional connection to hormonal crisis; this can be crucial when women have to decide to have a hysterectomy or seek an alternative methodology.

Estrogen dominance is prevalent in both men and women because of the many estrogenic chemicals discussed in previous chapters. The majority of estrogen-mimicking chemicals are in everything from our foods to our care. So, men are just as much in estrogen danger as their women. This is all due to a lack of more education.

According to some studies, more males between the ages of eighteen and twenty-five with testosterone levels one would typically find in fifty- to sixty-year-olds. According to hormone test, it was discovered that the young men who were tested had high percentages of phthalates and low testosterone.

Because of the unfortunate advent of industrial chemicals, EMF, Electromagnetic Force from cell phones, computers, Microwave ovens, HD TV, I-Pads, watches, soy derivatives, glyphosate, and endocrine disruptor's mature men are rapidly losing testosterone as they age. The boys of today's society are producing less testosterone during their growth and development. This can also cause premature balding and low sperm count. This crisis is attacking every family member and has been for decades, since plastics, Triclosan (as reported in "Scientific American," Triclosan is now detectable in human breast milk, blood, and urine samples.) Environmental Health (EHP) FOUND THE CHEMICAL IN %75 OF URINE SAMPLES TESTED FOR A STUDY FOCUSED ON TRICLOSAN, Center for Disease Control (CDC) and prevention detected Triclosan in %58 of U.S. waterways. According to the FDA," Animal studies have shown that Triclosan alters hormone regulations.

Other studies in bacteria have raised the possibility that Triclosan contributes to making bacteria resistant to Antibiotics. Parabens, Glyphosates, and GMO soy oil were introducing into commerce. Another antibiotic under sever watch, with even harsher side effects on the human Immune and Hormonal system, is "Fluoroquinolone or Levaquin. People who have taken Levaquin, even after one day, said, "my body was never the same after taking Levaquin, Pain, Immune deficiency, Thyroid issues   Now practically everything that our families and we consume are creating a hormonal travesty unless your household is entirely organic. Unfortunately, the entire grocery and personal care market are saturated with chemicals the increased estrogen dominance in us all.

As stated in previous chapters, another issue with estrogen dominance and toxicity is the development of fibroids. Fibroids can become such an uncomfortable issue; intimacy can become painful because of the growing fibroids along with inflammatory pain from "blood stagnation" or "blood stasis." The combination of fibroids and hormonal mood swings can result in not only an intimate crisis but a social crisis as well.

Spermicidal contraception and Cervical Cancer risks were examined by studying 479 cases of histologically confirmed invasive cervical Cancer cases and 788 random digit-dialing controls. It is the same with fibrocystic breast diseases and PCOS (Polycystic Ovarian Syndrome), endometriosis is undoubtedly a particular case, due to the excessive bleeding complications that can go on for as long as three weeks of the month due to extreme endometrial inflammation and tissue shedding.

Synthetic estrogens are also attacking men and boys, so it is not an option to wait, but to act now! Invest in a robust estrogen-free lifestyle and organic diet, along with becoming an investigator as to what are the real contributing factors of prostate cancer, male breast development, breast cancer, the elevated increase of estrogen, and the extreme drop in testosterone and progesterone. This is why testosterone therapy is in top demand all over the country, because men are unknowingly increasing the intake of exogenous estrogens through commercial meats and dairy that contains RBGH, GMO's, hidden unfermented soy ingredients, corn oil, vegetable oil, fast foods, and synthetic vitamins, protein shakes that contain traces of unfermented soy and Whey and commercial male care products. Read more to know more so that boys can become better men in future generations to come.

The best action for the husband or significant other to take when this crisis begins to develop is to get involved. Men should give moral support, along with supporting her visits to the doctor's office. Men who have a mate should also listen to and observed all details shared between one's mate and her physician so that one can participate in an action plan, whether it is a change in diet, exercise, or seeking an alternative approach. Couples must such for every modality that can deliver positive results.

Investigate the possible underlying causes ranging from the type of personal and body care that she is using to the type of food that is consumed. Get more holistically involved and seek alternative options instead of just settling for a more invasive procedure; there may be holistic options as well. According some conventional doctors and many holistic professionals, 75% of hysterectomies are unnecessary because of many alternative modalities including dietary and personal body care modifications. So, it would be wise to so seek a third opinion if one desires to prevent the ultimate contingency, which is surgery and HRT replacement. This is where men can play a vital support role in helping his mate make the appropriate decision.

There are many couples in the world loving one another dearly, but the disparities of estrogen dominance can take a toll on the once cherished love affair between couples.

The State of Men's Health Is A Great Risk as Well

Though there is a natural decline of testosterone in the average man, which is a contributing factor to weight gain, loss of muscle tone, loss of muscle strength, depression, bone degeneration, and even the compromise of sexual vitality. This is what we call "**Andropause**" the male menopause. Even though **andropause** is a natural aging phenomenon, the symptoms are not as pronounced as women who are experiencing menopause, but men will notice other symptoms during the aging process(what is referred to as Midlife crises is andropause). If exercise and proper diet are not a significant part of the male's lifestyle, weight gain, low stamina, mental drive, and virility will be enviable.

Because we are all vulnerable to this practical estrogen bombarded society through estrogen-mimicking chemicals in food, body care, and household products, we must take extra measures to maintain or rebuild **testosterone and DHEA levels**. Therefore bio-identical hormone testing is not an option. Through hormone testing, men can diminish the effects of andropause and return to youthful vigor with their mate.

It is essential to support one's spouse, or mate is becoming more educated on hormonal balance. Because a neglected lifestyle and unconscious diet will eventually convert testosterone to estrogen in men as they age due to the aromatase (an adrenal enzyme that converts androstenedione and **estrone to estrogen**. Inhibiting its action is one approach to breast cancer prevention and treatment) reaction. Aromatase is found most prevalently in fat cells, so the more body fat a man has, especially in the midsection, the more aromatase and hence the more estrogen.

While women are suffering from estrogen dominance, men are showing depleted testosterone levels. In fact, at the 2007 Summit on Environmental Challenges to Reproductive Health, it was reported that there is a worldwide decline of testosterone of one percent every year over the past 40-50 years. Furthermore, it has been revealed that testicular cancer now affects approximately one percent of European males who also have a one in six chance of having their sperm counts low enough to be considered infertile. This phenomenon, without surprise, is significantly more prevalent in urban areas than in areas considered rural.

Prostate cancer rates have soared over the last 25 years. As women seek lasting beauty and career advancement through breast enhancements, fuller lips, bio-identical hormone replacement, cosmetic surgery, and Botox injections, men are also joined this venture by using Botox , fillers , breast, check thigh and calve implants, taking measure that will boost sports performance, sex appeal , improve virility or physical appearance.

The general paradigm in medicine is to treat symptoms, not the cause. Research conducted at Ghent University Hospital in Belgium and reported in a 2008 issue of Clinical Endocrinology & Metabolism, found that body fat percentage and circulating levels of testosterone are partly controlled by the same genes. The objective of the study was to determine the effect of declining testosterone levels on body composition. The findings were that low levels of testosterone could lead to significant reductions in the quality of life, as well as disharmony between marriage partners. It may lead to erectile dysfunction, low libido, fatigue, malaise, loss of muscle mass, a feeling of weakness, drop in HDL levels, increased LDL, increased body fat percentage, depression, and decline in libido and sexual performance.

So, What Could Be Underlying Cause de-masculinity in Men?

- Lack of exercise
- Poor diet
- Obesity
- Insulin resistance
- Environmental toxins (hormone disruption)
- Food sensitivities
- Exposure to synthetic hormones
- Alcohol consumption
- Recreational drug use and Tobacco
- Certain medications (statins, anti-fungal, steroids)
- Infectious disease
- Radiation exposure

- Chemotherapy
- Testicular trauma
- Systemic disease
- Heavy metal toxicity
- Genetic predisposition
- Organ failure or insufficiency (liver, kidney, thyroid, adrenal)
- Inability to cope with stress
- Gastrointestinal diseases • Blood sugar
- Circulatory or cardiac disease (hypertension, CHF)
- Pulmonary insufficiency (asthma, COPD)

Bio-Identical Hormone Test Are Necessary for both men and women

In Clinical Physiology of Testosterone, the testes, the dominant male reproductive organ, secrete several male hormones, which are collectively called androgens. This group includes testosterone, dihydrotestosterone, and androstenedione. Testes produce from 5mg and 7mg of testosterone daily. By far, testosterone is the most dominant male hormone, accounting for about 95% of a healthy adult male's production. The balance is produced from dehydroepiandrosterone (DHEA), a precursor of testosterone, in the zona reticularis of the adrenal cortex. The stimulus for this production originates in the hypothalamic-pituitary axis, where gonadotropin-releasing hormone (GnRH) from the hypothalamus stimulates the release of two hormones, luteinizing hormone (L.H.) and follicle-stimulating hormone (FSH), in the pituitary gland. L.H. drives the production of testosterone in the testes, while FSH affects spermatogenesis.

Testosterone is abundantly produced during puberty and is responsible for the profound benefits throughout the body, such as:
- Promotion of libido and aggressiveness
- Stimulation of the growth and repair of muscles
- Supports the function of the heart
- Supports and reinforces the immune system
- Assists in the building of muscle, skin, and bone
- Stimulation of the production of sperm
- Nourishes the male urinary and reproductive systems
- Regulation of the production of prostaglandin, which controls the growth of the prostate
- Protects against neurodegenerative diseases
- May mitigate depressive disorders

As with all sex hormones, testosterone is a derivative of cholesterol Pregnenolone, the so-called "master hormone" is the first metabolite produced directly from cholesterol. Pregnenolone is also the precursor of DHEA, the most abundant steroid hormone in the human bloodstream. While DHEA is only a mild androgen, it is the precursor for androstenedione and androstenediol, which are both precursors of testosterone (and its metabolites) as well as estrogen and estrone (and its metabolites). Deficits in either the supply of DHEA or the efficiency of the enzymatic conversion of DHEA to the sex hormones can have a deleterious effect on the production of these sex hormone-dependent systems.

Noxious Chemicals Are Compromising

The Natural and Divine State of Man and Woman is paramount to acknowledge that there are **MILLIONS of TONS of SYNTHETIC ESTROGEN PRODUCING CHEMICALS**, such as dichlorodiphenyltrichloroethane (DDT), organochlorines, polychlorinated biphenyls (PCBs) and their metabolites are very active estrogen mimics and are ubiquitous throughout the world. These chemicals are used as pesticides on farms throughout the world and contain potent androgen antagonists, thus interfering with male androgen balances.

The common pesticide vinclozolin, used on **COMMERICAL/CONVENTIONAL** cucumbers, grapes, lettuce, onions, bell peppers, raspberries, strawberries, and tomatoes. This is a potent "androgen antagonist." One of the metabolites of vinclozolin is 100 times more potent than vinclozolin and is now being investigated as a possible male contraceptive. Other fungicides are so potent that they can inhibit all hormone production, like Pyrimidine carbinol, a systemic fungicide, is "known to block the synthesis of sterols, including cholesterol, from which all steroid hormones are made."

What could be more benign than bottled water? Unfortunately, the masses of people are now assuming that bottled water is safer than facet water. However, the masses don't realize that most plastics are made from petroleum and that plastics contains many toxic chemicals, such as phthalates and bisphenol-A which is only one of many Petrochemicals constituents, that has been scientifically prove to not only build up xenoestrogens in our bodies, but contributing to a myriad of health problems including depleting testosterone, shrink testicles, causing erectile dysfunction and compromising the natural state of "Manhood and Womanhood."

The production of normal sperm has been declining dramatically in developed countries like America over the last half-century: sperm count dropped an average of 42% from 1940 to 1990 along with significant decreases in sperm motility and the number of morphologically normal sperm." Given that there has been a parallel rise in the incidence of other abnormalities of male reproductive health (such as testicular cancer, undescended testes, and hypospadias, (the abnormal location of the urethra on the penis), experts are postulating that fetal or childhood exposure to environmental estrogenic or anti-androgenic compounds (including phthalates and bisphenol-A) or other hormone disruptors produces a **"Testicular Dysfunction Syndrome"** that links all of these abnormalities. The rising cases of impotency and erectile dysfunction, low libido and fatigue is practically due to the over exposure to synthetic estrogens.

It is predicted by researchers and concerned scientist, that this chemical fiasco will greatly impact of current levels of environmental estrogens will be manifest in males born today and beyond if we don't stand for a change now and stop buying anything and consuming anything that is contained in plastic.

In 2013, scientists from Brigham and Woman's Hospital Published findings showing that BPA exposure can affect egg maturation in humans. A review of previous studies published in 2015 found evidence that BPA can interfere with endocrine function involving the hypothalamus and the pituitary glands. The researchers suggested that this type of action can affect puberty and ovulation and that it may lead to infertility.

The authors add: " The detrimental effects on reproduction may be life-long and Transgenerational." Male impotence may be affected, according to a study that looked at the effect of men's exposure to BPA at work. Findings indicated that high-level exposure might increase the risk of erectile dysfunction and problems with sexual desire and ejaculation.

What Are Some Solutions?

One can substantiate any hypothesis using the scientific method. With virtually any therapeutic approach, some studies will confirm or deny the existence of "proof" of efficacy or denial. According to Abraham Morgentaler, M.D., associate clinical professor at Harvard Medical School, "there is not a shred of evidence that supplements and natural therapies offer any help for men with low testosterone.

Men do not have to be an OBGYN or primary care physician to find a solution, utilize the high science, which is proper intuition and common sense. If it is not organic, it is not natural, whether it be food, household products, laundry detergent, soaps, cosmetics, or any other consumer good. Most of all, Exercise. Eat more cruciferous foods like broccoli, cauliflower, collards, spinach. **Take super supplements that support testosterone and masculinity; maca, ashwagandha, Korean ginseng, DHEA (no more than 50mgs daily), systemic enzymes, serrapeptase, nattokinase, L-Arginine**, and quality supplements that support vitality. Stay away from; soy products and plastics, hand sanitizers, conventional poultry, and the magnificent meals featuring some hidden soy derivative.

There are a list of companies that have committed to reformulate products containing the harsh chemicals found to contribute to this crisis and eliminate the use of carcinogens, mutagens and reproductive toxins as required by the E.U. directive Environmental Working Group: The "EWG" is a non-profit, non-partisan organization dedicated to using the power of information to protect human health and the environment. The EWG offers several databases that allow consumers to research personal care and cleaning products to make educated decisions about what is used on the body and in the home.

As teenagers, men have high levels of testosterone and low levels of estrogen. As they age, testosterone levels in men decrease while their estrogen levels increase. Not surprisingly, high levels of estrogen in men usually correspond to low levels of testosterone. High estrogen levels in men contribute to prostate cancer and heart disease, as well as gynecomastia (enlarged breasts). As the testosterone is transformed into estrogen, the low levels of testosterone can cause many unpleasant symptoms, including loss of muscle mass, fatigue, low libido, erectile dysfunction. Furthermore, excessive estrogen in men raises body fat and can contribute to diabetes and high lipids.

Estrogen Mimicking Chemicals Is Feminizing Male Fish, Is Man Next? A Story by Stephanie Hemphill, September 14, 2009

The Mississippi River in Minnesota has the highest rate of feminized fish found in a study conducted by the U.S. Geological Survey.

Scientists are concerned when they find male fish with female sex organs. In the Mississippi River, near Lake City Minnesota, 73 percent of the smallmouth bass had characteristics of both sexes.

The feminization is thought to be caused by hormone-disrupting chemicals in the environment. They can include pesticides, PCBs, heavy metals, household compounds such as laundry detergent and shampoo, and many pharmaceuticals. Large and smallmouth bass seem to be particularly vulnerable to the chemicals.

The USGS study sampled fish in nine rivers around the country. The Yukon River basin in Alaska was the only one where researchers did not find at least one intersex fish.

Since the Industrial Revolution, humankind has practically ruined every natural state of nature. Within the last 150 years, he and his anti-life processes have created and released over **80,000 synthetic**, persistent chemicals into the environment, many of which model the hormone nature of estrogen inside the human body!

These chemicals are sprayed onto our crops, mixed in our foods, put into out body care, released in the air, and dumped into the rivers, lakes, streams, and aquifers all over our country. Keep in mind that these chemicals do not just disappear into thin air or some degrade. These estrogen-mimicking toxins will remain in the environment beyond our lifetime, for hundreds and even thousands of years.

Believe it or not, ladies and gentlemen, these chemicals are everywhere — found in **the new carpet, the new car, plastic containers, new makeup**, etc. — have estrogen-like activity in the human body. When men are exposed to **synthetic, toxic, poisonous estrogen daily**, get into their body; not only will they experience lower testosterone production, buy a compromised male offspring, along with a myriad of **health problems!**

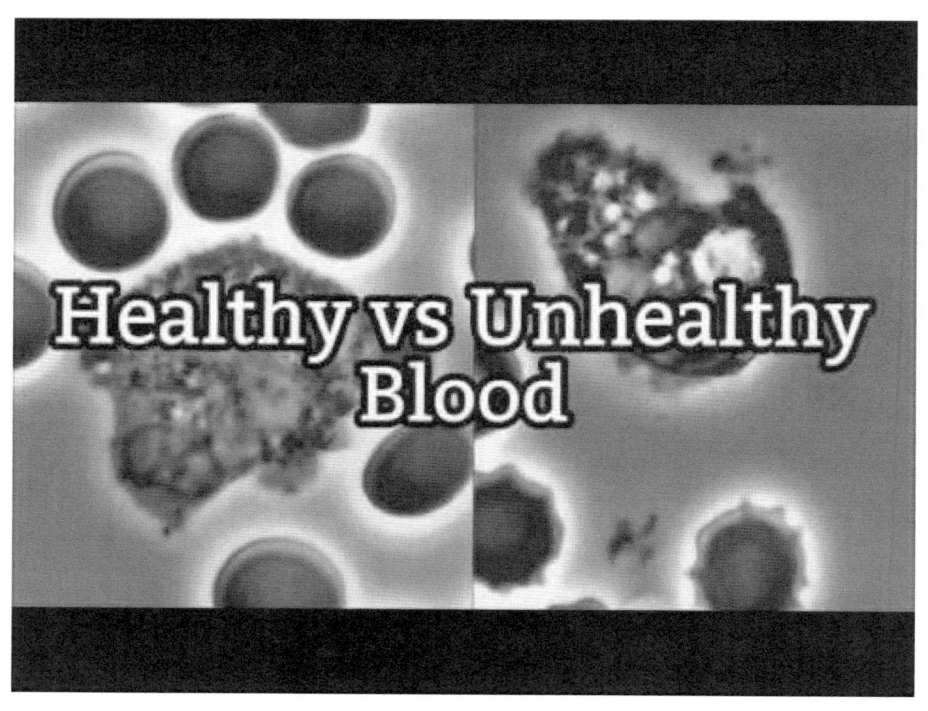

CHAPTER 17
DETOXIFY BEFORE YOU PURIFY

Everything we put onto our skin is absorbed into the bloodstream, passing through all our organ systems, thereby affecting the immune system. The average woman puts 515 synthetic chemicals on her skin every day.

There are many adverse effects of consuming the Standard American Diet (SAD) because of the thousands of chemicals that are used in the growth process, manufacturing process, and the preservation of the finished product. Practically all-commercial items that we consume put us in harm's way to some degree. The average woman absorbs 4lb/6oz. of chemicals from toiletries and make-up every year, according to research collected by In-Cosmetics, compiled just two years after the report from Bionsen. This natural deodorant company found that the average woman's daily grooming routine exposes her to a staggering 515 different synthetic chemicals each day.

WHICH DETOX PROGRAM IS RIGHT FOR YOU?

There are many detoxification programs. **Dr Anahitta Jafari's** is a "Kitchen Physician" and detox specialist that addresses many different conditions regarding chemical toxicity. Her clinic provides many modalities that can purify and nurture the human body. Food therapy is the absolute platform that the body needs to begin ridding itself of impurities that have been accumulating over the years. Dr. Jafari has a wide number of detox and rejuvenation protocols, derive, from spices, herbs, roots, soups, depending on your individual needs and conditions.

To thoroughly clean the body and household slate, we suggest the following types of detoxification:

Kitchen Detoxification

Start cleaning all your cabinets with organic cleaning material, marginally eliminate all of your toxic canned foods such as beanie BPA lined and aluminum canned vegetables, fruit cups in plastics, dehydrated packaged foods in plastics, bleached instant noodles, instant rice, beef jerky, pork rinds, potato chips cooked in vegetable oils, sodas, flavored instant oats, GMO popcorn, candy bars, and sugar-coated, artificially colored and flavored cereals.

Refrigerated Grocery

Due to the adulterated and commercial process of meat products, long term refrigeration or evening freezing can be a health risk. Do away with frozen commercial meats and pork products. Pasteurized beverages, artificially preserved fruit juices, and flavored waters has no nutritional value. Non-organic frozen fruits; all pastries, pies, pre-packaged cookie/pastry doughs made with white flour and sugar and chemicals, and fruit juices with high fructose corn syrup will certainly interfere with any detoxification program.

Bedroom

Eliminate artificial fragrances; they are full of chemicals; genetically modified synthetic oils permeate the air we breathe. Minimize the use of electronics as much as possible, because the electromagnetic frequencies they give off are not compatible with the natural electromagnetic current of either humans or other animals.

Wash the sheets or bedspread with organic, environmentally safe detergents to avoid headaches, insomnia, and skin irritation. Buy chemical-free soaps and cleaning products. If one likes adding a scent to laundry detergents or floor cleaner, try adding Organic Aromatherapy oils (not synthetic fragrance oils), such as Lavender, Lemon, or Orange!

Bathroom Detoxification

Bathrooms are usually where most people store all their toxic cleaners to clean toilet bowls, sinks, and showers. Synthetic chemicals, air fresheners, insect repellents, and otherwise could cause severe damages to our airway passages, and possibly cause asthma or other respiratory conditions.

Dry Skin Brushing

Dry brushing is an effective physical exfoliator. "Gently brushing the skin is a form of physical exfoliation, meaning it can slough away dead skin, leaving it smoother," **Melissa Kanchanapoomi Levin, M.D.**, NYC dermatologist and founder of Entière Dermatology, tells SELF. "When you exfoliate on dry skin, the friction is increased as opposed to when the skin is wet. When the friction is increased, exfoliation is more effective."

Organic Detoxification

When able, buy only Certified Organic fresh produce; replace sugary and salty snacks candy bars with fresh organic fruits, vegetables, and raw nuts. Most alternative products can be obtained at a natural product or a high-quality grocery store. Natural living and freedom are our birthright. The value of the health and happiness of the body and soul has no price tag, though unfortunately the powers that be have tried to assign it one.

Produce Patrol

Here is a List Produce That Contains A High Content of Pesticides and Sulfur Dioxide: Apples, Peaches, Bell Peppers, Celery, Potato, Cherries, Red Raspberries, Grapes (imported), Spinach, Nectarines, Strawberries, and Blueberries.

Lowest in Pesticides

Asparagus, Avocados, Bananas, Broccoli, Cauliflower, White Corn, Kiwi, Onions, Mangoes, Papaya, Pineapples, Peas.
If one can't get fresh organic produce, go to the closest farmer's market, and seek out locally grown produce. While canned foods are

unavoidable for many, those who can, should. The cans are lined with Bisphenol-A and other forms of plastics have been linked to reducing acetylcholine in the brain, leading to Alzheimer's disease, among many other conditions. It is also wise to avoid artificial sweeteners and chemical flavorings when possible, as those are also damaging to the body. Going further, as a rule, never microwave food in plastic containers. The rapid heating drastically increases the number of chemicals that leach out from the plastic into the food.

Storing water in a glass pitcher or bottle will prevent the leaching of xenoestrogen chemicals out of the plastic, however before storing it, be assured that it is free of impurities. Avoid buying plastic bottled water when able and purchase a countertop or faucet-mounted water purifier certified to remove pesticides, and other contaminants if possible.

If one cannot comprehend what is on the label or find out by using Google, also avoid all that contains parabens, phthalates, BPA, artificial colors, and synthetic fragrances. For those who use sunscreen, look for a sunscreen that relies on zinc oxide or titanium dioxide to block UVUV rays instead of xenoestrogens. Use only natural cleaning products in the home, and switch to unbleached paper goods if possible, due to bleached paper containing dioxin.

Toxic Overload

Did you know that 7 out of 10 deaths are due to chronic illness, often due to lifestyle circumstances, and many cases are due to over-exposure to environmental toxins? Consumer education is not an option due to the many toxic and adverse effects that are discovered months sometimes years after the product has saturated the market such as Glyphosate or Triclosan.

The body has three main excretion avenues to rid itself of burden and is as follows: Skin, Feces, and Urine. Urinalysis or urine metabolite testing generally provides the most favorable results, although, in the case of screening for heavy metals, fecal testing is also beneficial. Urine testing can be beneficial in determining the level of exposure to petrochemicals and their by-products, and in many cases, the source. Two commercial laboratories in the U.S. that has excellent testing protocols for toxins: **ZRT laboratory, Life Extension, and Genova Diagnostics.**

Juicing Is One of the Most Effective Detox Programs

This method has become one of the most popular ways to begin cleansing, detoxifying, and rejuvenating the body. An essential juicing combination for detoxification may consist of organic carrots, celery, beets, apples, or organic leafy greens juice. Always consume juice slowly to prevent any form of metabolic shock; most people consume between 6-12 ounces at a time. If one wants to enhance the nutritional benefit when juicing, one may consider adding an organic superfoods complex powder, which is GMF (Good Manufacturer Practicing, Non-GMO certified).

Though juices are sold in health food or grocery stores, it is much better to juice at home, because one can personally control the quality, and most are pasteurized. By pasteurizing fruit and vegetable juices, people miss out on the life-giving properties of live bioavailable nutrients and enzymes. These enzymes are crucial to the body and are readily available through fresh organic juices. As a rule, when juicing, slowing sip the juice right after making, as not to shock the body. It is best to consume fresh organic on an empty stomach (2 hours before or after eating)

People with ulcers should first consult a reputable holistic health practitioner who is familiar with juice feasting, or detoxifying. If one is diabetic, be mindful of fruits that have a high glycemic index. Be very cautious when juicing, especially if it is the first-time detoxing.

Diatomaceous Earth and Detoxification

The new supplement like source that is getting national notoriety is called Diatomaceous Earth. Though somewhat controversial, this powder is derived from fossilized seaweed deep within the ocean floor and is highly effective for many conditions. Diatomaceous Earth (DEDE) is an all-natural product that has a base ingredient of food-grade freshwater amorphous diatomaceous Earth. Diatomaceous Earth (DEDE) is not on Earth. It is the fossilized remains of microscopic shells created by one celled plants called Diatoms. Diatoms are one of the most abundant types of phytoplankton, occurring mainly in freshwater and marine habitats.

Diatoms absorb the minerals from the water and build a protective shell. As they die, the shells sift to the bottom of the water and form layers, sometimes hundreds of feet thick, called Diatomaceous Earth. Most deposits are so contaminated with foreign material as to be useless or even dangerous. Our DE is so pure; even as it comes from the ground, it meets FDA requirements to be called "food grade." This food-grade, non-crystalline diatomaceous Earth has been given a GRAS (Generally Regarded as Safe) rating by the FDA and has been approved by the FDA as a food additive.

Please make sure the DEDE is absolutely a food-grade quality. The two brands that are most popular Heritage or Luma Diatomaceous brand because they are an honest source of pure food grade D.ED.E. These brands can be purchased through All Health Concerns, LLC. Visit their website at www.allhealthconcerns.com or by calling 1.888.453.5526. Many people have testified that they have to experience anti-inflammatory results and even better weight management in addition to detoxification.

Health Benefits of Lemon and Lime Water

This is a very economical method of cleansing the blood, colon, and rest of the body. To avoid insecticides and pesticides, use only organic lemons or limes.
Squeeze at least a ½ lemon or lime in 6 ounces of room temp high-quality water from a container that is free from a Bisphenol-A plastic, consume 2-3 times daily on an empty stomach.

The value of eating lemons is reported by Jethro Kloss in his famous book Back to Eden: "The medicinal value of the lemon is as follows: It is antiseptic or is an agent that prevents sepsis [the presence of pathogenic bacteria] or putrefaction [decomposition of tissue]. It is also antiscorbutic, a term meaning a remedy which will prevent disease and assist in cleansing the system of impurities." For thousands of years and even today in the Persian culture, plates of lemons and limes are served at every meal. It was a part of the traditional cuisine of Persian to squeeze fresh lemons of rice, meat, fish, and stews. Dried lemon or lime is used for various dishes in Persian Cuisine.

High Mineral Salt Baths
These are simple and comfortable. HMSB Baths can help relax tired or tense muscles and release some poisons as well. Once or twice a week is a max when they are needed for tension.

Procedure: As you fill a bathtub, add around 2 cups of unbleached, non-iodized, high mineral salt to the bathwater, there are some very good chemical-free brands in the natural product stores. Water temperature should be hot, but not scalding for the most relaxing and effective treatment. Slowly submerge the body above the shoulders, in the bath. Remain in the water for between 20-30 minutes. Please make an attempt at this procedure if you are under any medication, intoxicated from alcohol or recreational drugs.

SAUNA THERAPY

Sauna therapy is one of the finest ways to remove toxic metals, chemicals, chronic pain, and other blockages in the body. Infrared sauna therapy, in particular, is highly effective for detoxification. There are three common types of saunas, Dry Sauna, Steam Sauna, and Infrared. To get more detail as to which would be most appropriate for you, you may Google or YouTube for more details or speak with a specialist or a physician before using. Before getting into the sauna, remove metals, jewelry for your body, and avoid heavy meals two hours before a sauna session. Also, avoid alcohol or other intoxicating substances.

Colonic Irrigation

According to research, it is safe and very comfortable for most people, even older people and people who are recovering from an illness. In traditional Persian medicine and other Eastern medicines, Herbal enemas are commonly used for children and adults, for constipation, high fever, and infection.

The Power of Castor Oil Packs

According to famous healer Edgar Cayce, this proven procedure can assist in lymphatic cleansing and circulation. Castor oil is rich in ricinoleic acid, accelerates rapid lymphatic drainage, has an immune-boosting fatty acid, and helps to reduce kidney stress. The finest castor oil in the world from Kerala, India (therapeutic quality) it is an ancient remedy often called the "Hand of Christ or the Palma Christi" and has been used for thousands of years by many cultures going back to ancient civilizations of India, China, Persia, Egypt, Africa, Greece, Rome, the Americas and in 17th Century Europe.

Castor oil must be "cold-pressed," certified organic, not solvent-extracted, or deodorized. It has known to be effective for many diverse types of pain, liver and gallbladder stimulation and cleansing/detox, digestive problems, lacerations, skin disorders such as eczema or psoriasis, menopause symptoms, to boost the immune system, as an emollient and skin softener and even if you are using the unique oil, make sure that it is certified organic and Hexane-Free. Some brands contain hexane, which causes more damage to the body, therefore purchase from the natural products store.

Ginger/soda bath:

1/3 cups each of dried ginger & baking soda for each bath tubful of tolerable, hot water (avoid excessive heat). Total amounts needed: dried ginger 1/3 cup baking soda 1/3 cup

Be sure the bathroom is warm—avoid getting chilled at any time. Have extra "oil" towels available.

Organic Body and Hair Care

Home Hair Therapy Recipes

1. Raw Organic Honey, Organic Goat Yogurt and Lemon Hair Mask: The basic of all hair masks. Fresh juice from an organic lemon and organic goat yogurt has been shown to eliminate dandruff. Add raw organic honey to this mask, because lemon juice tends to dry the hair because of its acidic nature. If you have very dry hair, add a few drops of organic sesame, almond oil to the hair mask so that it also nourishes your hair.

2. Aloe Hair Pack: Take the whole leaf of fresh Aloe Vera leaf. Cut it up in small pieces, place in the blender and pour a cup of high quality or clean filtered water, (do not use tap water). Blend several times until you get a milky texture. Then pour into a large glass jar, keep refrigerated, use each time after you wash your hair, towel dry and pour a half cup of the mixture on your hair, then massage into your scalp and hair, put a shower cap on and leave in between 6 and 8 hours. Rinse the following morning, (do not shampoo). It would be wise to invest in a quality shower/water filter. This is also very good for men who are going bald.

This is a nourishing hair pack filled with the goodness of nutrients to stimulate circulation, deep condition, restore strength and elasticity from root to tips for healthier, softer and lustrous hair. This special hair pack clears dandruff, detoxifies the scalp, prevents hair-fall, and adds life to dull and lifeless hair.

3. **Peppermint EO and Organic Green Tea Rinse**: Make a clarifying rinse by mixing a cup of certified organic green tea with a few drops of organic peppermint oil and a teaspoon of organic unfiltered apple cider vinegar. Dampen your hair and pour this rinse over it and leave on for five minutes. Follow it up with a mild shampoo and conditioner. The organic peppermint oil and green tea are excellent conditioners to control and keep dandruff at bay.

4. **Hibiscus Leaves and Flowers**: Hibiscus, especially the red hibiscus flowers and its leaves are very good for the hair because it is abundant in vitamin C. It doubles as an anti-dandruff hair mask or as a mask for voluminous hair. Soak the hibiscus flowers or/and leaves overnight, when ready to preparer slowly bring to a boil, turn off immediately, cover and let sit for an hour. After it cools down, place in the entire contents into the blend until it purees. Add warm extra-virgin cold press coconut oil to this paste and massage on the scalp. You don't need coconut oil on the stove to warm. Message vigorously into the scalp and leave it on hair for at least 45 minutes before you rinse your hair.

5. **Organic Banana, Raw Organic Honey, Organic Lemon Juice and Organic Sesame Oil Pack**: Blend two bananas with two teaspoons each of Organic sesame oil, raw organic honey and the organic juice of one lemon to create a paste, it should be a creamy paste. Apply this on your hair and scalp and let it stay for at least 30 minutes. Wash your hair with lukewarm water and follow up with a mild

shampoo and conditioner. This mask works best for people who have a combination of frizzy hair and dandruff.

6. **Apple Cider Vinegar** is very effective in getting rid of dandruff and psoriasis of the scalp. It is best to use ACV with the mother. It restores the pH balance of the scalp, thereby inhibiting the growth of yeast. It also helps work a natural clarifier and helps clean clogged pores and hair follicles. Take two tablespoons of apple cider vinegar. Add an equal amount of water and 15-20 drops of tea tree oil in it. Apply it onto your scalp and massage. Rinse your hair after a few minutes. Follow this natural treatment twice or three times a week.

7. **(Aluminum-Free) Baking Soda** can help reduce the overactive fungi that cause dandruff. With repeated use, it also helps restore the production of natural oils that keep your scalp from becoming dry and flaky. Wet your hair and rub some baking soda onto your scalp. Wait a few minutes and rinse your hair well with water. Do not shampoo your hair for a while after this treatment. Alternatively, you can add some baking soda to your shampoo when you wash your hair.

8. **Organic Cold Pressed Sesame Oil.** Scalp dryness can be cured with regular use of organic cold-pressed sesame oil, an effective natural moisturizer. Slightly heat about two tablespoons of organic cold press sesame oil until it is slightly warm. Massage it onto your scalp and then wrap your hair in a towel for half an hour. Brush your hair thoroughly to remove the dry flakes and then wash your hair.

Your FACE and BODY

Use only what you can consume by mouth. If it is not eatable don't use it on your face. Clean your body by taking a bath or shower in filtered water. Chlorine, Triclosan, and other toxins are bad for the skin; therefore, invest an advance shower filter. Scrub your body with a natural loofa sponge along with periodic dry skin brushing. Use only bar and shower soap made from organic material from brands found in the natural product stores. Safe sunlight exposure and eat fresh, organic dark green, leafy vegetables and fresh organic carrots. Use chemical-free, Organic shampoos, and conditioners. See the hair and scalp recipes above for hair maintenance.

Your MOUTH

Brush and floss your teeth after meals and snacks. Brush your teeth with a non-fluoridate toothpaste, and BPA-free toothbrush. If you take good care of your teeth, they can last your whole life. Healthy teeth have fewer cavities and less plaque build-up. Oil pulling is a very effective way to remove plaque from the teeth and clean the gums. In fact, using sesame and coconut oil, even in combination can certainly save your teeth and reduce expensive dental cost. We have found that **Bamboo salt** has phenomenal detoxifying properties.

Non-Toxic Brands Can Be Found in Health Food Stores

Albert's Organics, Aroma Naturals, Avalon Natural Products, Bath Petals, Canary Cosmetics, Carrot Tree Soaps and Essentials, Clearly Natural, LLC, Dead Sea Warehouse, Dr. Bronner's Magic Soaps, Dr. Huaska Essentials, Eco-Beauty Organics, Ecco Bella Botanicals, Eufora International, Exuberance, Farm aesthetics, Garden of Eve, Giovanni Hedgerow Herbals, Herbaria, Highland Heart Ltd., Holistic Skincare and Spa Therapy Co., Honeybee Gardens, Inc., Inky Girl Beauty, Kirk's Castille, Max Green Alchemy Ltd., Monave Mineral Cosmetics, Organic Truth: Mi Essence, Nubian Heritage, Osea Skin Care, Our of Africa, Out of Eden, Paul Penders Company, Shea Moister, Sunflower Essentials Bath & Body Care, Terra Essentials, Valhalla Essences, Wild Thyme Botanicals, and more.

Products and Cleaning Transitions

There are many non-toxic cleaning supplies, many of which are multi-purpose and can be easily made from basic ingredients. Natural cleaning products can be found in natural product stores. You may utilize The Environmental Working Group's database to research your preferred products.

Laundry Alternatives

• Add ½ cup organic vinegar to rinse as a fabric softener, soak white clothes for 30 minutes in 3% hydrogen peroxide, rather than using bleach. Surface cleaner: Mix 1-part apple cider vinegar with 1-part water. **Creamy soft scrub**: Mix 2 cups of baking soda with ½ - 2/3 cup of liquid castile soap and vegetable glycerin. (CANNOT contain sodium lauryl/Laureth-sulfate or SLS) In a sealed jar, this can last up to 2 years.

Bleach Alternatives Food Grade Hydrogen peroxide
(Please review instructions very carefully; it is a very powerful irritant). **Keep away from children and pets!**

Air Freshener
- Fresh flowers and Aluminum-Free Baking Soda or essential oils can be placed on untreated wood, place in the bathroom.

Glass/Surface
- Mix 1-part apple cider vinegar with 1-part water. Add 10-15drops of essential oil.

Ceramic Tile
- Mix ¼ cup vinegar in 1 gallon of warm water; generously apply a solution to tile with a sponge.

Floor
- Mix 1 cup of organic raw unfiltered vinegar with 2 gallons of hot water.

Kitchen Drain
- Pour ¼ cup baking soda followed by ½ cup organic vinegar, close the drain until it stops fizzing and flush with boiling water.

Garbage Disposal
- Grind lemon, orange peel and ice in the disposal.

Oven
- Make a paste using baking soda and water. Sponge onto stains and wipe clean.

Mildew
Make a paste using baking soda and water. Sponge onto stains and wipe clean (ideal for removing mildew stains). Apply full-strength hydrogen peroxide for at least 10 min., then wipe away.

Toilet
- Sprinkle baking soda into the bowl, drizzle with vinegar, scour with a toilet brush and rinse.

Insect Repellent
Ants: Spray pure lemon juice, lavender, or citronella with water, at entry points. Mosquitos: Fill spray bottle ½ full of distilled water. Add natural witch hazel to fill almost full. Add ½ teaspoon of vegetable glycerin. Add 30-50 drops of essential oils (choose from citronella, lemongrass, rosemary, tea tree, eucalyptus, lavender or mint).

CHAPTER 18
SUPER FOODS AND SUPPLEMENTS
FOR A BRAND-NEW WOMAN

Everyone should be shopping for organic produce and chemical-free grocery. One's produce selection should resemble a rainbow of colorful, healthy greens, peppers, stalks, carrots, potatoes, and cruciferous vegetables. One should also add essential nuts like walnuts, pumpkin seeds, raw almonds, and Brazil nuts. Then add superfoods like sprouts, buckwheat, wheat germ, rice such as (Gen Ji mai rice, black forbidden rice, red Bhutanese rice), kidney beans, black bean, lentils, and peas.

Note: Always take special precautions if a woman is pregnant or have a suspicion of being pregnant, seek the advice of a physician or holistic health practitioner before consuming a supplement or herbal formula outside of one's suggested food intake.

There is a philosophy, "Do not knock it until you try it." Everyone should experience the vegetarian, vegan diet at some point in their life. This lifestyle would not only ease the tension on the environment but help one's body purge more toxins and produce a cleaner state of health. Factory farming, the improper treatment of farm animals, antibiotic use, and the process of meats will wreak havoc on the human body, especially if the meat is not certified organic and grass-fed.

After years of consuming a combination of animal protein, white flour products, and adulterated foods, rest assured that there is an accumulation of accumulated amyloid plague in the colon wall, plaque in the arteries, the kidneys, and heart and liver is also taxed. Also, there is a percentage of undigested meat from years of daily meat consumption, depending on one's elimination function. There are different patterns of the vegetarian lifestyle, all of which produce some health benefits. FYI, before the Second World War that people limited themselves to about 4oz. of meat during a meal?

Types of Vegetarian Diets

There are several variations and definitions to distinguish between when talking about vegetarianism. Here are the most common types of vegetarian diets:

Vegetarian vs. Ovo-Lacto Vegetarian:
A "strictly" vegetarian diet consists of plant-based foods but may also include eggs and dairy. Typically, fish or meat of any kind is absent from the diet. The Ovo-Lacto diet includes eggs and dairy, and it is called an Ovo-Lacto vegetarian diet (hence the name Ovo, as in "ovum," and Lacto, as in "lactation").

Vegetarian vs. Pescatarian Diet

Pescatarian diets include fish and seafood, along with a variety of plant foods (vegetables, fruits, nuts, grains, beans). This dietary lifestyle includes eggs and dairy minus poultry, beef, or red meat. This dietary pattern will depend on the individual.

Vegetarian Diet vs. Vegan Diet:

Those following a vegan diet abstain from meat, fish, eggs, or dairy and consume only plant-based foods. Some vegans indulge in a completely "raw food diet." The raw diet may appear to be extreme, therefore quite beneficial, especially if one is in detox mode. People who live in colder climates such as Alaska may want to reconsider consuming just enough animal protein to survive the climate in the cold regions of the world. Very important note: For people who are challenged with digestive issues, such as Crohn's diseases, leaky gut syndrome, or acid reflux need to minimize their intake of raw. So which type of vegetarian or plant-based diet is healthiest?

As a vegetarian or pescatarian, one is still able to get plenty of amino acids and vitamin B12 without supplementation. If one is a vegan, it would be wise to supplement with vitamin B12, Ubiquinol (a reduced form of CoQ-10, and consume plant-based protein powder daily comprised of hemp, pea, brown rice, and quinoa. Additionally, be sure to get plenty of raw nuts, seeds, mushrooms, beans, seaweed, and higher protein grains like quinoa in one's diet. Whether one is vegan or vegetarian, the choice of foods should always be organic or privately farmed raised.

Dr. Botanica will be publishing the new consumer health book **MEDISINS AND NUTRISINS: A Consumer Protection and Supplement Guide** in December of 2019. This book will provide the readers with an array of education on nutrition and human health. This is a conscious reminder that the key to excellent Health and Vitality is right nutrients, abundance of proper rest, sufficient high-quality water, exercise, therapy, choosing empathy to frame our mindset, a willingness to be honest and do better, and the knowledge that every thought and word we have marks our mind and soul. We can either create joy or dysfunction in generations to come.

The health of all beings on this planet has been compromised by pollution. We suffer due to depleted nutrients in the soil, and overuse of deadly chemicals in our food, water, air, makeup, hygiene products, and even food containers. To reduce the risk of emerging diseases, we must not only elevate our awareness of what we consume— but take consumer action against what is unnatural and destructive in our daily lives. It all starts with us to educate ourselves and commit to the process of understanding. It is not only about us and what we want, but future generations to come. Will the generation after us, or even seven generations after us, be proud of the choices we made?

Nature provides us with a bounty of food and plants, all with the purpose of health and nourishment. If we put a bit of effort into learning, with these natural gifts, we can use our knowledge to eliminate many conditions that are considered diseases; but, are in fact manifestations of what we are breathing, using, consuming, and feeling.

Despite the aggressiveness of pollution, there is still a great deal that we can do to protect ourselves and our families from the numerous forms of toxicity in today's world.
First and foremost, be familiar with the product and brand that is purchased. If one cannot eat it, maybe it should not be used on the body. If it has a warning label, find an alternative.

Understanding why there is a desperate need to supplement us with at least one organic Superfood supplement formula is also necessary. Our modern ways of living have profoundly affected the health of us all on a cellular level; unless there is a mass return to our

Indigenous ways and thought (a return to our natural ways of living and being), there will be no escaping the need to take an organic dietary superfood supplement.

Choose supplements with knowledge, read labels carefully; if one does not understand an ingredient on the label, research the word.

Numerous organic supplements are manufactured only with foods, herbs, superfoods, and minerals that will help one to eliminate the toxins that have been accumulated and residing in the body over the years from chemical-filled foods and consumer products.

The body has a variety of defense mechanisms and can act against free radicals and toxic accumulations. When we are young, our defenses are highly complex, sophisticated, and can create a multifaceted web of defenses that attacks and eliminates pathogens as they enter our bodies. The same with chemical accumulation, it is because of the tenacity of the immune defense and elimination system that allows the human body to endure such abuse. The human body is both choosy and adaptable, it prefers quality, but it will adapt to the lesser quality for survival purposes.

After the age of 28, our immune response begins to decline regarding enzyme production marginally, plasmin (a genetic structure in a cell that can replicate independently of the chromosomes, typically a small circular DNA strand in the cytoplasm of a bacterium or protozoan. Plasmids are mostly used in laboratory manipulation of genes), another repair mechanism.

As we continue to consume toxic foods, use chemically based deodorants, toothpaste, mouth wash, shampoo, conditioner, hair straighteners, hair dyes, hair sprays, hair gels, conditioners, menstrual products, fragrances, and nail polish— the body slows down its elimination process because of the overload, causing more toxins to build up. This is when chronic and physical degeneration begins to manifest, such as a burst appendix. Some supplements can assist in the removal and transportation of these toxic chemicals from our bloodstream, lymphatic system, liver, kidney, and colon.

The body requires many nutrients to maintain balance, but unfortunately, the refined foods and other chemicals that pollute our bodies tax the ability to stay in optimal balance. For example, most people are deficient in magnesium. Magnesium is considered one of the essential macro-minerals to the human body because it is responsible for over 300 chemical reactions and metabolic functions. Magnesium has also been clinically proven to reduce the risk of heart attack and stroke, the number two cause of death among women, following cancer. Zinc has been scientifically shown to promote and regulate immune function, and along with the micro-mineral selenium, is found to be deficient amongst the general population.

Basic Nutrients are Very Important
Vitamins A, E, C, B-1 (Thiamine), B-5 (Pantothenic Acid), B6 (Pyridoxine), and Vitamin D-3 (an actual hormone) are other vital nutrients that are depleted from the body when we are overly exposed to chemical pollutants and free radical damage.

Please understand that each nutrient depends on a chain of other nutrients to be assimilated, transported and used by the human body, taking single vitamins or minerals will cause an imbalance in our bodies, it is vital to our health to purchase formulas that contain all the minerals in a synergistic chain of command.

EVERYONE NEEDS MAGNESIUM IN SOME WAY!

Magnesium - According to research, magnesium deficiency has been shown to not only increase the risk of heart attack and stroke but the development of leukocytosis, a persistent increase of white blood cells, which has been documented to lead to the development of leukemia and lymphoma (lymph tumor).

Magnesium is involved in at least 600 cellular reactions, from muscle contraction to making DNA. Low levels could also cause High Blood pressure or depression. Buckwheat, a gluten-free grain, has high amounts of magnesium— as do kelp, oats, almonds and cashews, cocoa or cacao, hemp nut seed, chia seeds, pumpkin seeds, sunflower seeds, dark leafy green vegetables, beans, legumes, black and brown rice, winter squash, sweet potatoes, and bananas! Locally it is preferable.

This mineral can stimulate macrophages (first line of white blood cell defense) to seek out and destroy invaders of the immune system. Natural sources of manganese are organically grown brown rice, oat bran, quinoa, rice bran, sprouted seeds/nuts, vegetables, spices, pineapple, sweet potato, green tea, lima beans, and millet. High levels can cause brain damage and violence in people in humans.

Selenium - A micro-mineral that is an "immunostimulant" and is a protective and therapeutic action against a variety of carcinogenic agents. Good sources include brown, black, and red rice (black and red rice is highly recommended for diabetic people), sunflower seeds, mushrooms (especially shiitake and reishi), mung beans, red kidney beans, brazil nuts, pecans, cashews, lentils, pistachios, Walnuts, Organic NON-GMO Oatmeal, Spinach, Organic Bananas.

Coenzyme nutrients

Ubiquinol - It is well-established that CoQ_{10} is not well absorbed into the body, as has been published in many peer-reviewed scientific journals.[4] Since the ubiquinol form has two additional hydrogens, it results in the conversion of two ketone groups into hydroxyl groups on the active portion of the molecule. This causes an increase in the polarity of the CoQ_{10} molecule and may be a significant factor behind the observed enhanced bioavailability of ubiquinol.

Ubiquinol promotes heart health by helping to provide the cellular energy needed to power the heart. Ubiquinol is critical in the production of ATP, the body's primary fuel.[1] This fuel is used for three basic yet critical heart functions:

1. Contraction - to keep the heart pumping consistently
2. Relaxation - to allow the heart to rest between beats
3. Molecular Synthesis - to maintain heart health by building important cellular components.*

Ubiquinol has anti-aging benefits and it has been shown to fuel the body and enhance energy. in addition to the normal aging process, Ubiquinol can help generate unstable molecules called free radicals that seek out healthy cells and ultimately damage them. This process of free radical damage is called oxidation.

Bee Products (honey, pollen, and propolis) — Bee pollen is the most complete food found in nature containing vitamin B-9 and all

21 essential amino acids, making it a complete protein. Honey, in its organic/wild, raw, unfiltered states is rich in minerals, antioxidants, probiotics, enzymes, and one of the highest vibration foods on the planet. A good source is Y.S. Bee Farms

Bio-Strath - Helps to promote well-being by decreasing fatigue and supporting the body during periods of physical and mental stress. Source of antioxidants.

Cacao (Raw Chocolate) – The seed of a fruit of an Amazonian tree, cacao is the highest
antioxidant food on the planet, the #1 source of magnesium, iron, chromium and is also extremely high in PEA, theobromine (cardiovascular support), and anandamide ("bliss chemical"). Raw Chocolate balances brain chemistry, builds strong bones, is a natural aphrodisiac, elevates your mood and energy.

Camu Berry — Highest Vitamin C source on planet. Great for rebuilding tissue, purifying blood, and enhancing immunity, and energy.

DHEA Is May Support Health and Vitality
Based on research, DHEA is one of the most recognized supplements for vitality. DHEA is vital for bone, joint health, and vitality and becomes depleted after the age of 30; therefore, it is suggested that one have a bio-identical test to confirm hormonal ranges too. DHEA, hormones, and blood chemistry should maintain balance and should not be above or below range, therefor should be tested through bio-identical hormone testing. DHEA is vital for joint health (Arthritis and Rheumatism v 40, 1997). There is still much-needed research on this "forgotten" hormone.

Maca — A staple in the Peruvian Andes for thousands of years, this adaptogenic superfood increases energy, endurance, strength, and libido. Dried maca powder contains more than 10% protein, nearly 20 amino acids, and 7 essential amino acids. As a root crop, maca contains five times more protein than a potato and four times more fiber.

Fish Oil and Omega-3 Fatty Acids. Acquire this supplement from the Health Food Store or your holistic health practitioner. Omega 3's are found in the fatty layers of cold-water fish, pants, Flax seeds, and nut oils. We suggest Omega 3-6-9 from a reputable brand source such as Carlsons' or Nordic Natural. This supplement can be rich in EPA (eicosapentaenoic acid), DHA (docosahexaenoic acid). Studies have shown that omega 3's support vascular flow, supports brain function, cardiovascular health, and promotes anti-inflammatory results. For people who have a vegan lifestyle, we suggest Flax, Black, Sea Buckthorn, Borage or Evening Primrose Oil. Omega Nutrition, Barlean's, or Amazing Herbs.

Ginger. It is a traditional treatment for stomachaches, and science supports the belief that it's good for your belly. The root speeds up digestion, moving food to the upper intestine from the stomach, and is also highly suggested for nausea. Ginger has also been found to have anti-viral and anti-bacterial effects. Prince of Peace Brand.

Goji Berries. According to medical news today, scientific research has found that Goji Berries supports the immune system by building resistance, promotes healthy skin, helps to balance glucose (blood sugar) levels, may protect the liver, and could even buffer depression and anxiety. Goji is a superb blood tonic, which makes it very precious to women, who are often somewhat blood deficient due to menstrual functioning. Goji is also a great immune tonic.

Hermits Mix by Dragon Herbs

This unique and absolutely delicious herbal food is both a powerful anti-aging tonic and a wonderful snack. Hermits Mix provides all three treasures, Jing, Qi and Shen. It is an amazingly satisfying herbal food and trail mix. Lycium is widely believed in the Orient to be a major anti-aging herb. Longan is an excellent blood tonic. The Lycium and Longan fruits mix perfectly and delectably with the walnuts and pine nuts. Walnuts are an excellent and important Yang tonic in Chinese herbalism. We use organically grown, peeled walnuts (the thin outer skin is believed to be slightly toxic and counter-productive). The pine nuts are an excellent source of energy. This mix gives you incredible energy. And, Hermit's Mix is an excellent beauty tonic. You've got to try this fantastic snack mix. You'll love it and you'll love to turn your friends on to it.

Medicinal Mushrooms (Reishi, cordyceps, maitake, shiitake, Tremella, lion's mane, etc.) — High in polysaccharides

and super immune enhancing components, medicinal mushrooms are one of the most intelligent adaptogenic herb/superfoods on the planet! They have also been proven effective in healing cancer and a variety of other ailments.

Mulberries. Super Food (This berries are pack with vitamins, antioxidants, and contains a usual source of protein. Mulberries have also been found to be a source of vitamin C and may lower your risk for heart disease. Very sweet and delicious with only 43 calories per 100 grams of berries, making them a great snack or side dish for those looking to lose weight

Quinoa. Super Food (Pronounced "keen-wah"), which is not a grain, but an edible seed, but it's used as a grain. The origin of quinoa dates back over 3,000 years indigenous to the Andean region of Bolivia, Columbia, and Peru. It was a major food source for the Incas and is referred to as the "mother grain." When cooked, quinoa has a nutty flavor and crunchy texture. Plus, it's high in protein, B-vitamins, fiber, magnesium, potassium, vitamin E, and essential amino acids like leucine, as well as many vitamins and minerals. Quinoa is an actual superfood and gluten-free.

Rhodiola: One of the most sought out adaptogens. Rhodiola rosea relieves stress by balancing the body's stress-response system. Rhodiola rosea helps re-establish balance by acting as an adaptogen—an agent that strengthens the body's response to physical, mental, and emotional stressors. **Rhodiola's** effects are particularly remarkable in the nervous system. According to Dr. Richard Brown of Columbia University, rhodiola is exceptionally beneficial because it "enhances the healing properties of one's own nervous system." He notes that the herb provides both "cognitive stimulation" and "emotional calming," which lead to improvement in cognitive and memory function, as well as contributing to the long-term upkeep of brain function.1

Caution: Rhodiola is not recommended for individuals with bipolardisorder. Always consult with your doctor, primary care physician, and a bona fide holistic practitioner before using.

Schisandra

Schisandra one of the most popular berry/herbs used in China today and by millions of people all over the world. It is called the "quintessence of tonic herbs" by Taoist masters. It was found to support the health of the liver, lungs, mental clarity, and even improve the functionality and health of the skin. According to research, it is the only herb known to contain a perfect balance of Yin and Yang. It is a profound adaptogen, Shen tonic, and sexual tonic for both women and men.

Spring Dragon Longevity Tea™ is a delicious herbal tea composed of the most famous tonic herbs in the Orient, all of which are renowned for promoting a long and healthy life.* The main herb is Gynostemma, a green leafy herb that is consumed throughout Asia to promote overall health.

Gynostemma is an adaptogenic, **dual-directional** herb. These unique properties support the body's response to change and stress, as well as promoting a situation-appropriate response from the central nervous system.* If you need to relax at the end of the night, then Gynostemma will **promote calmness, peace, and serenity.*** If you are just waking up in the morning and need to get your body started, Gynostemma will **promote clarity, focus, and energy**.

Gynostemma is soothing to the digestive system and **supports healthy aging.*** It promotes **heart, respiratory, and liver health**. In Asia, it has become increasingly popular as a component to **weight management programs**. When combined with a reasonable exercise program and healthy diet, Gynostemma has been shown to **promote fat loss**. It seems to act upon the metabolism and **promote healthy blood sugar levels**, as well. Additionally, the anti-cancer effects are still in beginning stages of research, but the effects appear to be very similar in many cell lines; some compound in the Gypenoside fragment may be an inducer of p53, a tumor suppressor gene, as the downstream events associated with p53 activity have been noted repeatedly.

Hemp Raw

Contains about 33 % pure digestible protein, rich in iron, amino acids, and vitamin E as well as omega-3's and GLA. A perfect food.

Hemp CBD

Hemp CBD will probably go down in American history as the most controversial health supplement. CBD stands for cannabidiol. It is one of many different cannabinoids found in the Cannabis genus of plants. Hemp is a species of cannabis, that is different from marijuana and hemp must contain 0.3% THC.

Once upon a time, cannabis-derived modalities were regularly prescribed by doctors – particularly for the relief of gynecological conditions. Going back even further into history around 4,000 years to Ancient Mesopotamia and Egypt/Acoupta cannabis was one of the most popular remedies in the medicinal kit of village herbalist, medicine women, and tribal shamans. Ancient manuscripts described different preparations used for difficult childbirth and other unspecified female challenges. There were also ancient texts discovered in Asian and Africa, which list numerous recipes containing cannabis seeds, flowers, stems, and/or extracts used in gynecology. This botanical must have had great health and healing potential, because it's gynecological use spread throughout Asia and Africa, eventually finding its way into Europe in the Middle Ages and later to the Americas.

Rarely was this natural botanical smoked –Most medicinal recipes were used for oral wounds, vaginal problems, intranasal, and topical applications. Fortunately, there is a much better understanding that is separating the misconceptions between Hemp CBD and marijuana THC. Through legalization of hemp products is allowing women to reclaim the long-lasting tradition of cannabinoid remedies – via extracts and topical preparations that are pure enough to be used gynecological. We certainly do not condone any botanical for psychoactive use.

There are even more modern-day Archival medical texts from the 1800s that describe different applications and formations for:
- Painful menstrual cramps
- Heavy bleeding
- Urinary irritation

- PMS
- Menopause
- Post-Partum hemorrhage

Within the female reproductive system, endocannabinoid receptors are broad. They have also been found to be quite dense in the uterus, but also found in the fallopian tubes, ovaries, and vaginal canal.

Royal Jelly is a phenomenal super Energy Food source. Royal Jelly is rich in traces of vitamins and amino acids and has been found to stimulate an immune response.

Sea Vegetables (seaweeds including: kelp, dulse, nori, hijiki, bladder wrack, chlorella, etc.) — Rich in life-giving nutrients drawn in from the ocean and sun, sea vegetables help remove heavy metals, detoxify the body, provide numerous trace minerals, regulate cholesterol, and decrease the risk of cancer. Seaweeds benefit the entire body and are especially excellent for the thyroid (high iodine), immune system, adrenals, and hormone function.

Spirulina and Blue-Green Algae — The world's highest source of complete protein (65%), spirulina provides a vast array of minerals, trace elements, phytonutrients and enzymes. Blue-green algae is a wild-grown superfood with a 60% protein percentage but is equally or exceedingly higher in other components. Both are vital superfoods, but make sure that you acquire these super foods from good quality sources like Parsi Herbs, Nutrex, Now Foods, Sun Chlorella, and Earth Rise.

Dr. Jafari's acknowledges Healing Touch Buddies for their great work.

Betty Ann Baker, CHTP, LMT
Executive Director
Healing Touch Buddies, Inc.
13901 US Hwy 1 Suite 10
Juno Beach, FL 33408

www.HealingTouchBuddies.org
www.facebook.com/healingtouchbuddies

Our Mission
"Healing Touch Buddies provides energy support, care and comfort to those diagnosed with breast cancer."

Healing Touch Buddies provides energy therapy in one-on-one supportive relationships with individuals diagnosed with breast cancer through our network of specially-trained volunteer energy therapy providers. Regardless of stage of diagnosis or treatment protocol, our Buddies offer consistent, reassuring and long-term therapeutic support for up to one year.

Healing Touch Buddies, Inc. is a Florida 501(c)3 non-profit organization

References

Chapter 1

1. CNN, Ny Times, announcements
2. Collins, Francis. "Henrietta Lacks' 'Immortal' Impact on Medical Research." Interview. Clip video, 07:04. PBS. Accessed December 5, 2017. http://www.pbs.org/video/henrietta-lacks-immortal-impact-on-medical-research-1383253 839/.
2. Jones, Howard W. "Record of the first physician to see Henrietta Lacks at the Johns Hopkins Hospital: History of the beginning of the HeLa cell line." *American Journal of Obstetrics and Gynecology* 176, no. 6 (June 1997): 227-28.
3. DOI:https://doi.org/10.1016/S0002-9378(97)70379-X. This first-hand account was interesting to see from the first person who ever examined Henrietta. If he had found something different, history of the HeLa cell line would have been rewritten.
4. Skloot, Rebecca. "Cells that save lives are a mother's legacy. (Deborah Lacks, who works on cells taken from her dying mother)." *New York Times*, November 17, 2001, A2. *Opposing Viewpoints in Context* (accessed December 13, 2017).

Chapter 2

1. The Long-Term Effects of Fluoride Consumption
Accelerated aging, Immune system dysfunction, Compromised collagen synthesis
Cartilage problems, Bony outgrowths in the spine, Joint "lock-up."
2. ATSDR/USPHS - "Toxicological Profile for Fluorides, Hydrogen Fluoride and Fluorine (F)" CAS# 16984-48-8, 7664-39-3, 7782-41-4 (1993), http://www.atsdr.cdc.gov/tfacts11.html
3. Health Effects of Ingested Fluoride, Subcommittee on Health Effects of Ingested Fluoride, Committee on Toxicology, Board on Environmental Studies and Toxicology, Commission on Life Sciences, National Research Council, August 1993, p.59
Analyses conducted by Parents of Fluoride Poisoned Children (PFPC) at Gov't -approved labs. Contact: pfpc@istar.ca
3. Jenkins GN - "Fluoride intake and its safety among heavy tea drinkers in a British fluoridated city" Proc Finn Dent Soc 87(4):571-9 (1991) Department of Oral Biology, Dental School, Newcastle upon Tyne, United Kingdom.
4. Diouf A, Sy FO, Niane B, Ba D, Ciss M - "Dietary intake of fluorine through of tea prepared by the traditional method in Senegal" Dakar Med 39(2):227-30 (1994)
History: Fluoride - Iodine Antagonism http://bruha.com/pfpc/html/thyroid_history.html
5. Lyche JL, Gutleb AC, Bergman A, Eriksen GS, Murk AJ, Ropstad E, Saunders M, Skaare JU. Reproductive and developmental toxicity of phthalates. JToxicolEnvironHealth B Crit Rev. 2009;12(4):225-249
6. Landrigan PJ, Goldman LR. Children's vulnerability to toxic chemicals: a challenge and opportunity to strengthen health and environmental policy. Health Aff (Millwood) 2011;30(5):842-850. doi: 10.1377/hlthaff.2011.0151.
7. Environmental Working Group: Roundup for Breakfast, Part 2, In New Tests, Weed Killer Found in All Kids' Cereal Sampled. https://www.ewg.org/release/roundup-breakfast-part-2-new-tests-weed-killer-found-all-kids-cereals-sampled?
8. Franks G. Fluoride in drinking water. Should you have it? How do you get rid of it if you don't want it? Denton, Tex.: Pure Water Products, LLC; 2005. Available at: http://www.purewatergazette.net/fluorideinwater.htm. Accessed Jan 3, 2005.
9. Foster M, Chu A, Petocz P, Samman S. Effect of vegetarian diets on zinc status: a systematic review and meta-analysis of studies in humans. J Sci Food Agric. 2013 Aug 15;93(10):2362-71. doi: 10.1002/jsfa.6179. Epub 2013 May 29. Review. PubMed PMID: 23595983. **https://www.ncbi.nlm.nih.gov/pubmed/23595983**

Chapter 3

1.1910 - U.S. Department of Agriculture Farmers' Bulletin 393 Habit-Forming Agents: Their Indiscriminate Sale and Use A Menace to the Public Welfare By L.F. Kebler, Chief, Division of Drugs, Bureau of Chemistry. --- Actual Author H.W. Wiley, Chief, Bureau of Chemistry.
2.According to a Government website - http://www.fda.gov/AboutFDA/WhatWeDo/History/CentennialofFDA/HarveyW.Wiley/default.htm
3.Garcia-Mayor, R. et.al. 2012. Endocrine disruptors and obesity: Obesogens. Endocrinol. Nutr. 59(4), 261-267.
4.Janesick, A. and Blumberg, B. 2011. Minireview: PPAR341as the target of obesogens. Journal of Steroid Biochemistry and Molecular Biology. 127, 4-8.
5.Grun, F., Blumberg, B. 2009. Minireview:The case for obesogens. Mol. Endocrinol. 23(8), 1127- 1134.
Campbell published an article in the *Journal of Clinical Nutrition* in 2000 in which he criticized a paper by Hu & Willett (2002) based on data from the Nurses' Health Study
6. Persistent toxic chemicals in the US food supply. [J Epidemiol Community Health. 2002]
7. Wiley, H. W. (1929). The History of a Crime Against the Food Law: The Amazing Story of the National Food and Drug Law Intended to Protect the Health of the People, Perverted to Protect Adulteration of Foods and Drugs. Self-published, Washington, DC.
8.Todhunter, E. N. (1966). Biographical notes from the history of nutrition: Harvey Washington Wiley—October 18, 1844–June 30, 1930. *J. Am. Diet. Assoc.*49 121.
9. Genuis S. J. What's out there making us sick? *Journal of Environmental and Public Health.* 2012;2012:10. doi: 10.1155/2012/605137.605137
10. Wynder EIL. And Gori GB. "Contributions of the environment to cancer incidence. An epidemiologic exercise." J. Natl. Cancer Inst. 58 (1977): 825-832.
11. TAREKE E, LYN-COOK B, ROBINSON B, ALI S: Acrylamide: a dietary carcinogen formed in vivo? *J Agric Food Chem* **56**: 6020-6023, 2008.12.TAREKE E, RYDBERG P, KARLSSON P, ERICSSON S, TORNQVIST M: Analysis of acrylamide, a carcinogen formed in heated foodstuffs. *J Agric Food Chem* **50**: 4998-5006, 2002.

Chapter 4

1.William G. Crook MD, *The Yeast Connection* (Future Health, 1984)
2.Leon Chaitow, *Candida Albicans* (Thorsons, 1991)
3.Jose' Fleming Researcher, Medisin: Causes and Solutions that are killing the World (Rising Sun Publications, 2005, 1st Edition)
4.Vazquez, Jose (2016-04-16). "Epidemiology, Management, and Prevention of Invasive Candidiasis". *Medscape.org.* Medscape. Retrieved 2016-04-16.
5.Martins N, Ferreira IC, Barros L, Silva S, Henriques M (June 2014).
6"Candidiasis: predisposing factors, prevention, diagnosis and alternative treatment". *Mycopathologia.* **177** (5-6): 223-240. doi:10.1007/s11046-014-9749-1 7.Brosnahan, Mandy (July 22, 2013). "Candida Albicans". MicrobeWiki. Kenyon College.
8.Novella, Steven (25 September 2013). "Candida and Fake Illnesses". *Science-Based Medicine.* Retrieved 4 July 2018.
9.Jarvis WT. "Candidiasis Hypersensitivity". National Council Against Health Fraud. Retrieved 18 January 2014.
10.Crook, William G. (1986). *The Yeast Connection: A Medical Breakthrough.* Vintage Books. ISBN 0933478062.

Chapter 5

1.Envtl. Working Grp., EWG's Skin Deep® Cosmetics Database, https://www.ewg.org/skindeep/.
2. Laura N. Vandenberg *et al., Hormones & Endocrine-Disrupting Chemicals: Low-Dose Effects & Nonmonotonic Dose Responses*, 33 Endocrine Rev. 378-455 (2012),

http://www.ncbi.nlm.nih.gov/pubmed/22419778.
3. Alyssa Katzenelson & Scott Faber, *On Cosmetics Safety, U.S. Trails More Than 40 Nations*, Envtl. Working Grp. (Mar. 20, 2019), https://www.ewg.org/news-and-analysis/2019/03/cosmetics-safety-us-trails-more-40-nations.
4. Food Additives Amendment of 1958, Pub. L. No. 85-929, 72 Stat. 1784.
5. Color Additives Amendment of 1960, Pub. L. No. 86-618, 74 Stat. 39
6. Food Quality Protection Act of 1996, Pub. L. No. 104-170, 110 Stat. 1489.
7.[13] Envtl. Working Grp., *Exposures Add Up- Survey Results* (2004), http://www.ewg.org/skindeep/2004/06/15/exposures-add-up-survey-results/.
8. European Union. Consolidated version of Cosmetic Directive 76/768/EEC, as amended, Annexes I through IX, 2010. Available at: http://ec.europa.eu/enterprise/sectors/cosmetics/documents/directive/#h2-technical-adaptations-to-be-incorporated-in-the-consolidated-text Accessed on 10/04/2018.
9. Orton F, Ermler S, Kugathas S, Rosivatz E, Scholze M, Kortenkamp A. Mixture effects at very low doses with combinations of anti-androgenic pesticides, antioxidants, industrial pollutant and chemicals used in personal care products. Toxicol Appl 10.Pharmacol 2014;278(3):201-8. doi: 10.1016/j.taap.2013.09.008. [PubMed] [Google Scholar]
11. Jung EM, An BS, Choi KC, Jeung EB. Potential estrogenic activity of triclosan in the uterus of immature rats and rat pituitary GH3 cells. Toxicol Lett 2012;208:142-8. doi: 10.1016/j.toxlet.2011.10.017. [PubMed] [Google Scholar]
12. Darbre PD, Harvey PW. Paraben esters: review of recent studies of endocrine toxicity, absorption, esterase and human exposure, and discussion of potential human health risks. J 13.Appl Toxicol2008;28(5):561-78. doi: 10.1002/jat.1358. [PubMed] [Google Scholar] Centers for Disease Control and Prevention. Overweight and Obesity. Centers for 14.Disease Control and Prevention Web site. Available at http://www.cdc.gov/nccdphp/dnpa/obesity/trend/index.htm.

Chapter 6

1. Cutlip, Scott M. *The Unseen Power: Public Relations. A History.* Hove, UK: Lawrence Erlbaum, 1994. ISBN 0-8058-1465-5
2. Bernays, Edward L. (March 1947). "The Engineering of Consent" (PDF). Annals of the American Academy of Political and Social Science. **250** (1): 113-20 at p. 114.
3. Bernays, Edward L. (March 1947). "The Engineering of Consent" (PDF).
4. *The Engineering of Consent* (Norman: University of Oklahoma Press, 1955)(contributor) OCLC 550584
5. Olasky (1985), p. 19.; Olasky (1984), p. 19, f. 40. "Bernays emphasized that in a large-scale society there were only two choices: manipulation or social chaos. He saw history moving in a certain direction and public relations practitioners obliged to climb on the locomotive".
6. Tye, Larry, *The Father of Spin: Edward L. Bernays and the Birth of Public Relations.* New York: Crown, 1998. ISBN 0805067892
7. Alix Spiegel. Freud's Nephew and the Origins of Public Relations, Morning Edition, 22 April 2005

Chapter 7

1. The Essential How-to Guide to Symptoms, Dosage, Timing, and More by *John R. Lee, M.D. and Virginia Hopkins,* Warner Books, 2006
2. How Hormone Balance Can Help Save Your Life, by John R. Lee, M.D., David Zava, Ph.D. and Virginia Hopkins., Warner Books, 2002
3. Meilahn E, De Stavola B, Allen D, et al. Do urinary oestrogen metabolites predict breast cancer? Guernsey III cohort follow-up. Br. J. Cancer. 1998;78(9):1250.
4. Rakel D. Integrative Medicine. 3rd ed. Philadelphia: Elsevier Saunders; 2012.
5. Warshowsky A. Uterine fibroids. In: Rakel D, ed. Integrative Medicine. 3rd ed. Philadelphia: Elsevier Saunders; 2012:515-528.

6.Bisphenol-A (BPA), BPA glucuronide, and BPA sulfate in midgestation umbilical cord serum in a northern and central California population. Environmental Science & Technology. 2013 Oct 7;47(21):12477-85.
8. Carson R. Silent Spring. Houghton Mifflin; Boston, MA: 1962. [Google Scholar]
9.Weiss G, Noorhasan D, Schott LL, Powell L, Randolph JF, Jr, Johnston JM. Racial differences in women who have a hysterectomy for benign conditions. Womens Health Issues. 2009;19:202-210.
Yang Q, Diamond MP, Al-Hendy A. Early Life Adverse Environmental Exposures 10.Increase the Risk of Uterine Fibroid Development: Role of Epigenetic Regulation. Frontiers in pharmacology. 2016;7:40.
11. Coelingh Bennink HJ. Are all estrogens the same? Maturitas. 2004;47:269-275

Chapter 8

1.An extensive bibliography on Consumer Concerns About Hormones in Food is available on the BCERF web site: http://www.cfe.cornell.edu/bcerf/
Renu Gandhi, Ph.D. BCERF Research Associate and
Suzanne M. Snedeker, Ph.D. BCERF Research Project Leader
2.WebMD Feature Reviewed by Michael W. Smith, MD on August 25, 2010
Source: Nationwide Children's Hospital.
Summary: A new study found that 64,686 children younger than five years of age were treated in US emergency departments for injuries related to personal care products from 2002 through 2016 -- that is the equivalent of about one child every two hours.
3.Lu C. Toepel K. Irish R, et al. Organic diets significantly lower children's dietary exposure to organophosphorus pesticides. Environ Health Perspect. 2006;114:260-263
4.vom Saal FS. Hughes C. An extensive new literature concerning low-dose effects of bisphenol A shows the need for a new risk assessment. Environ Health
Perspect. 2005;113:926-933
5.J Agric Food Chem. 2010 Oct 13;58(19):10356-63. doi: 10.1021/jf101688k. 2010 Oct 13;58(19):10356-63. doi: 10.1021/jf101688k. **Soybean toxin (SBTX), a protein from soybeans** that inhibits the life cycle ofplant and human pathogenic fungi. Morais JK[1], Gomes VM, Oliveira JT, Santos IS, Da Cunha M, Oliveira HD, Sousa DO, Vasconcelos IM.
6.Rackis et al, "The USDA trypsin inhibitor study", ibid
7. "Beefing Up Burgers with Soy Products at School", Nutrition Week, Community Nutrition Institute, Washington, DC June 5, 1998, p.2.

Chapter 9

1.WHO/UNEP. 2012. State of the science of endocrine-disrupting chemicals - 2012. Bergman A, Heindel JJ, Jobling S, Kidd KA, Zoeller RT, editors: United National Envirnoment Programme World
2.Diamanti-Kandarakis E, Bourguignon JP, Giudice LC, Hauser R, Prins GS, Soto AM, Zoeller RT, Gore AC. Endocrine-disrupting chemicals: an Endocrine Society scientific statement. Endocrine Rev 2009; 30:293-342.
3.Mouritsen A, Aksglaede L, Sorensen K, Mogensen SS, Leffers H, Main KM, Frederiksen H, Anders- son AM, Skakkebaek NE, Juul A. Hypothesis: exposure to endocrine-disrupting chemicals may interfere with timing of puberty. Int J Androl 2010; 33:346-359.
4.Vandenberg LN, Colborn T, Hayes TB, Heindel JJ, Jacobs DR, Lee DH, Shioda T.
5.Soto AM, vom Saal FS, Welshons WV, Zoeller RT, Myers JP. Hormones and endocrine- disrupting chemicals: Low- dose effects and nonmonotonic dose response. Endocrine Rev 2012; 33:378-455.
6.Rochester JR. Bisphenol A and human health: a review of the literature. Reprod Toxicol 2013; 42:132-155.
7.Jauchem, J. (2008, March). Effects of low-level radio-frequency (3kHz to 300GHz) energy on human cardiovascular, reproductive, immune, and other systems: A review of the recent literature.
8.*International Journal of Hygiene & Environmental Health*, *211*(1/2), 1-29. Retrieved March 3, 2010 from Academic Search Complete database.doi:10.1016/j.ijheh.2007.05.001.
9.Kava, R., Stimola, A., Weiser, R., & Mills, L. (2004). The top ten unfounded health scares of

2004: Cell phones cause brain tumors. American Council on Science and Health. Retrieved March 9, 2010 from http://www.acsh.org/healthissues/newsID.1010/healthissue_detail.asp
10.Neurological deaths of American adults (55-74) and the over 75's by sex compared with 20 Western countries 1989-2010:
11.Colin Pritchard, Emily Rosenorn-Lanng Surg Neurol Int 23-Jul-2015;6:123

Chapter 10

1.Lauren Wasser recovered from a near-death TSS experience and then debuted at the New York Fashion Week despite wearing a prosthetic leg.[32] She is now advocating for laws to require more research into the safety of feminine hygiene products.[33]

3,Ross, R. A.; Onderdonk, A. B. (2000). "Production of Toxic Shock Syndrome Toxin 1 by Staphylococcus aureus Requires Both Oxygen and Carbon Dioxide". Infection and Immunity. **68** (9): 5205-5209. doi:10.1128/IAI.68.9.5205-5209.2000. ISSN 0019-9567. PMC 101779. PMID 10948145.
4.Hanrahan S; Submission, Haworth Continuing Features (1994). "Historical review of menstrual toxic shock syndrome". Women & Health. 21 (2-3): 141-65. doi:10.1300/J013v21n02_09. PMID 8073784.
5.Lindsay, JA; Ruzin, A; Ross, HF; Kurepina, N; Novick, RP (July 1998). "The gene for toxic shock toxin is carried by a family of mobile pathogenicity islands in Staphylococcus aureus". Molecular Microbiology. 29 (2): 527-43. doi:10.1046/j.1365-2958.1998.00947.x. PMID 9720870.
6."Stayfree – FAQ About Toxic Shock Syndrome (TSS)". 2006. Archived from the original on 23 March 2007. Retrieved 13 October 2006.
Vitale, Sidra (1997).
7."Toxic Shock Syndrome". Web by Women, for Women. Archived from the original on 16 March 2006. Retrieved 20 March 2006.
8.What You Need To Know About Toxic Sjaock Syndrome, University of Utah Health. 2018-07-02. Retrieved 2019-10-19.

Chapter 11

1.July 2019 Interview with Ann Anderson concerning hear traumatic experience with hormonal imbalance, estrogen dominance and the experience of medical neglect.

Chapter 12

1. Curtis J, et al. Patterns of milk consumption and risk of cancer. Nutrition and Cancer 1990;13: 89-99.
2. Le MG et al. Consumption of dairy products and alcohol in a case-control study of breast cancer. JNCI 1986; 77: 633-636.
3. Zhang Y et al. A major inducer of anticarcinogenic protective enzymes from broccoli: Isolation and elucidation of structure. Proc Natl Acad Sci USA 1992; 89: 2399-2403.
4. Breslow RA et al. Long-term recreational physical activity and breast cancer in the National Health and Nutrition Examination Survey I epidemiologic follow-up study. Cancer Epidemiology Biomarkers Prevention 2001; 10: 805- 808.
5. Hilakivi-Clarke L et al. Maternal and prepubertal diet, mammary development and breast cancer risk. J Nutrition 2001; 154S-157S.
6. Allred CD et al. Soy diets containing varying amounts of genestein stimulate growth of estrogen- dependent (MCF-7) tumors in a dose-dependent manner. Cancer Research 2001; 61: 5045-5050.
7. Knekt P et al. Does antibacterial treatment for urinary tract infection contribute to the risk of breast cancer? British J Cancer 2000; 82: 1107-1110.
8. Blaylock R. A review of conventional cancer prevention and treatment and the adjunctive use

of nutraceutical supplements and antioxidants: Is there a danger or a significant benefit? J American Nutriceutical Association 2000; 3: 17-35.
9. Zhang x, Yee D. Tyrosine kinase signaling in breast cancer insulin-like growth factors and their receptors in breast cancer. Breast Cancer Research 2000; 2: 170-175
10. Mohammed, Hisham, et al "Progesterone receptor modulates ER-a action in breast cancer," Nature 2015; 523; 313-317.
11. Perks, Bea "Progesterone receptor could slow breast cancer growth," Pharmaceutical Journal, PJ 17 Jul 2015.
12. Ganmaa D, Sato A. The possible role of female sex hormones in milk from cows in the development of breast, ovarian and corpus uteri cancers. Medical Hypothesis. 2005;65:1028-1037.
13. Standish LJ. Greene K. Greenlee H, et al. Complementary and alternative medical treatment of breast cancer: A survey of licensed North American naturopathic physicians. Altern Ther Health Med. 2002;8:2-5. 68-70.

Chapter 13

1. Pang Huali, *Treatment of hysteromyoma with Gui Ling Xiaoliu Wan-A report of 30 cases*, Beijing Journal of Traditional Chinese Medicine 1989; (6): 31-31.
2. Zhang Zhuen, et al., *Clinical observation of 28 cases of hysteromyoma healed by integrated traditional and western medicine*, Chinese Journal of Integrated Traditional and Western Medicine 13.(3): 180-181.
4. Gui SQ, Yu J, Wei MJ, Yang SP, Shi DW. Experiment study on effect of tongifying kidney herbs on pituitary, ovary, and adrenal gland in androgen sterilized rats. J Chin Med Mater. 1998;4:189-193.[Google Scholar]
5. Highfield ES, Laufer MR, Schnyer RN, Kerr CE, Thomas P, Wayne PM. Adolescent endometriosis-related pelvic pain treated with acupuncture: two case reports. J Altern Complement Med. 2006;12:317-322. [PubMed]
6. Yang Shenshan, *A modified Ghuzhi Fuling Wan for the treatment of 100 cases of hysteromyoma*, Zhejiang Journal of Traditional Chinese Medicine 1984; 19(4): 180.
Du QY, Ding YL, Pan YH, Li YJ, Li W. Treating vaginitis with Chinese medicinal herbs: a review. Hebei J TCM. 2002;24:791-794.
7. Wang DZ, Wang ZQ, Zhang ZF. Treatment of endometriosis with removing blood stasis and purgation method. Zhong Xi Yi Jie He Za Zhi. 1991;11:524-526. [PubMed]
8. Zhang Q, He J, He S, Xu P. Clinical observation in 102 cases of chronic pelvic inflammation treated with qi jie granules. J Tradit Chin Med. 2004;24:3-6. [PubMed]
9. Jake Fraktin, Traditional Chinese Medicine Formula Book.
10. Bob Flaws, Blue Poppy
11. Dr. George Xavier Love, DOM, L.Ac., Presentation on Chinese medicine, Qi Gong Exercise. Blood, stasis, Inflammation, women's reproductive health. Blue Dragon Qi Gong Academy, Delray Beach Florida
12. Miljkovic D, Scorei RI, Cimpoiaşu VM, Scorei ID. Calcium fructoborate: plant-based dietary boron for human nutrition. J Diet Suppl. 2009;6(3):211-226.

Chapter 14

1. Peters ML, Leonard M, Licata AA. Role of alendronate and risedronate in preventing and treating osteoporosis. *Cleve Clin J Med*. 2001;68(11):945-951.
2. Schneyer CR. Calcium carbonate and reduction of levothyroxine efficacy. *JAMA*. 1998; 279:750.
3. Carpenter T, DeLucia MC, Zhang JH, et al. A randomized controlled study of effects of dietary magnesium oxide supplementation on bone mineral content in healthy girls. *J Clin Endocrinol Metab*. 2006;91(12):4866-4872.
4. Rude RK, Gruber HE, Norton HJ, et al. Dietary magnesium reduction to 25% of nutrient requirement disrupts bone and mineral metabolism in the rat. *Bone*. 2005;37(2):211-219.39

Rude RK, Gruber HE. Magnesium deficiency and osteoporosis: animal and human observations. *J Nutr Biochem*. 2004;15(12):710-716.
5. American Academy of Orthopedic Surgeons. Burden of Musculoskeletal Diseases in the United States: Prevalence, Societal and Economic Cost. Rosemont, IL: *American Academy of Orthopedic Surgeons*; 2008.
6. Davies JH, Evans BA, Gregory JW. Bone mass acquisition in healthy children. *Arch Dis Child*. 2005;90(4):373-378.
7. Wyshak G, Frisch RE. Carbonated beverages, dietary calcium, the dietary calcium/phosphorus ratio, and bone fractures in girls and boys. *J Adolesc Health*. 1994;15(3):210-215.
8. Di Daniele N, Carbonelli MG, Candeloro N, et al. Effect of supplementation of calcium and vitamin D on bone mineral density and bone mineral content in peri- and post-menopause women; a double-blind, randomized, controlled trial. *Pharmacol Res*. 2004;50(6):637-641.
9. Main KM. Mortensen GK. Kaleva MM, et al. Human breast milk contamination with phthalates and alterations of endogenous reproductive hormones in infants three months of age. Environ Health Perspect. 2006;114:270-276.
10. Dess, C. et al, "Dietary estrogens stimulate human breast cells to enter cell cycle", Environmental Health Perspectives (1997) 105 (Suppl.3):633-636.

Chapter 15

1. Davis, SR; Kruger J (2008-08-14). "2003 November 29 - Bioidentical hormones (troches) advice for doctors". Australian Menopause Society. Retrieved 2009-08-25.
2. What are bioidentical hormones? (2006, August). Retrieved from https://www.health.harvard.edu/womens-health/what-are-bioidentical-hormones
3. Head KA. Estriol: safety and efficacy. *Altern Med Rev*. 1998;3:101-113 [PubMed] [Google Scholar]
4. Carson R. Silent Spring. Houghton Mifflin; Boston, MA: 1962. [Google Scholar]
5. Dr. John Lee-pioneer and author of: What Your Doctor May Not Tell You about Premenopause, What Your Doctor May Not Tell You about Menopause, What Your Doctor May Not Tell You about Breast Cancer, and Hormone Balance Made Easy (Virginia Hopkins) www.johnlee.com
6. Website: www.womeninbalance.org advances research and education for natural solutions to women's health
7. El-Sakka AI. Impact of the association between elevated oestradiol and low testosterone levels on erectile dysfunction severity. Asian J Androl. 2013;15:492-6.
8. Northrup C. Estrogen dominance. Available at: http://www.drnorthrup.com/womenshealth/healthcenter/topic_details. php?topic_id=118. Accessed 12/16/13.
9. Allolio B, Arlt W, Hahner S. DHEA: why, when, and how much- -DHEA replacement in adrenal insufficiency. Ann Endocrinol (Paris). 2007;68:268-73.

Chapter 16

1. **Stephanie Hemphill: Study Finds Highest Rate of Feminized Fish in Mississppi River In Minn. St. Paul, Minn.** September 14, 2009 5:57 p.m.
2. El-Sakka AI. Impact of the association between elevated oestradiol and low testosterone levels on erectile dysfunction severity. Asian J Androl. 2013;15:492-6. [PMC free article] [PubMed] [Google Scholar]
3. Carani C, Rochira V, Faustini-Fustini M, Balestrieri A, Granata AR. Role of oestrogen in male sexual behaviour: insights from the natural model of aromatase deficiency. Clin Endocrinol. 1999;51:517-24.[PubMed]
Dean RC, Lue TF. Physiology of penile erection and pathophysiology of erectile dysfunction. Urol Clin North Am. 2005;32:379-95
4. Prins GS, Tang WY, Belmonte J, Ho SM. Developmental exposure to bisphenol A increases prostate cancer susceptibility in adult rats: epdegenetic mode of action is implicated. Fertility and Sterility. 2008;89(Suppl 1):41-42.

5. Risbridger GP, Ellem SJ, McPherson SJ. Estrogen action on the prostate gland: a critical mix of endocrine and paracrine signaling. J Mol Endocrinol. 2007;39:183-8.

Chapter 17

1. Kitchen physician School of Natural Healing, detox and whole food therapy, September 1995.
2. Supplement to the American Journal of Clinical Nutrition. Proceedings of the second international congress on vegetarian nutrition. May 1994;59 (5S): 1099S-1262S
3. The Human Body and How It Works, Exeter Books, NY 1979. Toxemia Explained, Tilden, J.H., M.D. 1926. Ultimate Colonies, Eldon L Lowder, 7835 South 1300 East, Sandy, UT.
4. Cecchini M. Chemical exposure at the World Trade Center: Use of the Hubbard sauna detoxification regimen to improve health status of New York City rescue workers exposed to toxicants. Townsend Lett. 2006;273:58-65.
5. Klein AV, Kiat H. Detox diets for toxin elimination and weight management: a critical review of the evidence. J H Nutr. 2015;28:675-86.
6. Genuis SJ. Elimination of persistent toxicants from the human body. Hum Exp Toxicol. 2011;30:3-18. doi: 10.1177/0960327110368417.
Campbel T.C. "The Dietary Causes of degenerative diseases nutrients vs. foods." In:
7. N.J.Temple and D.P. Burkitt (eds), Westerb disease: their dietary prevention and reversibility, pp. 119-152. Totowa NJ: Humana Press, 1994.

Chapter 18

1. Skerrett, Patrick J.; Willett, Walter C. (2010). "Essentials of Healthy Eating: A Guide". *Journal of Midwifery and Women's Health*. 55: 492-501. doi:10.1016/j.jmwh.2010.06.019. PMC 3471136. PMID 20974411.
2. Parker-Pope, Tara. "Nutrition Advice From the China Study", *The New York Times*, January 7, 2011.
3. California Proposition 65. Office of Environmental Health Hazard Assessment, 2016. Available online: http://oehha.ca.gov/media/downloads/proposition-65//p65single080516.pdf
3. FDA: U.S. Food and Drug Administration. Nail Care Products. U.S. Department of Health and Human Services, 2013. Available online: http://www.fda.gov/Cosmetics/ProductsIngredients/Ingredients/ucm127068.htm
4. Campaign for safe cosmetics. Chemicals of Concern. Toluene. Available online: http://www.safecosmetics.org/get-the-facts/chemicals-of-concern/toluene/ Accessed September 2016.
5. Hennig B. Ettinger AS. Jandacek RJ, et al. Using nutrition for intervention and prevention against environmental chemical toxicity and associated diseases. Environ Health Perspect. 2007;115:493-495.
6. Bland JS. Barrager E. Reedy RG. Bland K. A medical food-supplemented detoxification program in the management of chronic health problems. Altern Ther Health Med. 1995;1:62-71.
7. Hennig B. Ormsbee L. Bachas L, et al. Introductory comments: Nutrition, environmental toxins and implications in prevention and intervention of human diseases. J Nutr. Biochem. 2007;18:161-162.

INDEX

Adulterated Foods 44-45, 64-65, 227, 239, 264, 311, 324
Advertising 98-106, 108-119
Aboriginal Indigenous Women/African American Women Women 91,144, 147, 224, 244
American College of Toxicology 106
American College of Nutrition 180
Antonella Guzzonato 171
Anca Paghel 11
Ann Anderson 222
Anahitta Jafari iii, 312, 352-353
Aretha Franklin 9, R.I.P.
Asian Women
Aspartame 188, 192, 252
Atrazine 244
Arpad Pustai 47
Avicenna 276
Belly Fat 289-290, 283
Beyond Meat 52-50
Bioidentical 126, 239, 284, 289, 294

Birth Control 100, 136, 140, 155,158, 225, 249,
Bisphenol A129-131, 133,
Blood Sugar 58, 337
Body care 167, 183, 230, 241, 243, 247-248, 257, 285, 299-300, 309, 324
Bovine Growth Hormone 39, 55, 175, 176, 183, 189, 249
Breast Cancer 3, 75, 102, 107, 124, 123, 133,142, 161, 168, 176, 178, 192, 214, 229, 230-231-249, 252, 284-289, 298, 301, 340
Breast Cancer Fund 159, 174, 234
Breast Cysts 242
Brenda Buttner 14
Bt Cotton 278,
Bureau of Chemistry 64-67

Cancer 1, 3, 17, 18, 21-28, 31, 40, 49, 52, 61, 77-78, 80, 85, 89, 102, 106-109, 124-138, 143, 156, 159, 160, 166, 169, 171, 173, 177, 180, 183-187, 196, 204, 206, 223-239, 242-254, 261, 272-273, 284, 288, 289, 296, 298, 30, 306, 308, 331, 336, 337, 339, 3403m
Caucasian Women 144, 257, 259,
CDC 60, 82, 171, 171, 176, 215, 216, 219, 297
Campaign for Safe Cosmetics 91, 107, 161-165
Candida 70-74
Candida Remedies 75
Cell Phones 198-202, 212
Cereal 183, 189, 313
Cervical Cancer 16, 18, 122, 123, 298,
Chicken 42, 46, 49, 54-56, 175
Chicken Nuggets 191
Chicken Wings 57-58
China 35, 173,178, 179,186, 258, 259, 264, 320, 337
Chinese dairy Association 177
Cigarettes 24, 114-115, 118, 123, 237
Cloning 18
Collagen 265, 269, 271
Colonic Irrigation 320
Corn 27, 39, 45, 46, 49, 235
Corn oil 191
Coretta Scott-King12, R.I.P.
Cosmetics 19, 29, 76-92
Cotton 54, 159, , 268, 269, 273-280
Cotton Tampons 212
Dairy Cows 178
Dairy products 42, 44, 49, 52, 59, 70, 127, 155, 175, 185
DDT 107, 233, 248, 249, 251, 305
DES 55
DHEA 234, 279, 282, 295, 296, 325
Dioxins, 146, 209, 233, 273, 274, 275,

Deodorants 78, 79, 83, 87, 88, 90, 97-100, 105, 109, 122, 312
Diatomaceous Earth 73, 317-318
Detoxification 75, 95, 312, 313, 314
Diabetes 20-21, 33, 49, 60, 71, 109, 231, 154, 186, 231
Diane Oxberry 7
Diet for a New America 175
Dr. Botanica 271, 291, 294, 328
Dr. Devra Davis 201
Dr. Issac Eliaz 253 (MCP)
Dr. Franz Adlkofer 201
Dr. James K. Todd, 214
Dr. John R. Lee, 124, 125, 237-240, 235
Dr. Martin Cooper 196
Dr. David Zava 238, 240, 288, 289
Dr. Saenz 170
Dragon Herbs 335
Dysmenorrhea 150
East Indian Women 258
Edward Bernays 108-113
Elizabeth Garrett 8, R.I.P.
Endocrine Disruptors 28, 107
Endocrine System 83, , 101, 194, 211
Endometriosis 28, 124, 138, 144-146, 149, 164, 192, 205, 209, 218-221, 250, 266, 289, 291
European Descent, Women, (also see Caucasian) 146, 168, 169,169, 240-241, 251, 257, 264
EMF's 194-203
Estradiol 59, 127-128, 131, 132, 145, 257, 278, 279, 288, 308,
Estriol 127, 136, 1376, 141, 278, 279, 285
Estrogen 21, 25, 39, 54, 74, 75, 76, 93, 98, 100, 120, 122-128, 130, 133, 134-138,
Estrogen Dominance 122
Estrone 127-128

Environmental Working Group (EWG) 83, 161, 308, 324,
European Union 91, 105, 168,
Eye Liner, 9
Factory Farms, Farmers 42, 172
Fatima Ali 13
Farrah Fawcett 7, R.I.P.
FDA 31, 58, 59, 68, 80, 82, 83, 93, 96-99, 100, 107, 109, 162,190, 191, 192, 211, 216, 243, 297, 318
Fermented soy 179-180, 248, 299
Fish Oil 269, 334
Fibroids 122,123, 128, 133,140-148, 153, 210, 223-226, 256-257, 258, 259, 261, 263, 264, 272, 287, 296, 298
Fluoride 24, 29-36, 44, 75, 120, 132, 133, 168, 236-237, 249
Food Additives 190
Food Adulteration 43
Genetic Roulette 51
Goitrogens 177, 179
Gwen Ifill 14, R.I.P.
Genial Day 159, 212, 274-282
GMO's 2,19,50-55, 68. 75,127-130, 205, 243, 267, 272-274, 289-29, 304, 308, 324, Index
Gene Mapping 18
Glyphosate 25-30, 52-64, 182-183, 297
Goji Berries 335
Growth Hormones 19, 38-39, 54, 55, 62, 165, 166, 173,175, 237, 272
Gui Zhi Fu Ling 151, 254
Gwen Ifill 14, R.I.P.
Gynostemma 337
HBO 16
HRT 139-145, 243-234, 299
Hair 85. 92, 96
Hair Care 89
Hair Color 79, 94
Hair Dyes 76, 104, 106
Hair Products 84
Hair Shampoo 77
Hand Sanitizers 195, 281, 308

Harvard University College of Medicine 241
Harvey Wiley 64-68
Hemp 309, 328, 332, 338
HeLa Cell
Henrietta Lacks 16-21, R.I.P.
Hermits Mix 335
High Fructose Corn Syrup 191, 313
Hispanic Women 258
Hysterectomy 140-144
Hip Replacement 256
Hong-Yen Hsu 264
IGF-1 176-177, 185,191, 249
Impossible Burger 52-55
Industrial Chemicals 89, 160, 172, 237, 249, 285, 297
Industrial Toxicity 23
International Journal of Andrology 173
Iranian Women 258
Jade Russell 6, R.I.P.
Jeffrey Smith 50, 51
Juicing 316-317
June Jordan 10, R.I.P.
John Robbins 177
Katherine Textorm 15, R.I.P.
Kick Study (Samuel Chase) 32
Laura Ziskin 5, R.I.P.
Lauren Wasser 199-203
Leah Bracknell 15, R.I.P.
Linda McCartney 10, R.I.P.
Lipstick 78, 83, 87, 102, 163
Magnesium 73, 157, 178, 179, 252, 266, 267 269, 331, 332, 334, 336
Man Boobs 247
Marilou Diaz Abaya 8, R.I.P.
Maryam Mirzakhani 12, R.I.P
Modifed Citrus Pectin, (MCP) 253
Meat 41-42, 47-49, 52-53, 57, 62, 70, 136, 149, 155, 170-171, 175, 181, 188, 190, 191, 229, 235, 241, 248, 266, 313, 319, 326-327
Medicinal Mushrooms 335-336

Men 308-310, 322-302
Menopause 122, 128, 134-138, 140-141, 149, 150, 226, 242, 259, 260, 278-279, 284, 286, 292, 312, 330
Menstrual Bleeding 142-221, 255, 258, 261
Menstrual Cramps 151, 336
Menstrual Cycle 125, 135, 139-140, 151,154-156, 213, 224, 268, 274, 286, 329
Menstrual Flow 214-215, 219, 251-253, 254, 257, 326
Menstrual Pain 145
Menstrual Products 89, 209-211, 331
Moms Across America 53, 54
Monsanto 28, 29, 52, 184
Minnie Riperton 9 R.I.P.
Miso 181
Monosodium Glutamate 188, 191, 258
Mr. Mcguire (Walter Brooke) 28
Myeloma Cancer 108, 244
Myomectomy 143,146, 225, 226
Nails 84-87, 132, 164, 245, 250, 257, 295, 331
Natto, Nattokinase 182, 308
Neurotransmitters 195, 291
Nina Simone 13, R.I.P.
Noreen Fraser 5, R.I.P.
Obesity 22, 46, 59-62, 109, 132, 135, 168, 175-176, 239, 302
Obesogens 59. 60-63, 87
Oprah Winfrey 16
Ovarian Cysts 57-58, 100, 219
Para-Thyroid 194, 266
Parsi Herbs 76, 339, 356
PCOS 134, 135,15, 298
Phthalates 62, 79-94, 101, 104, 109, 132-134, 172, 185, 211, 250, 276, 297, 305, 315
Plastics 2, 62, 65, 69, 74, 105, 124, 129-134

135, 149, 167, 172-175 230, , 241, 242, 272, 297, 305-310, 313
Plastic toys 172-174
Poison Squad 65-69
Poultry 56-58
Premenstrual (PMS) 122,151, 155, 338
Progesterone 135-136, 143, 145, 149, 155, 229, 231, 238, 239
Prop-65 54
Prostaglandins 150, 296
Puerto Rican children, 56
Quinoa 332
rBGH 58, 185-186, 191, 237, 249,
Real Food 45-55
Rhodiola 336
Saliva Test 239, 286, 288
Samuel Chase 32
Sanitary Napkins 68-70, 119,156-157, 272-275, 277
Schisandra 335
Seeds of Destruction 150, 151
Selenium 333
Spirulina 337
Surgery 139, 141-142, 144, 175, 221, 254, 255, 256-257
Sharon McGhee R.I.P. 6
Super Foods 77, 336, 339
Sally Fallon 45
Smoking 115, 119, 168, 266
Spring Dragon Tea 337
Sodium Nitrate 190
Soybeans 63, 230
Soy 2, 31, 39, 46, 49, 50, 52, 66-67, 177, 178-180, 248, 297, 299, 308
Soy Infant Formulas 31
Soy oil 289

Steroids 54-55, 126, 302
Super foods
Sugar 58, 70, 157, 251, 313
Sugar Cravings 157, 290,
Susan Strasberg R.I.P, 11
Synthetic Chemicals 2, 4, 21, 25,46, 102, 130, 312, 314
Synthetic Estrogen 28
Talcum Powder 108, 249
Tap Water 28, 109, 314
Tampons 31, 72, 74, 92, 155, 159, 204-205, 208-218, 257, 272, 273
Tempeh 182
Testosterone 59, 62, 100, 105, 125, 128-135 154, 166, 172, 175, 176, 180, 187, 195, 239, 242, 247, 266, 286-288, 290, 296, 297, 298, 300, 301, 302, 303, 304, 307, 308, 310
The Immortal Life of Henrietta Lacks 16-21
Thyroid 3, 32, 34, 36, 60, 92, 95, 167, 178, 180, 181, 189, 194, 195, 266, 286 , 287, 289, 290, 291, 292-293
Thyroid Cancer 30
Thyroid Disease75, 290
Toothpaste 33, 39, 79, 87, 88, 92, 105, 106 108, 121-122, 169, 196, 249, 257, 324, 331
Tourmaline 274-276
Toxic Shock Syndrome (TSS) 205, 207, 208, 214-220
Traditional Chinese Medicine 258, 260 261, 264
Triclosan 98, 105, 195, 297, 307,316

Unfermented Soy 2, 179-181
University of Melborne 139
University of Ottawa 173
Vanity products 21, 118
Vegan 45, 49, 73, 156, 177, 269, 326, 328
Vegetarian 45, 67, 177, 179, 327, 328,
Weed Killer 28, 52, 182-183-184, 250
Weight 41, 58-62, 108, 124, 130, 173, 179, 181, 204, 240. 259, 286-289
Weston Price 44-46
William Carter 66-67
Xenoestrogens 42, 79, 127, 129, 149, 166129, 130, 146, 166, 167, 242, 247, 266, 272, 282, 307, 315j
ZRT 279, 281, 287, 288, 289, 291, 316

About the Authors

Dr. Anahitta Jafari

About Anahitta Jafari, Ph.D., Iridologist, and Master Herbalist

Anahitta Jafari, Ph.D., is a seasoned veteran in nutritional science and herbalism. She began studying traditional Persian medicine at the age of 13, carrying on the legacy passed down to her from her maternal grandmother and great-grandmother. She is a certified iridologist, 6th-generation traditional Persian herbalist, bodily purist, professional food therapist and is officially recognized in the holistic profession as the "Kitchen Physician."©

Dr. Jafari has researched and studied the medical philosophy of one of the most significant and prolific physicians in history, Persian Polymath Avicenna, and remains an avid student of his teachings to this day. She holds a medical degree from Iran as a general practitioner (non-practicing physician), has studied Homotoxicology at the International Society of Homotoxicology and Antihomotoxic Therapy, and has a degree in Homeopathy. She has hosted her health talk show, in addition to appearing on a myriad of radio and television talk shows. She is also internationally renowned as an expert on holistic health and spirituality.

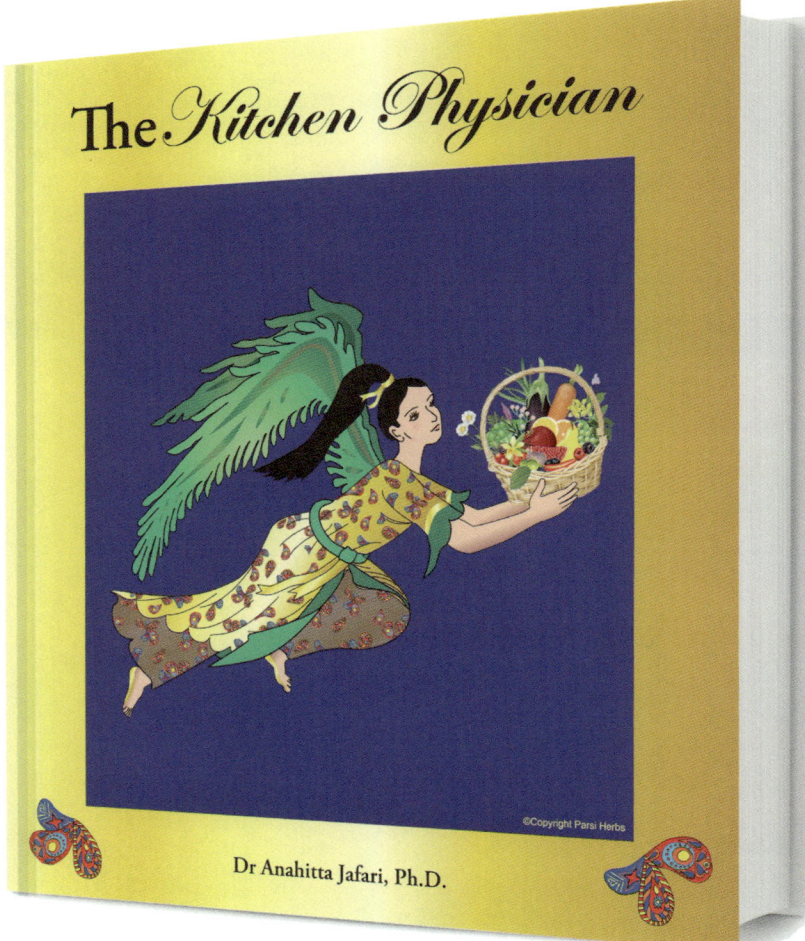

Parsi Herbs
Signature PRODUCT LINE

Nutritional Bioavailability is the most important component when it comes to supplements. The Parsi Herbs is product line that is made from organic, super foods, herbs, vitamins, mineral, enzymes and food state ingredients. This one of the purest whole food supplement lines in the natural product industry.

About Dr. Botanica©.
Hon. Ph.D., Researcher, Master Herbalist, Nutritionist

Dr. Botanica© has worked in various areas of the Natural Product Industry for a total of 26 years and continues his research on many modalities of health, wellness, and disease prevention. He began his journey on the path of holistic health at the age of 11 and developed a passion for nature, wildlife, and the environment. As a hobby, Dr. Botanica© began to acquire various new articles from National Geographic, Time, and Life Magazine concerning the environment, health, and diseases. This spectrum of intrigue soon became a religion for Dr. Botanica©, and natural living became his lifestyle. He was also motivated by the unfortunate passing of his father, grandfather, both grandmother, aunt's cousins, and whom all perished from cancer.

In 1979, Dr. Botanica© began studying the work of several pioneers of the holistic and natural sciences of health industry like Bernard Jensen, Paul Bragg, Jethro Kloss, and Dick Gregory. In 1994, the late health guru, activist, and comedian, Dick Gregory embraced, befriended and mentored Dr. Botanica. Dick Gregory soon acknowledged him as a master of natural health when he witnessed the immaculate recovery of a patient who was diagnosed with Stage-IV Non-Small Cell Lung Cancer in 2000 that used Dr. Botanica's Adjuvant Nutritional protocol to compliment his Traditional medical treatment, in 2006 the patient was announced by his physician as cured and was considered and "miracle patient".

In 1994, he opened his first full line health food store called Grass Roots, and several years after All Health Concerns, totaling 20 years of health food and wellness retail. In 1999, Dr. Botanica© earned a diploma in Chinese Herbology from the International College of Traditional Chinese Medicine. In 2014, he received an Honorary Doctorate for his research and the award-winning work of a book titled MediSin. Dr. Botanica© has also received training in Bio-Identical Hormone Testing, Metabolic Therapy, Orthomolecular Medicine, and Bio-identical Hormone Testing.

Dr. Botanica©

Dr. Botanica's book "Nutrisins" will be published in January 2020